D1487458

MALCOLM, WILLIAM

A BLASPHEMER AND
REFORMER

A BLASPHEMER & REFORMER

TEN MODERN SCOTTISH NOVELS
Isobel Murray & Bob Tait

GRAMPIAN HAIRST
An Anthology of Northeast Prose
Edited by William Donaldson and Douglas Young

LITERATURE OF THE NORTH
Edited by David Hewitt and Michael Spiller

A BLASPHEMER & REFORMER

A study of
James Leslie Mitchell/Lewis Grassic Gibbon

William K Malcolm

ABERDEEN UNIVERSITY PRESS

First published 1984
Aberdeen University Press
A member of the Pergamon Group
© William K Malcolm 1984

The publisher acknowledges subsidy from the
Scottish Arts Council towards the publication
of this volume

British Library Cataloguing in Publication Data

Malcolm, William K.
 A blasphemer and reformer
 1. Gibbon, Lewis Grassic—Criticism and
 interpretation
 I. Title
 823'.912   PR6025.I833Z/

 ISBN 0-08-030373-0

PRINTED IN GREAT BRITAIN
THE UNIVERSITY PRESS
ABERDEEN

Contents

In memory of my father;
and for my mother,
John, Annie and Stuart

Preface and Acknowledgements

As the half-centenary of Leslie Mitchell's death approaches, it is gratifying to reflect that his writing has not only endured the passing of the years, but has established him firmly as one of the finest literary talents to emerge from Scotland in recent times. The work published under the pseudonym of Lewis Grassic Gibbon has earned Mitchell a special place in the popular imagination, and the television adaptations of three of his short stories and of his masterpiece, *A Scots Quair*, have won many new admirers for his writing. Publishers have responded to this in recent years, by bringing out in their turn some of his lesser known work while the major titles are now available in various editions. All things considered, therefore, Leslie Mitchell's reputation is higher now than it has been at any other time since his death in 1935.

Despite his widespread appeal, however, illuminating criticism of Mitchell's writing is very much at a premium, with the result that he remains a much praised but little understood figure. A certain amount of scholarly misunderstanding has arisen from a basic error of approach, and all too few of Mitchell's critics have resisted the temptation to confine him to a purely Scottish context, some even going so far as to acclaim him as a purveyor of some kind of national myth. While Mitchell undeniably held both his country and countrymen dear and found them a constant source of strength and inspiration, any attempt to do justice to his work and thought must establish a wider frame of reference altogether. We must not ignore the cosmopolitan range of influences at play in his writing, nor deny the universality of its appeal. Very much as in MacDiarmid's early poetry, the Scottish medium in the Grassic Gibbon fiction sustains art of the highest order; the author works through this to address themes of the greatest consequence to all men.

Mitchell's reputation rests upon a small part of his total output, yet his whole literary canon is of considerable interest, not least for the insight it gives to his artistic and intellectual development. As I feel that an understanding of Leslie Mitchell's personal ideology is vital for the true appreciation of his writing, I propose to preface my appraisal of his fiction works with a brief study of his most deeply held beliefs. I am convinced that Mitchell's achievement appears even more remarkable when his work is examined from this point of view. *A Scots Quair* in particular emerges as one of the most stimulating and profound novels of the twentieth century.

I would like to thank the following people for giving so generously of their time and wisdom to help me in my research: Dr Cuthbert Graham, Dr Douglas Young and Dr Ian Campbell, authorities on Mitchell who put their specialist knowledge at my disposal; Dr David S Hewitt, whose consistently sound advice as supervisor of my studies has helped greatly to ease my manuscript through its various evolutionary stages; and other members of the English Department at the University of Aberdeen, in particular Dr Isobel Murray, Dr J Graeme Roberts and Mr Graham Trengove, who responded graciously to my requests for assistance, and Mr Matthew P McDiarmid and Mr Thomas Crawford, experts on Scottish literature who have influenced my thinking from my days as an undergraduate. I would also like to express my appreciation to Dr R Cairns Craig, now of the Department of English Literature at the University of Edinburgh, whose stimulating lectures on the modern Scottish novel helped warm me to my task in the early stages of my postgraduate research.

Additional acknowledgements should be made for the sterling work done on my behalf by staff at Aberdeen City Libraries, Aberdeen University Libraries, The British Library in London and The National Library of Scotland in Edinburgh; and I am especially grateful to Mr Stanley M Simpson, Assistant Head Keeper of Manuscripts at the latter, for his willing help and cooperation. Thanks are due to the Trustees of The National Library of Scotland and to Mrs Rhea Martin for allowing me to quote from manuscript material, and to Curtis Brown Ltd, on behalf of the Estate of James Leslie Mitchell, for granting permission to quote from his copyright works.

I am indebted to John Reid ('David Toulmin'), Jessie Kesson, George Mackay Brown and William McIlvanney who, in giving me the benefit of their practical expertise in literary matters, helped to clear up for me various questions relating to the modern fiction writer's craft in general, and concerning Leslie Mitchell's art in particular. Mr John Fraser, Rector of Mackie Academy, Stonehaven, and Rev Ian G Gough, Minister of the Parish of Arbuthnott and Kinneff, saved me much time and trouble in my endeavours to clarify certain biographical details; I am pleased to have had the chance to meet Mr and Mrs Jeams of Stonehaven and Miss Nellie Riddoch and Mr Andy Robertson of Arbuthnott, whose intimate knowledge of Leslie Mitchell and of the history and traditions of the Mearns afforded me a sharper view of my subject. Betty Reid of the Communist Party of Great Britain and Finlay Hart of its Scottish Executive patiently helped me in my efforts to uncover Mitchell's official political movements. Latterly, the practical help and advice of Colin MacLean, managing director of publishing at AUP, proved invaluable. And I must not forget the loyalty of my family and friends by whom I have been fortified (in more ways than one) throughout my six years of research upon Leslie Mitchell.

Above all, however, my thanks are due to Leslie Mitchell's family, and to Mrs Rhea Martin in particular, whose friendship, support and assistance has contributed immeasurably to the completion of my work. I feel especially privileged to have known Mrs Ray Mitchell, who deepened my understanding of her husband as only one of her singular devotion could have done, and I preserve happy memories of the idyllic week I spent with her at her home in Welwyn Garden City shortly before she died, in September 1978.

WKM
Aberdeen 1983

Abbreviations

Novels by Mitchell

SR Stained Radiance (London 1930)
TD The Thirteenth Disciple (London 1931)
TGB Three Go Back (London 1932)
LT The Lost Trumpet (London 1932)
IS Image and Superscription (London 1933)
Spart Spartacus (London 1933)
GH Gay Hunter (London 1934)

Novels by Gibbon

SQ A Scots Quair (London 1976)
  (This edition follows the typesetting of the single-volume version of the trilogy published by Jarrolds in 1950, with the minor revision that it is consecutively paginated.)

Other works by Mitchell and Gibbon

Hanno Hanno: or The Future of Exploration (London 1928)
Niger Niger: The Life of Mungo Park (Edinburgh 1934)
CM The Conquest of the Maya (London 1934)
NAU Nine Against the Unknown (London 1934)
SH A Scots Hairst (London 1967)
  (All Gibbon material originally published in *Scottish Scene* will be cited as it appears in this volume.)
NLS denotes a manuscript located in The National Library of Scotland, Edinburgh

Critical works

Munro Ian S Munro, *Leslie Mitchell: Lewis Grassic Gibbon* (Edinburgh and London 1966)
Young Douglas F Young, *Beyond the Sunset: A Study of James Leslie Mitchell (Lewis Grassic Gibbon)* (Aberdeen 1973)

Introduction

In September 1929, the month after his discharge from the Royal Air Force, Leslie Mitchell wrote to his old teacher in the north of Scotland from his home in Hammersmith proclaiming proudly, 'I'm now a professional writer-cratur'.[1] Considering the writer had only one slim volume on the history of exploration and a handful of stories published in various places to his credit at the time, this statement seems rather presumptuous, but Mitchell's subsequent publishing record over the following five and a half years until his lamentably early death on 7 February 1935 provides impressive testament to the industry and dedication of a man determined to earn a living by the pen.

Mitchell came to a writing career relatively late in his life and died when he was just reaching the heights of his powers, but he left an impressively large body of work behind him, the full extent of which is still not widely appreciated. The grand total of seventeen books produced in the last seven years of his life, ranging from historical studies and biography to short story collections and novels, is supplemented by a wealth of lesser products. Although most of his stories have been preserved in book form, either in the two English collections or in *Scottish Scene*, the final total is augmented by various fugitive pieces printed in newspapers and periodicals such as *TP's and Cassell's Weekly* and *Reynolds's Illustrated News*. In the course of my search in *The Millgate Monthly* for Mitchell's profile of William Perry, I discovered that he also had a short series of five stories published in its pages between 1931 and 1934. When all these fragments have been taken into consideration, therefore, it transpires that Mitchell had no less than thirty-nine separate stories published in all. His biographer Ian Munro and bibliographer Geoffrey Wagner also cite between them fifteen non-fiction articles by him which appeared in assorted journals and newspapers, ranging from scholarly essays on archaeology submitted to well-respected periodicals, to facetious letters written to newspapers in the heat of the moment protesting against criticism that had been made of his work. To this number may be added three book reviews which I discovered in *The Free Man*, and an article called 'The Prince's Placenta and Prometheus as God' which languished anonymously among Mrs Mitchell's papers, and which I subsequently traced to the Anarchist journal *The Twentieth Century*. Mitchell also worked as a publisher's reader in his later years, in which capacity he wrote introductions for English translations of two European novels, Heinrich Mann's *The Blue Angel*, and *Mala the Magnificent* a novel by the Danish anthropologist and explorer, Peter Freuchen. Mitchell's bibliography thus fully justifies his earlier claim to be 'a professional writer-cratur'.

[1] Notes start on p 192.

Although James Leslie Mitchell remains very much a name to conjure with in the context of Scottish literature, the eleven major volumes which emerged under his own name are now largely forgotten. Two of his English novels have been republished in recent years, but it is significant that the fine historical novel *Spartacus* should have been resurrected by Hutchinson in 1970 under the pseudonym of Lewis Grassic Gibbon, and that Paul Harris should promote their recent reprint of *The Thirteenth Disciple* under both Mitchell's own name and his assumed name. It is for the smaller body of work which appeared under his pen name that Leslie Mitchell is best remembered. This is wholly appropriate, for the trilogy of novels collectively known as *A Scots Quair* is undoubtedly his crowning achievement.

The publication history of the Grassic Gibbon novels and stories shows that Mitchell's reputation as a writer has grown steadily over the years, and it is particularly heartening that he has begun to win recognition outwith his native land, with Raymond Williams[2] and David Smith[3] both acclaiming him recently as a major figure in the radical tradition of British literature. Despite these encouraging signs, however, Mitchell's work has yet to receive its critical due. References to both Mitchell and Gibbon in newspapers, journals and magazines are legion and, although many articles have been devoted to him, unfortunately these tend to be of limited scope and leave the bulk of his *oeuvre* largely untouched. Even more disappointing is the fact that only two extensive studies of Leslie Mitchell have been published to date, although this situation was slightly improved by the appearance in April 1983 of Douglas Gifford's compact comparison of *Gunn and Gibbon*. However, I mean no disrespect to Dr Gifford's typically invigorating study when I voice a preference for his appraisal of Gunn; the value of his assessment is impaired by the fact that he restricts his attention to Mitchell's major works. While the two principal critical works on Mitchell contrive to give a fuller picture of the man and his writing, neither book manages to do full justice to his achievement.

Ian S Munro provides the main details of the author's life and work in his vivid and sympathetic biography, *Leslie Mitchell: Lewis Grassic Gibbon*, which remains the authoritative reference work upon him. However, Mr Munro's book does not give Mitchell's fiction the informed critical attention it deserves, and thus Douglas Young's *Beyond the Sunset* remains the only full-length critical study of Mitchell's writing published to date. Yet, while Dr Young's broad commentary on the published works is most valuable, I suggest that his basic approach is rather singleminded and that he exaggerates the importance of diffusionism by claiming a dominant position for this historical theory within Mitchell's thinking and writing.

The diffusionists believed that, far from evolving naturally, civilisation had its origins in the one freak happening, the discovery of agriculture in the Nile valley several thousand years before the birth of Christ; and from this focal point the distinctive features of the new society (such as war, religion and class divisions) 'diffused' throughout the primitive world. This historical vision was useful to Mitchell in that it supported his anti-religious stance and encouraged him in his denunciation of social inequality. Nevertheless, while diffusionist doctrine provided an 'objective correlative' for his personal political and philosophical opinions, it does not lie at the heart of either his personal philosophy or his art. Indeed, much of the success of *A Scots Quair* in particular is due to the fact that in this volume Mitchell penetrates beyond the superficial and relatively arid theories of diffusionism to those principles which moved him most deeply as a man.

In the first two chapters I propose to define these principles as they are reflected in Mitchell's writing, using the evidence of letters and manuscripts as well as his published work. Leslie Mitchell's intellectual preoccupations developed in a relatively straightforward manner throughout his life, and this is made abundantly clear when one compares him with his friend Hugh MacDiarmid whose own ideals, like those of his intoxicated visionary who expressed the desire to 'aye be whaur/ Extremes meet',[4] encompassed a bewildering diversity of unrelated and downright contradictory viewpoints. In marked contrast, Mitchell only really courted the one extreme in both his political and religious opinions throughout his life, and therefore I intend to define the ideological base upon which his work is founded before moving to an appreciation of the fiction itself.

My *modus operandi* in this elucidatory section will be to concentrate upon the two main thrusts of Mitchell's personal philosophy, the one basically religious and the other essentially political, and to signify the principal ways in which they developed. These two impulses will be considered under the headings 'blasphemer and reformer'[5] which Mitchell employed in his eulogy of Quetzalcoatl, a legendary figure from ancient American history; the Scots author evidently identified wholeheartedly with the values which the Toltec demi-god embodied. The words 'blasphemer and reformer' seem to me to provide a particularly useful shorthand for Leslie Mitchell's own philosophical disposition, for not only do they represent the twin edges of his personal credo, but they also indicate the positive and negative—the constructive and destructive—attitudes which each of these viewpoints embraces. When he hails Quetzalcoatl as a 'blasphemer', therefore, Mitchell is praising him on account of his opposition to the established forms of religious observance and the gory rites of the ancient American theocracies, and also on account of the rationalistic creed that he introduced in their place. Likewise, when he acclaims his subject as a 'reformer', Mitchell is celebrating both the positive and negative aspects of Quetzalcoatl's social campaign, which involved both the destruction of the existing system and the establishment of a worthy alternative. At their most mature, Mitchell's political and religious opinions strike this delicate balance between negative and positive criticism.

Throughout his adult life, Mitchell devoted himself to a campaign in search of greater freedom in the political and religious spheres. He maintained a radical political stance as revolutionary 'reformer' from the time when he was a cub reporter in Aberdeen, and this radical bent is consequently one of the dominant features of his writing. He also argued in a typically outspoken manner that a more enlightened attitude should be adopted in modern society towards religion. His writing is thus distinguished also by its tendency to 'blaspheme', to demonstrate vigorously, indeed belligerently, against the traditional religious modes which he felt to be both socially redundant and philosophically insecure. This destructive criticism provided the springboard for a more positive quest for an alternative, empirically valid form of religious experience.

I would not make any extravagant claims for Mitchell's originality as either a political theorist or a philosophical thinker, but then it seems to me unfair to expect this quality from the artist in the first place. Matthew Arnold observed over a hundred years ago in 'The Function of Criticism at the Present Time':

> Creative literary genius does not principally show itself in discovering new ideas, that is rather the business of the philosopher. The grand work of literary genius is a work of synthesis and exposition, not of analysis and discovery; its gift lies in the faculty of being happily inspired by a certain intellectual and spiritual atmosphere, by a certain order of ideas, when it finds itself in them. . . .[6]

Mitchell's work possesses this greater validity, for it is comprehensively true to the spirit of its age. In fact, Victorian ethics and ideals are formally and categorically renounced in the immensely powerful episode in *The Thirteenth Disciple* dealing with the bonfire which Malcom [sic] Maudslay witnesses at midnight on New Year's Eve at the turn of the century. The bonfire is graphically apprehended as a symbolic conflagration signifying the advent of a new age, with the celebrants systematically 'burning out the nineteenth century' (*TD* p. 25). Accordingly, Mitchell's own writing has a conscious and quite startling modernity.

The inter-war years were a particularly traumatic period in modern European history, and rapidly deteriorating social conditions made unique demands upon the artist at this time. By the early thirties, art had acquired a stern political aspect, and the general increase in political awareness is reflected in Leslie Mitchell's writing. The First World War itself had an even more profound effect upon the intellectual climate in the early part of the century, leading many people to revise their deepest thoughts and beliefs; in fact, this may be regarded as the cataclysm which finally cut modern man off from the comparatively stable values of Victorian society, releasing him into a godless universe ruled by the principle of chance rather than design. Although it took another World War to produce a literary school which consciously exploited this vision of the Absurdity of existence, the First World War appears as a particularly potent leitmotiv in Mitchell's writing, and the crisis of faith which this event precipitated is also very much in evidence in his work. Indeed, so highly attuned was he to these pressing philosophical issues that later developments in European thought, especially the sense of the Absurd as elaborated by the French Algerian Albert Camus during the Second World War, are anticipated in Mitchell's work.

Leslie Mitchell's writing thus reflects modern intellectual developments, but it is motivated by thoughts and feelings which were distilled from personal experience. The bulk of his work, including the trilogy, reveals the author's moral fervour, his passionate social concern and his philosophical integrity, and these qualities can all be traced back to their source in the sensitive nature and the insatiably curious intellect which were his birthright. Given the qualities which stamped Mitchell's character as a boy, it is not difficult to appreciate how he gradually acquired an interest in radical politics, in scientific progress and in philosophical speculation when he was still a young man, and how these themes eventually came to the fore in his writing. And although these ideas are only brought to full fruition in the splendid art of *A Scots Quair*, nevertheless Mitchell's whole literary corpus merits examination because at the very least it gives fascinating insight into the artistic and ideological factors which combine to make the trilogy such a magnificent achievement.

Mitchell has yet to be given full credit for the care and deliberation with which he moulded his trilogy, and I will later consider the reasoning behind the work. However, it is important to understand at this juncture that the author conceived the *Quair* as a uniform whole, and as such its integrity deserves to be respected. Thus, Mitchell can be said to have written only one major work of lasting importance, but in the magnitude of this single achievement I feel he ranks above Neil Gunn, his only modern Scottish compeer in the genre of the novel, even though Gunn has justly been acclaimed as the more consistent craftsman.[7] Therefore I will devote a major part of this study to a critical appreciation of *A Scots Quair*.

The relationship between art and ideology is complex. Mitchell himself never seemed quite sure as to the precise function of art, including his own. Indeed, he appears to have swung from one extreme to the other on this matter, for his early work projects the purist view of the artist as an élite figure working from a cloistered and self-indulgent viewpoint, whereas latterly he subscribed to the opposite opinion, identifying art as propaganda created with some ulterior didactic motive. Happily, this revision does not significantly affect the quality of Mitchell's own writing—although some of the later works benefit from their exceptionally pragmatic character—and in *A Scots Quair* the author finally rises above the diverse literary and philosophical influences integrated within the book to make great art from the ideological forces by which he himself was motivated. This, to my mind, as Mitchell's novelist hero John Garland declares in *Stained Radiance*, represents the ultimate responsibility of the artist in this society, for finally the most that can be asked of him amidst the fluctuating values of the modern world is that he remains true to himself and presents his own deepest thoughts and beliefs in his work, on the initial understanding, as Garland observes, that they themselves are 'worth the having' (*SR*, p 88).

A Scots Quair is both Leslie Mitchell's personal manifesto and his literary masterpiece, the product of an age which has witnessed the evolution of 'confessional' and 'philosophical' modes of fiction.[8] The trilogy deserves to be analysed within the frame of reference which Mitchell establishes for it, in the book itself and elsewhere in his writing, as an experimental novel which capitalises upon established modes and conventions, but which finally remains distinctly *sui generis*; for the eclectic qualities ultimately prove to be of secondary importance to the central themes and techniques which are the volume's greatest strengths.

ONE

'Reformer':
Mitchell's Political Thinking

FORMATIVE EXPERIENCE AND EARLY INTEREST IN SOCIALISM

Disagreement has been rife over Leslie Mitchell's political beliefs, and there has been a particularly stong tendency for those who have volunteered opinions on the matter simply to cast him in their own image. Thus, both George Blake and John Paton have identified him as a moderate socialist, while James Barke has acclaimed him as a practising Marxist.[1] Hugh MacDiarmid, meanwhile, remained gloriously true to character by contradicting himself several times on the subject over the years, hailing his friend in 1946, for example, as 'a Scottish Communist-Nationalist à la John MacLean [who] abandoned his earlier facetious attitude to the Scottish Renaissance Movement',[2] and then claiming in an interview broadcast several years later that he was 'a Socialist Internationalist of the type whose politics emphatically did not begin at home'.[3] In fact, A Scots Quair has been subjected to both nationalist and Marxist interpretations, and while this can be taken as an indication of the broad appeal his work possesses, it also reflects the general uncertainty that exists concerning the author's political beliefs.

Mitchell himself contributed to the uncertainty by using different terms—principally those of anarchist and communist—to describe his personal standpoint, and definition is made more complicated by the keen interest he also took in Scottish affairs. The main problem here is one of terminology rather than ideology, however, for Mitchell's interests and ideals remained constant throughout his life, despite the fact that he pursued his political goals under various headings. While MacDiarmid swung between the political extremes of fascism and communism during his life Mitchell stuck resolutely to his radical role of left-wing 'reformer'.

There are important circumstantial factors to be taken into account when considering the consistency of Leslie Mitchell's political beliefs. For instance, he lived in a time of increasing poverty, of record unemployment and international bankruptcy, but, dying before the full facts had come to light concerning the Stalinist purges which took place in the USSR in the mid thirties, he was able to respond directly and spontaneously to these deteriorating social conditions without becoming too deeply involved in heart-searching questions of political ethics. I feel certain that Mitchell's political ideals, based upon the humanistic principles of communism, were strong enough to withstand the disappointment and disenchantment resulting from the Stalinist regime—which he would have dismissed as a tragic and deplorable perversion of the true Marxist system. In any case, events later in the decade, in Spain, Italy and Germany, would undoubtedly have renewed his faith in the communist struggle. Had he lived to learn the truth about Stalin's Russia, however, his political vision would in all likelihood have lost some of the romantic idealism which was a feature of his political outlook from his youth.

While historical circumstances thus had a certain bearing upon the character of Mitchell's political vision, naturally the most telling reasons for the stability of his political disposition are personal ones. Less concerned with the mechanics of social organisation and economic theory than with basic moral issues and human ideals, his political standpoint was largely determined by his personal temperament and experience.

The adage that the child is father to the man rings especially true when one considers Mitchell's political role of 'reformer', for his adult sympathies can be traced back to his boyhood. Although he has been represented as a lonely and introspective child who preferred to read books rather than participate in the more energetic ploys of his schoolmates, his schoolmaster at Arbuthnott remembered him as 'a kindly boy',[4] and he seems to have been peculiarly sensitive towards all signs of suffering and cruelty. This compassionate streak in Mitchell's nature is well illustrated in one particular passage in 'The Land' in which the author confesses—

> When I hear or read of a dog tortured to death, very vilely and foully, of some old horse driven to a broken back down a hill with an overloaded cart of corn, of rats captured and tormented with red-hot pokers in bothies, I have a shudder of disgust (SH, p 79).

However, Mitchell kept this response in perspective, for he carries on in this essay to subordinate his interest in animal welfare to his preoccupation with his fellow men.

Mitchell's Arbuthnott School essay books are obviously of limited importance to an understanding of the work he produced as an adult, yet they reflect the simple affection he felt for the people of the Mearns, expressed in richly observed cameos and pen-portraits of the local folk.[5] Mitchell came to sympathise with the hard-pressed tenant crofters who farmed the area around his home on the Reisk, and his own family's social circumstances coloured his subsequent political attitudes quite substantially. As a result of that occupational vulnerability which accompanied their lowly station as tenant farmers, when Leslie was only seven years old the Mitchells had been forced to forsake a tolerable holding in Auchterless for a much less hospitable tenancy in the Mearns, which committed the whole family to the effort, as the author put it in one of his most heavily autobiographical works, to 'grub a livelihood from hungry acres of red clay' (TD, p 23). While the Howe o' the Mearns is by no means a poor farming area in general terms, it is safe to assume that here the Mitchells came to appreciate the full truth of the country dictum that the world is 'illy pairted', for Bloomfield was an especially unprofitable concern at the start of the century, being too small to be considered even a 'sma' holding', and being badly drained, isolated and exposed into the bargain.[6] For Leslie Mitchell as for Chris Guthrie, therefore, books offered a welcome means of escape from harsh social reality, but like his heroine, he also found this an inadequate solution, for his political sympathies were already firmly engaged with those whom he later called simply the 'common folk' (SQ, p 269).

Many years later, in his essay on 'The Land', Mitchell could still call forth Crabbe-like images which were burdened with the pain of personal experience—as in 'a bewildered labourer in pelting rains and the flares of head-aching suns' who is promised 'years of a murderous monotony, poverty and struggle and loss of happy human relationships' (SH, p 69). Ten pages later in the essay, the writer goes on to affirm personally, 'I am concerned so much more deeply with men and women, with their nights and days, the things they believe, the things that move them to pain and anger and the callous, idle cruelties that are yet undead.' This philanthropic bent which was to become one of the hallmarks of Mitchell's writing was thus an integral part of his character by the time he reached his mid-teens. And under the influence of Robert Middleton, the neighbour and friend who was later to become his father-in-law and inspire the portrait of Long Rob of the Mill, these sentiments had probably acquired a political edge by the time Mitchell turned his back on the rigours of crofting life in 1917 in order to start work as a cub reporter with The Aberdeen Journal.

Although Mitchell spent less than two years in Aberdeen, this urban experience in general, and in particular the squalid harbour beat he was assigned, confirmed his sense of social commitment. This stimulated an early interest in left-wing organisations which moved him to address political meetings and culminated finally, as he relates in his essay on Aberdeen, in his election to the council of the new Aberdeen Soviet (SH, p 100). His political ideas at this time would have had an infectious quality of youthful romanticism redolent of the attitude expressed by Malcom Maudslay, the autobiographical hero in The Thirteenth Disciple, who describes his early reaction to socialist authors such as William Morris as follows:

> Here were people who, like himself, had shuddered in sick horror at sight of the dehumanized and wandering crucified; people who also had known the challenge of the winters' stars and seen solution of all the earth's bitter cruelties in a gigantic expedition against the World's Walls . . . though they seemed vaguely in dispute over plan of campaign. He discovered with them a splendid, romantic hope which coloured his days and nights; he had no vision of his sardonic self fifteen years in the future (TD, p 60).

Malcom subsequently speaks in more practical terms of the precise correlation between political activity and social welfare, and this may be regarded as a direct expression of Mitchell's own humanistic preoccupation, his protagonist considering how:

> All his life the people of the abyss, the cheated of the sunlight, were so to haunt his happiest moments and dreamings: these, the eternally crucified, who are not of Demos, who challenge in mindless hopelessness every scheme of reform or revolution . . . (TD, p 77).

This passage goes some way towards explaining the variety of political headings under which Mitchell exercised his role of 'reformer', for in his mind political means were always strictly related, and subordinated, to the social ends which they were designed to achieve. And it is revealing that Jack London's most enduring social study, *The People of the Abyss*, should be echoed here, as the American author reveals exactly the same set of priorities in his book.

In the profile of Aberdeen, Mitchell looks back upon his boyish idealism with a mixture of nostalgia and embarrassment, but his Glasgow experiences were evidently much more traumatic, as his essay on the city testifies. In this depressed area he encountered poverty and hardship on a scale and in an intensity that he could not have imagined previously, and his horrified reaction to these extreme conditions is very much on a par with Edwin Muir's as detailed in Chapter Three of *An Autobiography* and in the novel *Poor Tom*. The legendary militancy of Red Clydeside between the wars was no mere case of political opportunism but, as Nan Milton's biography of John MacLean and the autobiographical volumes by Willie Gallagher and Harry McShane all attest,[7] a direct product of the intensely deprived social conditions prevailing at the time. Almost inevitably, therefore, Leslie Mitchell's own political ideas were tempered by his short stay in Glasgow, his experience here heightening his awareness of the class struggle and hardening his political allegiances also, again inspiring him to join a group with strong communist sympathies. Many years later he wrote in one of his letters, 'I am politically a pessimist':[8] in fact the sense of despair in this statement dates from the period of less than six months that he spent amidst the destitution of post-war Glasgow.

The marked difference of tone and pitch between Mitchell's essays on Aberdeen and Glasgow bears full witness to the power of remembered experience, for there is little humour, either of an affectionate or a sardonic kind, in the latter essay, written fifteen years after this gruelling episode in his life. This piece has a trenchancy and vehemence absent in the portrait of Aberdeen, the author launching into a bitter tirade against the dehumanising phenomenon of the Glasgow slums, which ultimately deprive the inhabitants of their basic right of freedom, 'the clean anarchy which is the essence of life' (*SH*, p 88). And there is a distinctly pathological quality in the vision represented four pages earlier, of how:

> The hundred and fifty thousand eat and sleep and copulate and conceive and crawl into childhood in those waste jungles of stench and disease and hopelessness, sub-humans as definitely as the Morlocks of Wells—and without even the consolation of feeding on their oppressors' flesh.

Mitchell's fondness for William Morris's *News From Nowhere* is eminently understandable in this context, for this gentle utopian tract—hailed by the Russian Anarchist Peter Kropotkin as 'perhaps the most thoroughly and deeply Anarchistic conception of future society that has ever been written'[9] —contains a forthright and emotional denunciation of the desperate conditions persisting in the British slums of the nineteenth century, condemned as 'places of torture for innocent men and women', in which the victims are 'degraded out of humanity'.[10] Mitchell's criticism of conditions in Glasgow has a similar, almost Swiftian, intensity, and although the belief he expressed in the resultant essay in the basic human ideals of 'decency, freedom, justice' (*SH*, p 92) survived this disturbing urban experience, the harsh social reality of Glasgow purged the more wistful elements from his political vision and introduced a greater sense of urgency to his demands for social reform.

Having been abruptly dismissed from his job with *The Scottish Farmer* for embezzling company funds—interestingly, for political uses—Mitchell's fortunes hit rock-bottom, and the few depressing months he spent out of work towards the end of 1919 ultimately forced him, like many others at this time, to seek a livelihood in the armed forces. This experience wielded both a direct and indirect influence upon his political opinions. Thus, while he did indeed find financial security in the Army, predictably he found the destruction of war extremely harrowing, and, as the recurrent motif in his fiction indicates, this spell only served to reinforce his guilty obsession with the more cruel and brutal aspects of modern existence. Whatever his attitude was to the Army experience itself, however, Mitchell never fully won free from the idea that his enlistment was attributable to the social conditions of the time. John Garland views this situation from an orthodox socialist point of view, observing in *Stained Radiance:*

> He hated the Air Force. Like ninety per cent of those in the ranks, he had enlisted under the compulsion of hunger and unemployment. His stomach had conscripted him more surely than any Man Power Act could have done. He had never forgiven the Service the fact of its feeding him (*SR*, pp 30-1).

For a brief time following his release from the Army, Mitchell tried unsuccessfully to find a way of earning a living outwith the forces, but hunger and unemployment soon 'conscripted' him again, and he joined the Royal Air Force on 31 August 1923. As a clerk he was stationed in various parts of England. Yet escape from the immediate social and economic problems of civilian life evidently offered little comfort to him at this time either, for he subsequently confessed (in a letter written to his future wife) to an acute awareness that, 'We are, nearly all we soldiers, failures in life.'[11] The additional responsibilities which Mitchell acquired with his marriage two years after he wrote this laid him even more open to financial pressures, and the failure of his efforts to earn much-needed extra income by writing must have proved an added burden. Far from offering an escape from everyday realities or encouraging him to suspend his political activities, Mitchell's experience of the forces actually gave him greater cause to criticise the structure of contemporary society.

Consequently, while Mitchell's first book does not have an overtly political character, most probably because of the sober and restrained spirit of the series to which it belongs, muted socialist sentiments can be detected in the text, as in the prophesy that, 'Science and order will rule that [future] world, the snarling buffooneries of competition have given place to the sanities of universal co-operation' (Hanno, p 23), and in the sarcastic reference to Australia as 'a progressive state, with slums, strike-breakers, and imperial aspirations' (Hanno, p 47). This book gives a brief glimpse of things to come, therefore, for from this time Mitchell continually reaffirmed his devotion to the cause of the underprivileged classes; increasingly so, in fact, as the situation gradually deteriorated throughout the twenties and early thirties towards the deplorable figure of a record three and three quarter millions unemployed in Britain which was finally reached towards the end of 1932.

Mitchell's indignant reaction to this was not remarkable at the time; it reflected fairly accurately the generally resentful mood and attitude of the 'New Left' movement of the day. And yet his personal response has a special ardency as his famous outburst in a letter to Helen Cruickshank proves: he confesses candidly that, 'horrors do haunt me', and he explains:

> That's because I'm in love with humanity. Ancient Greece is never the Parthenon to me: It's a slave being tortured in a dungeon of the Athenian law-courts; Ancient Egypt is never the Pyramids: it's the blood and tears of Goshen; Ancient Scotland is never Queen Mary: it's those serfs they kept chained in the Fifeshire mines a hundred years ago. And so on. And so with the moderns: I am so horrified by all our dirty littly cruelties and bestialities that I would feel the lowest type of skunk if I didn't shout the horror of them from the house-tops. Of course I shout too loudly. But the filthy conspiracy of silence there was in the past!—and is coming again in Scotland, in a new guise, called Renaissance, and Objectivity, and National Art and what not. Blithering about Henryson and the Makars (whoever these cretins were) and forgetting the Glasgow slums. . . . [12]

The invective directed at Scottish culture may be largely unwarranted, but there is no doubting the sincerity of Mitchell's sentiments in this passage. He recognises the confines of neither time nor place; his sympathy embraces the persecuted slaves of ancient Greece as well as those of his contemporaries consigned to the Glasgow slums. The maxim that charity begins at home has a compelling political significance, and yet evidently Mitchell was forced to adopt a more cosmopolitan outlook by the very intensity of his social sympathies. Thus, his late widow wrote to me, 'I can say that he, like many others, passionately desired for all—a better world' [her emphasis], and she added by way of reinforcement, 'There is no doubt, had he lived, he would have worked to that aim.'[13]

Leslie Mitchell's background and experience thus confirmed him in his role of 'reformer' and committed him to the quest for social improvement. However, as he pursued this goal under different political banners, I move on to consider his own understanding of the two main creeds with which he associated himself—those of anarchism and communism—after considering further the actual scope of his political vision.

NATIONALISM, INTERNATIONALISM AND COSMOPOLITANISM

Many of the arguments put forward in the thirties both for and against nationalism seem dogmatic and unenlightened nowadays. Scottish writers such as Gunn, Muir and MacDiarmid were constantly leaping either to attack or defend the political and cultural attitudes of the Scottish Nationalists during this period. In order to understand the importance of the nationalist question during the thirties, however, it is necessary to appreciate the general political climate of the time.

Whereas the most prominent political distinction made in Britain nowadays is that between totalitarian and democratic regimes, the most important political choice facing Europe in the thirties lay between the poles of fascism and communism. The gradual increase in imperialist expansionism which had culminated in the First World War thus combined with events in Germany and Italy in the early thirties to encourage popular distrust in Britain of strongly nationalistic and patriotic sentiment. I have already indicated how Leslie Mitchell was naturally inclined to look beyond his native land, but his critical attitude towards the cause of the Scottish Nationalists apparently gained strength from the contemporary tendency to equate nationalism with fascism, for in his essay on 'Religion', he warns that, 'the various Scots nationalist parties have large elements of Fascism within them' (SH, p 170), and later that same year, he wrote to Neil Gunn:

> . . . I'm not really anti-Nationalist. But I loathe Fascism, and all the other dirty things that hide under the name. I doubt if you can ever have Nationalism without Communism.[14]

This last condition is crucial, for in his essay on 'Religion', Mitchell defines the two political extremes, the black and the white respectively, as 'fascism and communism' (SH, p 164). This blind fear of fascism informed and conditioned Mitchell's attitude towards nationalism, demonstrating that, at the most, he was capable only of achieving MacDiarmid's early depiction of him as a 'Communist-Nationalist à la John MacLean'. On one of the rare occasions when he does tend to favour the aim of national independence, in the essay on 'Glasgow', he looks upon it from a socialist point of view, contemplating the idea of Scotland winning its freedom from England 'by the obvious and necessary operation—social revolution' (SH, p 91), and viewing this act as part of a greater political scheme. Thus, two pages after he makes this tentative endorsement of the aim of Scottish independence, Mitchell feels obliged to confess, 'I am a nationalist only in the sense that the sane Heptarchian was a Wessexman or a Mercian or what not: temporarily, opportunistically.' In fact, by this stage in the essay he has already firmly established his attitude towards nationalist causes in general, particularly in an unjustly severe passage explicitly directed against nationalism and small nations, in which he complains:

> What a curse to the earth are small nations! Latvia, Lithuania, Poland, Finland, San Salvador, Luxembourg, Manchukuo, the Irish Free State. There are many more: there is an appalling number of disgusting little stretches of the globe claimed, occupied and infected by groupings of babbling little morons—babbling militant on the subjects (unendingly) of their *exclusive* cultures, their *exclusive* languages, their *national* souls, their *national* genius, their unique achievements in throat-cutting in this and that abominable little squabble in the past (SH, p 91).

George Malcolm Thomson, the dedicatee of *Cloud Howe*, thus seems totally justified in the confident statement he made to me when he wrote of Mitchell, 'I am sure he was not a Scottish Nationalist.'[15] Certainly in the essay on 'Glasgow', Mitchell is quite vitriolic in his criticism of political and cultural nationalism, the same sentiments being expressed in slightly milder form in his open letter to *The Free Man* titled 'News of Battle: Queries for Mr. Whyte'.[16] And yet although he was unreasonably prejudiced against nationalist movements, unquestionably Mitchell retained a spontaneous and genuine affection for his native land.

Mrs Mitchell told me that her husband 'was truly a Scot and as such proud of his country',[17] and the letters now held in The National Library of Scotland show that despite the wanderings which effectively separated Mitchell from his homeland from his early twenties until his death, he never finally burned his bridges for, as shown in his regular correspondence with his friend George MacDonald in Aberdeen and with Alexander Gray at Echt, his thoughts frequently turned to home. One particular letter written in 1929 gives a vividly explicit sense of Mitchell's yearning for his native land, the author observing, 'In five days I'll be in Scotland. And, though I keep a flippant tone, I do feel rather like a pilgrim to holy ground'; and this provokes the exclamation, 'What romantics we Scotsmen are!'.[18]

Mitchell's fiction also illustrates his pride in his country of origin, as an example of the process identified by Edwin Muir when he observed in *Scottish Journey* that, 'natural description, though a pleasant art, has something of make-believe in it; it pretends to reproduce a scene or a locality, but really expresses the writer's emotions'.[19] In this sense, *Sunset Song* constitutes just as emotional and explicit a tribute to his native Mearns as Mitchell's 1934 essay on 'The Land'; similarly, it is surely beyond coincidence that he should resort to this kind of landscape description throughout even his earliest published work, in the early novels *Stained Radiance, The Thirteenth Disciple* and *Image and Superscription*—all, significantly, boasting Scottish interludes. Occasionally Mitchell represents his feelings more directly in his English stories, referring knowingly in 'A Footnote to History' to 'that aching land-love inherited from generations of hillmen-peasants',[20] which surely harks back nostalgically to his own roots in the Mearns. And in 'The Epic' Mitchell sympathises with his expatriate narrator's innate sense of 'the quiet, secure things' of life, which he romantically defines as, 'autumn and stars and . . . English [sic] fields, and smell of ploughed lands, and kindly peasant song'.[21]

Thus, although he was not a Scottish Nationalist at any time in his life, Leslie Mitchell never ceased to feel emotionally and romantically attached to his native land.

A brief investigation of his views on art, language and history provides an especially useful pointer to his political opinions. As the poetry of MacDiarmid, Lewis, Spender and Auden and the drama of Yeats and O'Casey testifies, art was particularly closely linked with politics, both of a nationalist and a socialist character, in Britain in the early decades of this century. Mitchell's art was also largely politically orientated, and his political beliefs can be detected in his general artistic precepts.

In March 1934, in 'News of Battle: Queries for Mr. Whyte', Mitchell depicted himself 'living furth of Scotland, non-Nationalist, and yet interested in this new revival of cultural and political Nationalism', and throughout his life he remained basically neutral with regard to the idea of Scottish independence, with his interest in Scottish culture being restricted to similarly modest proportions. His mature opinions on cultural matters are largely traceable to the education he received as a child at the capable hands of Alexander Gray, for his school essay books indicate the solid grounding he was given in English and History in particular, and these essays also attest to the encouragement he received to write on cosmopolitan and universal themes, as well as purely local ones. This contributed significantly to the catholicity of the tastes he displayed later as an adult.

Mitchell's surviving library bears witness to a pervasive interest in those authors belonging to revolutionary, or at least innovatory, literary movements which consciously challenged traditionally accepted standards, such as Shelley and the Romantics, Rossetti and the Pre-Raphaelites, Gorky and the Socialist Realists, Morris, Wells, Shaw, and even, latterly, MacDiarmid himself. This, however, is the only uniform theme discernible throughout Leslie Mitchell's reading, and, apart from complimentary volumes from James Barke, Neil Gunn, Eric Linklater and MacDiarmid, his book collection contains only a few stray volumes by Scottish writers.

The simultaneous creation of the alter-ego of Lewis Grassic Gibbon and the publication of *Sunset Song* naturally had the effect of strengthening the connection between Mitchell and his native land, but this did not significantly affect his attitude to art or to politics. The celebrity of Grassic Gibbon put him in touch with the major luminaries of the Scottish Literary Renaissance in the thirties, including MacDiarmid, Gunn, Linklater, Compton MacKenzie, George Malcolm Thomson and Helen Cruickshank, and indeed, under the latter's influence, Lewis Grassic Gibbon eventually became a 'distinguished member' of the Scottish PEN Club.[22] Miss Cruickshank also tried to stimulate Mitchell's interest in Scottish culture by helping him to acquire books listed in James Thin's Scottish catalogue,[23] and her efforts appear to have been rewarded to some extent, for in his last year Mitchell worked as editor and coordinating force behind the series of books eventually published after his death by Routledge and Kegan Paul, under the general imprint of 'The Voice of Scotland'.

Although he became more interested in Scottish literature in his later years, Mitchell's own political and cultural attitudes remained firmly 'non-nationalist'. Thus, while he expressed the opinion in 1933 that 'There's still great poetry in Scotland',[24] he was unrelenting in his criticism of the Scottish Literary Renaissance. In one of his book reviews for *The Free Man*, for example, Mitchell comes dangerously close to biting the hand that was then feeding him, disparaging 'the funny little quarterlies which keep up an illiterate ape-chatter at the heels of the Scots Renaissance'.[25] He is just as forthright in the essay on 'Glasgow', in which he lambasts the self-indulgent Scots littérateur who 'turns to culture for comfort' and 'cultivates aesthetic objectivity as happier men cultivate beards or gardens' (*SH*, pp 84–5); and the author is even more outspoken in his private correspondence, when he refers to the Scottish cultural revival in his much-quoted—and much toned-down—letter to Helen Cruickshank (*See* n 12). For this reason, MacDiarmid elicits praise in *The Free Man* as the fearless maverick who spurned the insular comforts of the established Scottish literary fold in the bold attempt to force his native land out of itself and connect it with broader universal standards. And Mitchell's approval of this endeavour can be seen in his quietly nostalgic account of his first personal meeting with Grieve himself, which presents them as kindred spirits attempting 'to form a section of the Revolutionary Writers of the World'.[26]

The sins of ideological complacency and social dishonesty which both Mitchell and Grieve most vehemently denounced in their respective attempts to raise modern Scottish literary standards are twin targets in an unpublished manuscript by Mitchell, in which he systematically attacks the stereotyped figure of Wallace Mongour, as dilettante representative of the contemporary Scottish literary establishment, by subjecting him to cruelly satiric caricature. This multi-racial literary editor of a London Magazine is condemned for exploiting Scottishness in a mercenary and patronising fashion, by regularly producing novels 'dealing with Scots life and based on intimate study of the works of the minor German dramatists, with which he is well acquainted'. The satire continues remorselessly:

> Every three years [he] produces a new book of verse. As literary editor of the "London Looker-on" he has done more than any other to keep alive interest in the Scots Renaissance, and in his charming home in Hampstead [he] has become the centre of the movement.
> His opinion on Lowland Scots as a literary medium is considered and definite. Relating it, I wish it were possible to reproduce the speaker's pleasing, if slightly sheep-like voice. "Heh-eh. An excellent medium (bleat) for describing the ruder humours of the bothy, heh-eh! But quite inadequate to deal with the more subtle problems of the emotions (bleat) because it has not the necessary exactitude."[27]

Wallace Mongour is a fairly savage creation, and yet there is more than a grain of truth in the satire, for thinly veiled references to some of Mitchell's eminent contemporaries in the field of Scottish letters can be identified in the portrait. Edwin Muir was particularly renowned for his interest in German literature. George Malcolm Thomson was a possible butt for the jibe directed at the organiser who conducts his campaign on behalf of Scots literature from 'his charming home in Hampstead'. And Eric Linklater, who was rebuked by Mitchell in 'Literary Lights' for his '*ex cathedra* judgement upon it [Scots] as "inadequate to deal with the finer shades of emotion" ' (*SH*, p 145) is the most likely target of Mitchell's linguistic criticism.

More importantly, however, this satirical composite emphasises Mitchell's enduring pride in Scottish culture, the inference being that Scotland *is* still capable of producing great art, although the author sees this emerging from a more spontaneous and indigenously Scottish source than, to his way of thinking, the self-conscious and rather insincere attempt being made at that time to foster a Scottish literary renaissance. In this way, Mitchell the radical and scholarly cosmopolite can, with little ideological modification, transmute into Grassic Gibbon, the quintessential but equally demanding Scot. Like

MacDiarmid, Mitchell was at times fiercely Scottish, and the ardency of this feeling prevented him from merely wallowing in Scottish cultural traditions, but encouraged him to extend and update them, to seek MacDiarmid's famous Precedents, with the aim of bringing literary Scotland into line with the rest of the world.

Mitchell never allowed his interest in Scottish literary matters to interfere with his political opinions, however, and even when he was writing to C M Grieve on the publisher's plans for the forthcoming 'Voice of Scotland' series, he defined his political stance of 'reformer' in completely unambiguous terms, informing his friend:

> You and I, alas, are the only communists. I tried to foist James Barke upon them, but they wouldn't have it. However, I imagine we'll keep the red flag flying pretty efficaciously. . . .[28]

In fact, Mitchell's general views on art reflect his overriding concern with radical political movements and his personal detachment from nationalist affairs. Although he himself wrote certain novels and stories of an escapist character, he relentlessly pilloried all basically trite or superficial art forms, whether literary or visual, and whether of an escapist or an esoteric nature. His own aesthetic aims were firmly harnessed to contemporary reality, and accordingly in 'Literary Lights' he praises MacDiarmid and Lewis Spence as true poets, 'in the sense that life, not editors or anthologists, demand [sic] of them their poetry' (SH, p 152). In his final published work, Mitchell denounces the contemporary cinema for this very reason, for its tendency either to ignore or pervert and distort reality: he follows his characteristically idealistic definition of the function of art—to present 'the free and undefiled illusion'—with a vituperative description of the cinematic muse as being 'clad not even in reach-me-downs', and he goes on to extend the metaphor, contending that, instead, 'she is tarred and feathered or sprayed with saccharine in the likeness of a Christmas cake; and unendingly, instead of walking fearless and free, she sidles along with her hands disposed in a disgustingly Rubens-like gesture'.[29]

The honesty of portrayal which Mitchell calls for inevitably centres upon social reality, and he focuses particularly sharply upon the dichotomy between the rival social states of freedom and oppression. Again in his article criticising the modern cinema he complains that the viewer is never shown either heaven or hell as it exists for him on earth, in the shape of 'the Punak of Borneo, a quarter of a million of them, naked, cultureless, happy, the last folk of the Golden Age; or the dead cities of Northern England, cities of more dreadful night than that dreamt by Thomson'.[30]

In his essay on 'The Antique Scene', this social concern promotes the conclusion that 'all art is no more than the fine savour and essence of the free life' (SH, p 137), and this celebration of freedom is envisaged being performed either positively, by idealistic representation, or negatively, by the condemnation of oppression. Social and political issues thus lie at the very heart of Mitchell's work, and in the statement of faith which the social destitution of Glasgow elicits from him in his profile of the city, aesthetic concerns are firmly subordinated to social ones, with the welfare of the individual and of the poor folk of the slums in general being given top priority:

> There is nothing in culture or art that is worth the life and elementary happiness of one of those thousands who rot in the Glasgow slums. There is nothing in science or religion. . . . For the cleansing of that horror . . . I would welcome the English in suzerainty over Scotland till the end of time. I would welcome the end of Braid Scots and Gaelic, our culture, our history, our nationhood under the heels of a Chinese army of occupation if it could cleanse the Glasgow slums, give a surety of food and play—the elementary right of every human being—to those people of the abyss . . . (SH, p 87).

This is the uncompromising attitude of the humanist for whom his own literary endeavours are, along with all other aesthetic considerations, of minor importance in comparison with social concerns. In fact, Mitchell constantly emphasised the priority of life itself over art, and he considered that to ignore the demands of life in art was the ultimate abuse of its power. Eventually he came to regard art as a highly demonstrative tool, a valuable social weapon, and this idea culminated in the belief expressed in his portrait of C M Grieve, that 'all good art is propaganda'. Seventeen months later, he expanded this observation in a letter written to *The Left Review* in which he proclaimed, 'I am a revolutionary writer', explaining, 'I hate capitalism; all my books are explicit or implicit propaganda', although he added the proviso that, 'because I'm a revolutionist I see no reason for gainsaying my own critical judgement'. Despite these reservations, however, Mitchell made a noble effort to streamline the manifesto of the British revolutionary writers, and his plan of action contains the committed aim, to 'be a shock brigade of writers'.[31]

Leslie Mitchell thus came to view his art as an expression and an extension of his radical political opinions, and therefore his functional approach to literature stands in stark contrast with the attitude held by Neil Gunn, for whom art represented a heightening of reality rather than the propagandist act of candid simulation favoured by Mitchell.[32]

Mitchell's views on art thus establish the importance he attached to his political role of left-wing 'reformer', indicating that he placed Scotland within a commendably wide political and cultural context.

In 'Literary Lights', Mitchell presents English as a language which is unnatural to Scotsmen, and he shows the demands that the effort of writing in orthodox English makes upon Scottish writers, commenting, 'it is as though the writer did not *write* himself, but *translated* himself' (SH, p 144). In addition to his interest in Scots literature, as the fiction of Grassic Gibbon clearly indicates, Mitchell was also naturally fond of the Scots language, and in his first novel he looks upon Scots as the appropriate medium for the description of the experience of Scots life itself. Thea Mayven remarks how:

> She found herself remembering long-forgotten words of the good Scots, canty, lightsome words and jingles, things with old laughter and the smell of the peats and sea in them; darksome old words like clamjamfried and glaur and greep, words

wrought for the bitter winter nights by the plodding peasants of the Eastern seacoast . . . (*SR*, p 215).

As a Scottish writer, Mitchell personally appreciated the general condition subsequently analysed by Edward Sapir and Benjamin Lee Whorf (and embodied in the theory which has become known as the Sapir-Whorf hypothesis) which preserves the basic idea of the semantic inviolability of individual languages, and which finally makes a philosophical connection between the structure of individual languages and the attitudes and behaviour of individual races.[33] In his Scottish fiction Mitchell actively sought to overcome the stultifying artificiality of English and create a more responsive prose style by the measured use of native Scots words and phrases. Thus, the author describes his technique in 'Literary Lights' as being 'to mould the English language into the rhythms and cadences of Scots spoken speech, and to inject into the English vocabulary such minimum number of words from Braid Scots as that remodelling requires' (*SH*, p 154). Grassic Gibbon's linguistic approach succeeds because rather than constituting an insular, static act of aesthetic withdrawal, it involves a dynamic and inventive process of compromise.

In his Scottish fiction, therefore, Mitchell is not retreating from English or trying to create a Scottish alternative as such to English prose. Rather, his aim is to stimulate English by imparting to it distinctive Scots words and phrases which have no semantic parallel. His attitude to English is completely free of hostile nationalist sentiment, indeed he invariably praised the English language, describing it in 'Glasgow', for example, as, 'that lovely and flexible instrument, so akin to the darker Braid Scots' (*SH*, p 92). In his prefatory note to *Sunset Song*, Mitchell shows deference towards 'the great English tongue', politely asking for 'latitude', 'forbearance' and 'courtesy' in prospect of his impending experiment to 'import into his pages some score or so untranslatable words and idioms', and confining this exercise to limits which are felt to be 'in fairness to his hosts' (*SO*, p 14).

The American edition of *Sunset Song* emphasises that, far from being obscurantist, Mitchell's linguistic enterprise was designed as an aid rather than a hindrance to universal expression and comprehension. The author professes the hope in his initial 'Note the reader is advised to read' that his dialectal innovations will prove self-explanatory and will finally provide an 'enrichment' of the English language for his American readers.[34] Accordingly, he apologises for the hundred-word glossary appended to this edition of the book, which is itself introduced later on in the volume as a rather spurious and redundant feature, the author commented tersely:

> As implied in the note at the beginning of this book, most of the Scots words are untranslatable except in their context setting. Otherwise there would have been little point in using them: English would have served, as elsewhere. So the following "translations" are very faulty—the English a mere approximation to the Scots.[35]

However, although this Scots vocabulary is presented as 'untranslatable', in the prefatory note the author expresses the hope that it will nevertheless prove to be readily understandable even to American English speakers, advising:

. . . should the context refuse to give up the meaning of a Scots word used, the reader may turn to the Glossary. But the author hopes that that will be seldom: the author, indeed, has quite failed in his purpose if the Glossary proves a pressing need.

Finally, Mitchell stresses again that his exploitation of the Scots vernacular is not gratuitous, but that potentially his native language is of value to English in general as a complement and an embellishment, 'For the author . . . can be best regarded as a sagaman arrived in the house of the English with the salvage of his own ruined house of words; and the tongue of his hosts, so it seems to him, may be yet enriched with this salvage of words that are only half-alien.' The theory certainly seems to have worked in practice, as the vernacular used in the Grassic Gibbon fiction is readily accessible, especially in comparison with the obscure idiomatic constituents of a poem such as MacDiarmid's 'A Drunk Man Looks at the Thistle', or the difficult Doric dialogue of William Alexander's *Johhny Gibb of Gushetneuk* and William P Milne's *Eppie Elrick*.

Leslie Mitchell's intentions in deploying and promoting his native Scots tongue are certainly not nationalist, although they do reflect his general fondness for Scotland. True to character, his attitude to Braid Scots is ultimately—to employ the author's own terminology—cosmopolitan.

Mitchell showed a lasting interest in scientific experiments geared towards the creation of an international language. Ravelston, the hero of the story 'Cockcrow', works diligently towards this end, and *Gay Hunter* contains passing references to Esperanto and Volapuk (*GH*, p 134), the two famous attempts to create an artifical language of international standing. Similarly, Mitchell's own aim, to create a universally intelligible prose style which retained a distinctively Scottish flavour, was itself part of a greater scheme of a polyglot character. In the long term, he saw this experiment as an elementary step towards his ideal of a cosmopolitan language, which is finally foreseen, in the essay on 'Glasgow', as a synthesis incorporating the best features of the individual tongues of the world, the ultimate objective being to create the conditions whereby man 'sings his epics in a language moulded from the best on earth' (*SH*, p 93). Mitchell's natural affection for his native tongue subsequently manifests itself in a typically cosmopolitan manner, the author ascribing to the Scots language a major role in this universal hybrid, affirming, 'I think the Braid Scots may yet give lovely lights and shadows not only to English but to the perfected speech of Cosmopolitan Man: so I cultivate it, for lack of that perfect speech that is yet to be.'

Mitchell's attitude to language thus confirms his tendency to look beyond Scotland and indicates the universal scope of his vision. His championing of Scots has a more precise significance as a pointer to his political opinions, however, in signifying the proletarian character of his sympathies. For just as MacDiarmid pointed out in his introduction to *The Golden Treasury of Scottish Poetry*,[36] so Mitchell also appreciated the importance of Scots in modern times as the language of the lower classes, identifying Braid Scots in 'Literary Lights' as 'the speech of bed and board and street and plough' (*SH*, p 145). Thus, class questions were uppermost in his mind even when he was considering Scotland itself.

While MacDiarmid contrived to be both a Communist and a Nationalist —sometimes even simultaneously—Mitchell's patriotic feelings actually existed in a degree and form permitted by the Manifesto of the Communist Party itself. According to this tract, nationalist sentiment is not wholly incompatible with communism, Marx and Engels conceding that:

> Though not in substance, yet in form, the struggle of the proletariat with the bourgeoisie is at first a national struggle. The proletariat of each country must, of course, first of all settle matters with its own bourgeoisie.[37]

This was probably one of the few political works with which Mitchell was intimately acquainted, and subsequently he obeyed the decrees of the Manifesto to the letter with regard to the national assertion of communism. The doubts he voiced to Neil Gunn as to whether 'you can ever have Nationalism without Communism' evidently reigned supreme; and this is confirmed by his attitude to Scottish history.

Leslie Mitchell showed great interest in all world history, as his book on the ancient Mayan civilization, his final published book on international feats of exploration and his unfulfilled aims to write a *History of Mankind* all demonstrate. Throughout these projects, Mitchell pursues, or intended to pursue, a liberally Marxist approach (although this is modified by his diffusionist sympathies), the author concentrating in particular upon class struggles, upon acts of tyranny and upon the welfare of the lower classes in general. In fact, his assertion in the synopsis for the final chapter of his *Story of Religion* that, 'human history is the history of class war'[38] paraphrases the opening sentence of *The Communist Manifesto* itself: 'The history of all hitherto existing society is the history of class struggles.'

Mitchell's historico-political stance is most concisely represented in 'The Antique Scene', a summary of the development of the Scots nation. The summary is dominated and determined by an acute sense of class consciousness; famous people and events from ancient to modern times are judged in accordance with their ultimate effect upon the 'common folk'. This essay is more important as a vehicle for a political thesis than as an objective historical review. Thus, while Scotland's birth as a civilised nation is introduced with a degree of cynicism orthodox for a confirmed diffusionist, early primitive disputes are resolved in a straightforward socialist manner, with the Kelt being derided on class grounds, as 'a typical aristocrat' who enslaved the Pictish people (*SH*, p 129). Indeed, the Pictish and Celtic races are both glibly apprehended as the antagonists in the historical conflict between slave and oppressor.

These priorities persist in Mitchell's judgement of more modern events. The War of Independence is presented as the individual high-water mark of Scottish history, prompting the author to enthuse that 'Scotland was the home of true political nationalism (once a liberating influence, not as now an inhibiting one)'. A qualification is imposed by Mitchell's revolutionary and egalitarian sympathies: 'not the nationalism forced upon an unwilling or indifferent people by the intrigues of kings and courtesans, but the spontaneous uprising of an awareness of blood-brotherhood and freedom-right' (*SH*, p 131)—the proletariat of Scotland 'settling matters with its own bourgeoisie' in true Marxist manner. Thus the author signifies the relevance of the title of Wallace's force, 'Army of the Commons of Scotland', and proclaims the leader, newly dubbed Guardian of Scotland, 'a great republican with the first of the great republican titles' (*SH*, p 132) who completely overshadows his successor, the aristocratic self-seeker, Robert the Bruce. The ideal of a Scottish Republic is not an end in itself, however, for six pages later it is sublimated into an expression of the 'Greater Republicanism' which is presented as a transitory stage towards the ultimate aim of cosmopolitanism.

Recent history is treated in much the same vein. The Highland Clearances and the Industrial Revolution are both denounced for 'enriching the new plutocracy and brutalizing the ancient plebs' (*SH*, p 141). And the conclusion of the essay, dealing with Scotland from early Victorian times to the time of writing, builds up to a passionate Marxist condemnation of the whole capitalist system as its exists not just in Scotland but throughout the world. Mitchell observes sadly:

> It is a hundred and fifty years of unloveliness and pridelessness, of growing wealth and growing impoverishment, of Scotland sharing in the rise and final torturing maladjustments of that economic system which holds all the modern world in thrall (*SH*, p 141).

Two of the main unfinished projects that Mitchell was working on immediately before his death involve major Scottish themes, and examination of the surviving manuscripts for the projected study of Wallace and the planned fictional trilogy about the Scottish Covenanters confirms that the author's spontaneous affection for his native land was always kept firmly in check, especially when he came to consider social and political issues.

The ten-page sketch which is all that remains of the Wallace biography corresponds almost exactly with the portrayal of Wallace given in 'The Antique Scene'. This highlights the author's affiliation with Marxist-Leninism in his overwhelming desire for a supreme champion to lead the mass rebellion, and it also demonstrates the main area of Mitchell's interest, for Wallace, like Spartacus or Ewan Tavendale or even Lenin himself, emerges as a people's champion whose aim is not just national independence but social equality, and who is therefore represented directing his army not against the forces of national subordination, but against those of social oppression. Wallace, then, is a 'popular' hero in the true sense of the term, for 'the nobles hated him because of his love of the lowly, the peasant folk who flocked by his stirrup'.[39] His following, therefore, his 'army of commons', is presented as quintessentially proletarian.

However, Wallace is not merely associated with the lower classes; like Spartacus and Ewan, he is identified with them symbolically, and he also receives a heightened awareness of his political mission, realising:

> Yet though the nobles surrendered, he might not, he was the Commons' man, every face he looked at in the opening of an earth-house was the face, it seemed to him, of

a wronged and bitter brother, it seemed to him every starving woman he met in the lee of a burned and ruined toun was mother of his, her breasts his succour in childhood's blood, night and day nothing to him of it left him not free for the love and ease of his ain countree. And they hid him and loved him, hated him also, he was to them that quenchless spirit that would not die, that would not let them cry "Enough! We surrender; we'll turn to ease and peace and leave your Southron men the land to call yours."

Thus, although Mitchell is here pursuing the idea of freedom within a Scottish setting, Wallace's compassion is identical to that of Spartacus, and the theme remains primarily social, and universal. Hence, the Wallace biography, far from being nationalist, promised to be egalitarian, proletarian, and essentially Marxist.

The contrasting views expressed by two of his compeers on this subject help to clarify Mitchell's own position. Neil Gunn, who argued regularly in his correspondence with Mitchell over the respective merits of nationalism and communism, makes no distinction at all in his short tale 'The Ghost's Story' between Wallace and Bruce, who are simply united under a nationalist banner as champions who both fought for the cause of Scottish indepen-dence.[40] Thus, Gunn's patriotic leanings lead him to ignore the class differences between Wallace, the bona-fide altruistic leader of the Scottish people, and Bruce, the aristocratic leader of the Scottish nobles who subsequently assumed monarchic power by fairly undemocratic means. However, to James Barke, a devoted Communist whose immediate ideological affinity with the author of *Spartacus* and *A Scots Quair* was readily acknowledged by Mitchell himself, this social contrast is of paramount importance. Thus, in his autobiography, Barke apportions a substantial share of the blame for the decline of the Scottish nation to 'the Anglo-Norman adventurer Robert de Brus', who 'defeated the Scotland of William Wallace'.[41] His tack, like Mitchell's, is that Scotland's most famous heroes are pitted against each other, and the final conclusion is inevitable, Barke proclaiming, 'William Wallace was our greatest national hero, a hero who had struggled for our national independence at the head of the common people.'[42]

Mitchell's concept of freedom as embodied by Wallace is thus a projection of his egalitarian sympathies and an expression of his communist principles. And his interpretation of the story of the Covenanters seems destined to have followed a similar course, with the author inclining towards a distinctly proletarian point of view. The working title for this Grassic Gibbon novel, 'Men of the Mearns', intimates the author's primarily socialist interest in his material, and indeed the Covenanters are introduced in the Wallace manuscript rekindling the very same torch as that which was brandished by Wallace himself, Mitchell describing how he 'rode from that field [Falkirk], and not again, tell on the tale, did the Commons of Scotland gather to battle under their ain folk till the Covenanting times'.

Although the two main fiction works which Mitchell happened to be involved with at the time of his death both concern Scottish historical themes, the line of approach the author indicated he intended to take is very much in keeping with the attitudes he expressed in his published work. Mitchell's campaign for human rights included, but extended beyond, his native land.

Nevertheless, there seems to be some element of truth in Hugh MacDiarmid's allegation to Douglas Young that, just before he died, Mitchell 'declared himself an out-and-out Scottish Republican'.[43] Early in 1933, Mitchell told a reporter semi-jocularly that he would return to his homeland 'when there's a Scots Republic',[44] but in his profile of C M Grieve published six months later in *The Free Man*, he looks forward confidently and seriously to the time 'When we have our Scots Republic'. However, the essay on 'The Antique Scene' indicates that this aim of a Scots Republic was more important to Mitchell for its radicalism than for its nationalism, and the aim of the Scots Republic is presented as a local manifestation of the spirit of 'the Greater Republicanism' which Mitchell apprehended as the corollary to the Covenanters' struggles, as an ideal of a universal dimension.

Mitchell's world view is not internationalist, however, for in the essay on 'Glasgow' he observes that his social and political objectives can be realised only upon the complete abolition of national boundaries. As Jean Renoir reflected in his stirring pacifist feature film from 1937, *La Grande Illusion*, internationalism still preserves the idea of national identity. Mitchell rejects this attitude as well, concluding:

> Glasgow's salvation, Scotland's salvation, the world's salvation lies in neither nationalism nor internationalism, those twin halves of an idiot whole. It lies in ultimate cosmopolitanism, the earth the City of God, the Brahmaputra and Easter Island as free and familiar to the man from Govan as the Molendinar and Bute. A time will come when the self-wrought, prideful differentiations of Scotsman, Englishman, Frenchman, Spaniard will seem as ludicrous as the infantile squabblings of the Heptarchians. A time will come when nationalism, with other cultural abberrations, will have passed from the human spirit, when Man, again free and unchained, has all the earth for his footstool . . . (*SH*, pp 92–3).

This rather romantic vision evidently had a strong hold upon Mitchell's imagination for in 'News of Battle: Queries for Mr. Whyte' he goes through exactly the same procedure of rejecting out of hand the more extreme demands made by the Scottish Nationalists before proffering in their stead 'the vision of Cosmopolis, the City of God'. And although this vision of Cosmopolis has an idealistic quality, nevertheless it is firmly sustained by the two political creeds which Mitchell promotes within this universal context—those of anarchism and communism.

ANARCHISM

The work of the nineteenth century Anarchist philosophers like Proudhon, Kropotkin and Bakunin may lack the scientific discipline of Marxist dogma, yet their writing is arguably as important as Marxist literature in its impassioned defence of the basic human values of freedom and equality. The radical doctrines of anarchism have proved especially attractive to modern Scottish writers, Neil Gunn and Hugh MacDiarmid both having drawn inspiration from this source in the fight against poverty and oppression. Indeed, in *The Serpent* Gunn quotes Michael Bakunin—or 'St. Bakunin', as Mitchell canonises him in 'Glasgow' (*SH*, p 89)—on the count that 'liberty without socialism means privilege, socialism without liberty means slavery and brutality'.[45] While Bakunin himself became progressively more critical of Marxist theory, however, anarchism is more often acclaimed as a radical political alternative, or a complement, to communism, and this is the sense in which Leslie Mitchell understood it, for in the role of social 'reformer' his egalitarian sympathies went hand in hand with his libertarianism, with a sensibility which can loosely be termed anarchist. Quite simply, Mitchell's ideal of universal equality was sought in full recognition of the rights of the individual.

In *Scottish Scene*, MacDiarmid accepts the compatability of anarchist and communist dogma, calling himself 'an Anarchist', but confessing, 'equally, of course, I am at present a member of the Communist Party'.[46] The Communist Party itself would disapprove of this association, but communism and anarchism are undeniably closely related, both in their criticism of the capitalist system and in the objectives they outline for the future organisation of society. The communist ideal of a classless society as it is embodied in the vision of the millennium has an obvious correspondence with the anarchist aim of social freedom, and Bakunin's theoretical realisation of this objective has an exceptionally strong affinity with the Marxist model, the Russian author writing:

The future organisation of society should be carried out entirely from below upwards, by the free association and federation of the workers, in associations first of all, then in communes [*sic*], in regions, in nations, and, finally, in a great international and universal federation. It is then only that the true and invigorating order of liberty and general happiness will be established, that order which, far from denying either of them, affirms and brings into harmony the interests of individuals and of society.[47]

As Peter Kropotkin observed, the importance of Morris's *News From Nowhere*, highly regarded by Mitchell, is that it offers a vision of an anarchist utopia, of the 'days of freedom' lurking in the future. Yet Morris called himself a socialist—indeed he had strong Marxist sympathies—and accordingly, like Mitchell later, he sought both to encourage social equality and to safeguard the freedom of the individual. These two ideals are in evidence in Mitchell's work in one particular paragraph in 'The Antique Scene' in which first the Scots people are applauded for the traditional protection of 'the rights of the individual' and then the clan system operating in the Highlands is commended as 'a communistic patriarchy' (*SH*, p 133). Mitchell, in fact, was interested in anarchism both for providing a model for the perfect society and as a creed which asserted the rights of the individual.

Dorothy Tweed remembers that 'Mitchell forecast that Fascism would probably sweep the world, then Communism, and Anarchism would follow that'.[48] This anarchist ideal figures prominently in Mitchell's work. In his non-fiction especially, he promotes the ultimate aim of freedom exhaustively, celebrating in his essay on 'Glasgow' (SH, p 88), 'the clean anarchy which is the essence of life', and condemning in Nine Against the Unknown, the atrocities hypocritically carried out in the name of civilisation by such illustrious historical figures as Lief Ericsson, Cabeza de Vaca, Magellan and Columbus—this in stark contrast with his enduring belief in 'the philosophy of Anarchism' (NAU, p 125).

As Douglas Young has shown in his study, Mitchell's political credo found substantial relief in the diffusionist view of history. Indeed, the diffusionist concept of the Golden Age offered Mitchell a concrete model for the ideal society. Unlike Edwin Muir's utopia which is described in Muir's auto-biography as some kind of psychic state, Mitchell's Golden Age has a strong physical property, finally embodying the twin social aims of universal freedom and equality. In this vision of the past, the communist ideal is accommodated by the ideal of anarchy. Mitchell writes in the Anarchist periodical The Twentieth Century in 1932:

> And they [primitive men] co-operated in matters of mutual group life as a colony of modern anarchists might co-operate—without the merging of individuality in any group-consciousness.[49]

However, diffusionism is not merely a retrospective vision, Edwin Muir himself, for example, observing its constructive capacity when he recalled his own interest in it as a historical vision which lay behind many ideologies, 'up to modern Socialism'.[50] Similarly, Mitchell also applies the diffusionist perspective to the present and the future, envisaging his anarchist utopia with particular clarity in the concluding paragraph of the Twentieth Century article quoted above, in which he proclaims—

> [Prometheus's] social state was anarcho-communism, not communism. Prometheus —the Natural Man of the world's future—will plant his trees and gaze at his stars and explore his atom, apart, alone, unafraid, no half-wit mental hermaphrodite with his consciousness mislaid in some fast-glued intertidal human scum a-squatter on the beaches of the universe. His benevolence towards his fellow-beings will be natural, individual, thalamic. His kingdom will be Self.

Mitchell may describe this vision as anarcho-communist, but his anarchist principles all but engulf his communist sympathies in this instance.

The political ramifications of diffusionist doctrine were not lost on Mitchell, and its ethnological principles actually did much to confirm him in his modern role of 'reformer'. Thus, the vision of the utopian society of the future provided in Gay Hunter is virtually synonymous with the past arcadia represented in Three Go Back. The chief tenets of diffusionism conform with the political directives of both anarchism and communism, and yet it would be misleading simply to cast Mitchell as an anarcho-communist, for he did not hold the two creeds in equal respect. His priorities, in actual fact, have much in common with those of MacDiarmid, who reflects in Lucky Poet that for him Communism represents 'a stage on the way to Anarchism', albeit 'a necessary and indispensable stage'.[51]

Mitchell's aims likewise extend beyond the promises of communism, again to anarchism. His ideal, in which all men live in happy communal freedom, endures unchanged throughout his work. Thus he, like Kropotkin, ultimately demands the abolition of property rather than the Marxist redistribution of wealth, and finally, in accordance with the original meaning of the word anarchy, he calls for the abolition of all constitutional and legislative ruling, eventually seeking what is effectively an apolitical state. In 'The Antique Scene' Mitchell thus surveys the anarchistic order of the early Scottish hunters with his customary sense of longing, yearning for a wholesome form of existence which, like theirs, is 'without religion or social organization' (*SH*, p 125). And in a fairly orthodox idealisation of primitive society which appears in *The Lost Trumpet*, not even communism is tolerated, Dr Adrian including this in his catalogue of social disorders resulting from the chance discovery of agriculture (*LT*, p 138). As a formal political dogma, therefore, not even communism escapes Mitchell's abolitionist wrath; in the final analysis, it must disappear from the ideal society of the future along with all the other maladies of modern civilisation.

Thus Mitchell's ideal state, in which all men are both free and equal, endures unchanged throughout his work. And yet the means he considers for achieving this state tend to fluctuate. The early novels are inconclusive on this score, and the imaginative romances are downright evasive. Sometimes, as in *The Thirteenth Disciple*, the goal seems attainable only through individual effort, but in *Spartacus* and *A Scots Quair*, Mitchell considers the possibility of a universally liberating concerted effort; and this effort he identifies as communism. So it is paradoxical that, although the author's ideal is apolitical in essence, he finds it necessary to adopt a militant political stance to bring this aim of universal freedom into being, to call for the enlargement of the powers of the State in order to produce its abolition. Hence Mitchell advocates Marxist violence, as opposed to Proudhon's pacific methods, to destroy capitalist society as a necessary prerequisite to the eventual establishment of an anarchist state. As Kleon the political theorist says to Spartacus, 'We must destroy before we build' (*Spart*, p 125).

COMMUNISM

Leslie Mitchell's connection with the Communist Party goes back to his days as an impressionable young reporter in Aberdeen, when the enthusiasm generated by the Russian Revolution encouraged him to join the first Aberdeen Soviet. Inevitably, his attitude to communism changed over the years, but Mitchell retained an active interest in communist ideology until his death.

The idealism latent in Mitchell's early involvement with radical politics appears to have subsided when he encountered the full force of urban decay in Glasgow, and although he evidently recaptured his earlier optimism in later years this was mostly confined to the implicitly anarchist sentiments expressed in his diffusionist apologias. Accordingly, communism became more important to him as a system offering the means to achieve his personal political objectives than as a vision embodying these ends themselves.

Mitchell's moral sensitivity and his social awareness were the sustaining forces behind his political attitudes, and the extremism of his political stance is largely attributable to the intense compassion he felt for the poor and downtrodden. The letters he wrote to Mr and Mrs Gray and to George MacDonald show that he remained emotionally and intellectually committed to the cause of the 'common folk' throughout the twenties and thirties. After the initial euphoria of the Bolshevik Revolution had died down, and even following his disturbing experience of post-war Glasgow, he expressed his enduring faith in 'the ultimate coming of Communism',[52] and in the same letter, written in 1924, he recorded his sympathy for striking transport workers in the south of England. In addition, Mitchell's poems, most of which probably date from the twenties, reveal that although he was never deeply read in socialist literature he was well acquainted with socialist lore and history, and his interest in the Paris Commune of 1871, and in Lenin, Rosa Luxemburg and Karl Liebknecht, and indeed in Spartacus, provides telling evidence with regard to his political sympathies at this time (see Appendix A).

The letters written to the Grays are of a similar temper, with the author condemning the Tory government in December 1926,[53] and three years later the sobering effect of the failure of the General Strike in 1926 is still strongly felt in his denunciation of the Labour Party, the author asking his old teacher disdainfully:

> What do you think of those snivelling Labourists? Safety first! Keep out M. Trotsky —a dangerous revolutionist, and whatever would the *Morning Post* say? Keep down the school-leaving age—the dear industrialists will still require cheap labour. Persecute the unemployed like criminals—good for them. . . . Swine![54]

Deteriorating social conditions and the failure of the General Strike combined to boost the Communist Party in the late twenties, and Mitchell's own response to these events was in line with this wider pattern. His essay on 'Glasgow' fully captures the distress he felt at contemporary social conditions, while the profile of Ramsay MacDonald records his disillusionment with the Labour Party. And although it was not really until the early thirties that Mitchell fully regained his belief in the communist struggle, this response can still be attributed in large part to the social and political conditions prevailing in Britain from the late twenties onwards.

The essays in *Scottish Scene* provide proof that Mitchell's political allegiances hardened in his later years, for Marxist ideas are at work in 'The Antique Scene', 'Glasgow', and even the study of 'Religion'. It is in this latter essay that his Marxist sympathies can be seen most clearly threatening to outgrow his diffusionist sentiments. His confidence in the inevitability of the disappearance of the traditional religions from the modern scene has moved away from the diffusionist conviction of their absence from the Golden Age of the past, to the fundamental Marxist belief in their transience within the universal dialectic of change, 'immutable and unstayable' (*SH*, p 170). And although Mitchell supports the major British socialist movements in general in his portrait of Ramsay MacDonald, he constantly evokes scorn for all political moderatism. Socialism is tolerated for its ideals but affably rejected on account of its mildness, lacking as it does the incisiveness of communist method.

It is unlikely that the precise details of Mitchell's involvement with the official Communist Party will ever be known now, and I have been completely frustrated in my efforts to trace his movements, even with the aid of both the Communist Party of Great Britain and the Scottish Communist Party themselves. Finlay Hart could offer no concrete proof, but told me he felt that, 'had he been a member of the Party in Scotland [I] would have known'.[55] And Betty Reid, of the British Executive, also handicapped by the lack of records concerning membership, was forced to resort to personal memory, observing to me that, 'I did have a firm impression that he had been a member of the Party at some time, and that there were some problems which I have now forgotten which caused him to leave the Party.'[56]

.I have already shown the unreliability of Mitchell's acquaintances as witnesses for his political views, but his own work provides some indication of his mounting interest in communism. *Stained Radiance* considers radical political involvement as a means of solving the pressing social problems of the late twenties, and although the author adopts a rather ambiguous approach to both communism and anarchism, there is a perceptible hardening in his attitudes as they appear in this book especially when compared with the mild socialist sentiments expressed two years earlier in *Hanno*. In the early portions of his first novel, Koupa, who calls himself 'a child of Change' (*SR*, p 95), and Storman, the hard-line Leninist who condemns one woman as a 'Morrisy revolutionary' (*SR*, p 139), are Marxist pedagogues. Midway through the book the Communists are dissociated from the Labour Party, whose members are condemned in a series of sardonic political cameos reminiscent of portions of *Grey Granite*, expressing the author's general disenchantment with the traditional political parties. At this point, the Bolshevik model offers the inspiration for the 'accurate blue-printing of a project' (*SR*, p 166), but towards the end of the novel Storman's disenchantment with communism encourages him to view this experiment very differently, as he sadly relates in his letter of resignation:

In Russia, a Communist state, I saw the same purposeless disorder as rules in capitalist England; I saw the same aimless enslavement to an archaic economic machine; I saw a ruling-class—the Communist Party—in power—a class differing in no fundamentals from those ruling elsewhere. I saw Communism in operation as merely one more refutation of the belief that betterment is a thing capable of achievement by any mass action (*SR*, pp 275–6).

Such a passage is not far away from the post-Stalinist response articulated from the late thirties onwards by novelists like Arthur Koestler and George Orwell but, although Mitchell habitually kept his communist sympathies on a tight rein, it is well to remember that Storman's opinion does not necessarily represent Mitchell's own viewpoint. Indeed, Storman's individualistic perspective is finally counterbalanced, if not actually outweighed, by Garland's acceptance of the communist mandate; and in *Image and*

Superscription the Russian Revolution and its aftermath are seen in a much more praiseworthy light, Gershom Jezreel relating enthusiastically how 'In Russia Revolution had come, the officers done down, the fighting finished, peace, rest, and ease from the fear of death had come there for all men' (*IS*, p 210).

Spartacus and *A Scots Quair* are obviously Mitchell's two most intensely political works, and I will deal with these in full when I turn to his fiction. However, these works do reflect what we know of the author's political persuasion at this time. Mitchell's closest friends from the thirties have all observed the severe edge to his character in his later years, Dorothy Tweed remembering 'how perturbed he would be at stories of distress, and how intolerant he was of movements which sought to patch up instead of purging the social system of its evils',[57] and Neil Gunn venturing the opinion in a letter to Mitchell that, 'You sound intolerant of all gradualism.'[58] Similarly, Cuthbert Graham remembers that, 'his attitude to communism and the idea of revolution [was that] it was something utterly painful but necessary'.[59] In his essay on 'Glasgow', Mitchell himself formally represents the thirties as a time when political 'fantasies' must be put aside (*SH*, p 86), and for this reason Marxist ideology proved particularly attractive on account of its stern and disciplined approach to the major social problems of the day. This is the inference in the skeleton of one of his last projects, the mammoth *Story of Religion*, the climactic chapter of which was to be devoted entirely to the reverend study of 'Karl Marx and the Kingdom of God on Earth'. In this hagiographic extract Mitchell praises his subject for tempering the socialist creed as it existed before him, describing how:

> ... Liberalism, fathered by Rousseau, and Socialism, fathered by d'Holbach and Owen, enshrine this new belief [Humanism]. But both, as with early Protestantism, are handicapped for lack of the discipline and faith-inspiration of a rigid dogma. This is to be supplied by Heinrich Karl Marx. ...[60]

Mitchell's essays in *Scottish Scene* and books like *Spartacus* and *A Scots Quair* confirm that he favoured the Marxist plan for a revolution of the united forces of the proletariat to take place in order to overthrow the ruling classes of the present capitalist system, assume control and set up a communist state which would guarantee equality and freedom for all. He also shared Lenin's concern for the appointment of an élite body to coordinate this mass effort, and Trotsky's desire to establish the new society internationally. His thinking was contrary to the rigid line laid down by the Party, however, and consequently Mitchell's relationship with the official executive was, at the least, variable. The synopsis for another of his unfinished projects, the autobiographical *Memoirs of a Materialist*, has a reference to a specific incident in his life which may suggest that he was an official Communist agitator in the early thirties, the author focusing his attention upon 'General Election, 1931: Shots of the author and his wife as Communist agents in a general election'.[61] However, it is likely that this reference, like a scenario in the same work of 'The author mapping in Yucatan', is apocryphal; indeed the bulk of the work Mitchell did in his later years to promote the communist viewpoint seems to have been performed outwith the Party itself.

Leslie Mitchell's communist sympathies endured until the end of his life. One of his last published articles concerns his interest in forming a group of revolutionary writers, and as late as January 1935 he was still receiving amicable correspondence from T H Wintringham, editor and secretary of the radical periodical *The Left Review*.[62] And yet while he described himself as a communist in his communication with MacDiarmid over the 'Voice of Scotland' series, this was not recognised by the official Party. In a letter written in reply to Neil Gunn's gentle arguments against his Leninist views, Mitchell observed, 'By the way I'm not an official Communist', and he explained that, 'They refuse to allow me into the party!'.[63] Almost a year before this time, Mitchell had indicated the clandestine nature of his relationship with communist politics, for he told Alexander Gray, 'I'd love a heart to heart talk on Communism—but for the fact that the Communist papers frequently attack me as a "disruptive Anarchist"!'.[64] Indeed it transpires that these newspapers were completely justified in their criticism, for the month after he had told Mr Gray of the antagonism of the Communist press, Mitchell declared in *The Free Man*, 'I am a Scotsman, an artist, and—an integral part of my being—an anarchist', and for good measure he added the claim that, 'My art is implicit anarchy.'[65]

In the final analysis, therefore, Mitchell's writing shows that he would never have submitted to the narrow dogmatism of any individual party, for his stance of political 'reformer' involved the integration of anarchist idealism with the more practical approach of Marxist ideology to the destruction of capitalist society. This political unorthodoxy is no weakness; indeed it bears witness to the compassionate motives underlying Mitchell's search for social improvement. As Mitchell stated in *The Left Review*, 'because I'm a revolutionist I see no reason for gainsaying my own critical judgement'.[66] Even when his enthusiasm with regard to the communist effort was at its most pronounced, therefore, he retained a creditable sense of critical objectivity.

'Blasphemer':
Mitchell's Philosophical Thinking

GOD AND RELIGION

In 1924 D H Lawrence complained that 'The adventure is gone out of Christianity', which convinced him that man 'must start on a new venture towards God'.[1] This was not a new idea, but Lawrence's diagnosis is representative of much of the intellectual climate prevailing in western society between the wars. Leslie Mitchell's views on God and religion also fit in with the general mood of scepticism that existed at that time.

It was only in his later years that Mitchell's 'blasphemy' began to manifest itself in constructive ways, but he criticised the Christian view of God relentlessly throughout his life. He was brought up in a fairly orthodox Presbyterian household in which the father, James Mitchell, was a 'God-fearing' Christian, although his mother was the only member of the family who was a regular attender at the local church.[2] Mainly under his father's guidance, Leslie and his brothers received a strict indoctrination into the teachings of the Christian faith contained in the Authorised Version of the Bible, which in his essay on 'Religion', he called 'a book that can be as painfully wearying as it can be painfully enthralling' (*SH*, p 167). This ambivalent attitude was expressed frequently in his later years, Mitchell's writing revealing his simultaneous appreciation of the poetry of the Bible and his opposition to its theology.

Two other devotional works figured in Mitchell's vast reading programme as a boy, both of which evidently reinforced his critical attitude towards the traditional Christian view of God. The first, R H Benson's extreme Catholic apology *The Dawn of All*, must have been off-putting for its fanatical projection of Catholicism as the panacea for all the world's problems. The other, Foxe's *Book of Martyrs*, had a more distressing effect upon him, for in his school essay book he describes this lurid account of Catholic atrocities as 'a recipe for nightmares'.[3] Coincidentally, the same book loured over the childhood of the radical Irish playwright Sean O'Casey, who remembered it with equal vividness in the first volume of his autobiography as a book 'full of fire and blood and brimstone'.[4]

Mitchell takes a fairly conventional line of approach in the essays he wrote at school on the subjects of 'Religion' and 'Superstitions', but his essay on 'Christmas' is more interesting. This study indicates that even in his early teens, Mitchell's opposition to the traditional theist stance was symptomatic of a contradictory materialist attitude. He shows commendable acuity for one so young and of such limited experience when he observes in the course of his narrative that—

26

Today—for the last twenty years—it is an undeniable fact that the Christian religion is declining. 'Tis not before the Indian Buddha, the Chinese Confucius, or the Arabian Mohammed, but the cold, cool demon, with its undefeatable energy, and heavily entrenched facts—Science.[5]

As well as criticising the Christian standpoint, therefore, from his early teens Mitchell embraced the opposing viewpoint, that of scientific rationalism. The reference in *The Thirteenth Disciple* to Malcom Maudslay's having 'secured books by Huxley and Haeckel and rejoiced with them at the discomfiture of the Deity' (*TD*, p 38) is undoubtedly autobiographical. In addition, at a comparatively early age Mitchell came under the influence of socialist writers like Shaw and Wells, whose work no doubt encouraged him in this rationalist approach. And from his late teens he must have been further influenced by the official policy of the Communist Party, with which he consorted until his death.

The concept of atheism thus features particularly prominently in Mitchell's mature writing. It is unfortunate that *The Story of Religion* never developed beyond the blueprint stage, for this study would have been especially illuminating. However, the surviving précis is still extremely telling with regard to the author's religious views, the opening chapter containing the typical aim to prove 'that Natural Man was fundamentally irreligious'. Mitchell explains:

He had no gods, he did not bury his dead, he neither feared hell nor hoped in heaven. He was an animal unvexed by the mystery of existence. For him the mystery had no existence, and existence had no mystery.[6]

Even more revealing is the plan for another of Mitchell's unrealised projects, that of the *History of Mankind*, in which a derogatory reference to 'the origin and development of the idea of immortality' is directly juxtaposed with a contrastingly favourable allusion to 'atheism'.[7] And in *Image and Superscription* Mitchell concentrates his religious cynicism within the single supremely destructive definition of the religious philosopher, represented as 'a blind man seeking in a dark room for a black cat that isn't there' (*IS*, p 170).

Although Mitchell makes few direct references to atheism in his published work—most probably for commercial reasons—the manuscripts of works destined for one reason or another to remain unpublished testify to a sustained interest in the subject. Thus the plan for a story called 'Domina', involving the same liberated heroine from *The Thirteenth Disciple*, carries typical 'irreligiousness' in the plan for a section concerning 'Domina about men as the god-makers', which asserts that 'Women had always more sense.' In another, untitled, manuscript fragment, Simon Mogara, presented as the author of a work entitled 'Philosophy of Heresy', expounds a theory which he calls succinctly the 'illusion of disillusion' which wavers between the sardonic and the nihilistic. And yet another untitled fragment expresses similar atheistic sentiments within the idiotic ramblings of a heavily satirical mother figure, who babbles:

Mind you . . . I'm not a Socialist. Such funny people, and with such strange ideas. Many of them are atheists, the Rector says, and that man Bernard Shaw, whose [sic] one of them, writes such funny plays, and says rude things which one must laugh at. But atheism is so silly, when you look at things, I always think. There must have been a creator, I always say to Pompy, or else the sun would be square and the moon made of cheese, just like in the nursery rhymes. Neffy was never taught any nursery rhymes. She was always a funny child. . . .[8]

Mitchell's atheism also receives more direct expression. In Chapter Eight of the 'Brief Synopsis of A HISTORY OF MANKIND', for instance, he evinces scorn for all organised state religion and its basis in the mistaken idea of immortality, preferring to it the 'atheism and belief in a mechanistic world' of the early Ionian thinkers like Thales and Anaximander.[9] But finally, most positive of all his references to atheism is the plan for a chapter in his proposed autobiography which promises both objective intellectual consideration and personal confession:

Reel III: Scenario Script (viii)—*Anti-God*: Essay on religions; on the Christs, their origins, their messages; on atheism as a religion.[10]

The bold proclamation 'Anti-God' brooks no argument concerning Mitchell's personal endorsement of atheism.

The diffusionist account of human evolution lent support to the idea of the inherent redundancy of formal religious observance. Mitchell was greatly attracted by the pre-civilised period in human history as signifying a time when man lived in harmony with nature and when he was completely free of the political and religious constraints which arose with the haphazard discovery of agricultural methods. In his article on 'Religions of Ancient Mexico', he summarises the diffusionist position as follows—

. . . the case of the diffusionist is that many primitive peoples have no gods at all: they hear the thunder and disregard it, they neither bury, cremate, nor eat their dead: they leave them where they lie.[11]

As with his political beliefs, Mitchell's religious opinions found substantial relief in the diffusionist vision of the freedom of life in its natural state. For this reason, Akhnaton, the Pharaoh of Egypt from 1375BC is applauded for proclaiming 'a reign of naturalism in all relationships, human and divine' in an attempt to win back to this natural norm.[12] In 'The Antique Scene' the first Maglemosian Scots are hailed as 'men naked, cultureless, without religion or social organization' (*SH*, pp 124–5), and in *The Conquest of the Maya* a similarly undeveloped people are eulogised for the same reason, the author remarking—

It is impossible to call these groupings clans or tribes: they were the freest of assemblies and associations, for there was no rule, no authority, no chief, no council of elders, no law, no sexual problems, no wives, no husbands, no gods, no devils, no science, no war . . . (*CM*, p 43).

Within the diffusionist scheme the development of social classes and religious hierarchies is seen as a single process, and thus Mitchell frequently denounces religious practice on moral, as opposed to philosophical, grounds. Again in his last book he places 'that benignity that was an attribute of Natural Man' in direct contrast with the code of behaviour which the Christians observe when he refers to 'these heathens of the great lost continent kinder that Christians, heathen though they were' (*NAU*, p 152). Similarly, towards the end of the book Nansen, who is accorded the most flattering portrait of the nine explorers and who thus tends to represent the author's own viewpoint, perceives the eskimos to be 'unsavage, unspoilt, Christians it seemed to him without Christianity' (*NAU*, p 299).

In purely ethical terms, therefore, Christianity has nothing to offer natural man which he does not already possess in a higher form. This is most emphatically stated in *Nine Against the Unknown* when Mitchell makes his criticism of Marco Polo's Venice by measuring it against a high moral ideal, observing that, 'religion was a Name, a fast, a gesture, a supplication, a horrifying Fear or a comforting Hope: never a fine distillation of exultant altruism or passionate pity' (*NAU*, p 55).

Mitchell also criticises organised state religion for the active part it plays in maintaining the social order. Strictures imposed upon religious conduct undermine the freedom of the individual to a greater or lesser degree, and thus Thales earns praise for the antipathy he shows towards this theocratic system, being heralded as 'a single blasphemer'—a familiar encomium —whose rationalism promoted 'the envisagement of the world and all the terrors of life and death and time through individual eyes and independent reasoning' (*NAU*, pp 50-1). By breaking with tradition and flouting the rigid decrees laid down by the state regarding religious conduct, Thales is implicitly criticising the existing social order. In one way, then, religion is an alien development which has the pernicious power to influence the structure of society. However, Mitchell also condemns it on the deeper grounds that it is ultimately irrelevant to the human condition.

Throughout his work, Mitchell constantly compares natural man with his civilised counterpart, and the contrast is extremely pointed in reference to religion. In his essay on 'Religion' in *Scottish Scene* he ridicules 'the Scot who had mislaid original thought for a dour debating of fine theological points' (*SH*, p 167), and he criticises the Bible on the same page on account of its 'dull and unintelligible theological chatter'. Elsewhere in the volume he laments the 'Christian ritualism and superstitious practice' instituted during the Scottish Reformation (*SH*, p 135), and expresses a preference for 'the tides of irreligion and paganism' which he sees gaining strength in modern times (*SH*, p 165).

This pagan standard is most obvious in 'Glasgow' and in 'The Antique Scene', in which the author uses the vehicle of an ancient pictish peasant to reject theocratic reform as superfluous to 'the essentials of existence—his fields, his cattle, his woman in the dark little eirde, earth-house', further observing that, 'the peasant merely exchanged the bass chanting of the Druid in the pre-Druid circles for the whining hymnings of priests in wood-built churches; and turned to his land again' (*SH*, p 128).

More directly, Akhnaton is acclaimed in the 'Synopsis of THE STORY OF RELIGION' for his affirmation that 'There can only be the God that is Joyous Life',[13] and this pragmatic pagan spirit dominates the essay on 'Religion', in which the contemporary Presbyterian is characterised as someone 'who mislaid beauty and tenderness and love of skies and the happy life of beasts and birds and children for the stern restraints, the droning hymns and the superhuman endurances demanded of the attendants at Kirk service' (SH, p 167). And two pages later Mitchell condemns the Free Church for similar reasons, for debasing both the sensuous and sensual qualities which are essential components of his own ideal, complaining that, 'It looks upon all the gracious and fine things of the human body . . . with sickened abhorrence, it detests music and light and life and mirth.' The ideal presented here is thus an even more liberated one, promoting the idea of hedonistic indulgence in the physical experience of life, the pagan principles of 'light and life' being backed up by a Dionysian sensibility which savours the joyous qualities of 'music' and 'mirth'.

Under the influence of diffusionism, Mitchell's antipathy to religious thought became even more pronounced. Indeed, to his personal conviction of the irrelevance of religious discipline to the ordinary concerns of life the diffusionist perspective added the further criticism that the growth of religion as part of the origin of civilisation in general was itself adventitious. Mitchell's article on 'The Prince's Placenta and Prometheus as God' summarises the official diffusionist standpoint on the subject of religion:

> The view-point on religion of every archaeologist and anthropologist who has come under the influence of Diffusionism may be focused into two axioms: (a) Natural Man is naturally irreligious; (b) Religion is a survival of archaic science.[14]

This formal diffusionist approach is also to the fore in the essay on 'Religion' in which the author repeats the hypotheses that 'a religion is no more than a corpus of archaic science' and 'Man is naturally irreligious' (SH, p 157), before again condemning his subject thirteen pages further on as 'a cortical abortion, a misapprehension of the functions and activities of nature'. And in Nine Against the Unknown, Mitchell accepts the official diffusionist explanation of the accidental inception of the idea of an afterlife, tracing it to the seemingly miraculous capacity of the dry Egyptian soil to preserve a dead body. Yet again, then, metaphysical consideration is opposed to the natural order of things, the author apprehending 'the idea of immortality' as 'a play and a counter-play of thought and surmise upon a very prosaic happening' (NAU, p 16).

In his article upon 'Religions of Ancient Mexico', Mitchell again repeats the idea that Caliban-like divine speculation is not an indigenous part of human behaviour, and he goes on to suggest that the norm is an unquestioning preoccupation with the physical concerns of existence, to the exclusion of all theological 'fancy'. Thus, the Golden Age natives encountered by Columbus on the island of Guanahani in AD1492 are admired for possessing 'no discernible beliefs whatever regarding those supernatural agencies which most peoples have postulated as necessary operatives behind the mask of the natural'.[15] Such 'supernatural agencies' played a scant part in Mitchell's own philosophical vision.

The ideal that Mitchell subsequently formulates in his study of 'Religion' is of a situation in which human behaviour is ultimately completely untrammelled by religious discipline:

> One sees rise ultimately . . . in place of Religion—Nothing. To return to clinical similes, one does not seek to replace a fever by an attack of jaundice. One seeks the fields and night and the sound of the sea, the warmth of good talk and human companionship, love, wonder in the minute life of a water-drop, exultation in the wheeling Galaxy. All these fine things remain and are made the more gracious and serene and unthreatened as Religion passes. Passing, it takes with it nothing of the good—pity and hope and benevolence. (*SH*, p 171).

Mitchell's philosophy thus has a secular bias which affirms the irrelevance of theological speculation to ordinary life, but it also has a directly atheistic quality in that it refutes the very idea of the existence of God. Again in his essay on 'Religion' he portrays himself as a champion of science as opposed to religion—a role which has much in common with that of Brecht's hero in *The Life of Galileo*. Mitchell acknowledges the benefits which paradoxically accrued from the Industrial Revolution, of which he says:

> This brought Scotland its slums and its Glasgow, its great wens of ironworks and collieries upon the open face of the countryside; but its final efflorescence broke the power of the Church and released the Scot to a strange and terrible and lovely world, the world of science and scepticism and high belief and free valour—emerging into the sunlight of history from a ghoul-haunted canon (*SH*, p 162).

This Brechtian conjunction of 'the world of science and scepticism and high belief' is most apposite. For in the light of his atheistic view of existence Mitchell's abiding interest in scientific progress—and particularly in the science of exploration—acquires a considerably deeper significance.

Mitchell's interest in exploration was an enduring one, for both his first and last published books concern this theme, and this is also a recurrent topic in his English novels, with the main protagonists of *The Thirteenth Disciple* and *Image and Superscription* themselves being explorers. The author's treatment of the theme of exploration in these books confirms that his religious cynicism, evident in his essays on 'Religion' and 'Glasgow' and throughout his work in general, is symptomatic not just of his overriding concern with the practicalities of life, but of an alternative, essentially materialistic belief in the physical nature of reality.

In *Nine Against the Unknown* Mitchell condemns acquisitive explorers like Lief Ericsson and Cabeza de Vaca on obvious moral grounds and also for the part they played in spreading the forces of civilisation throughout the world. But, in its most elevated form, scientific exploration represents to him a process of almost spiritual potential. According to Mitchell, life possesses no ulterior meaning, and therefore the unknown elements of the universe remain a mystery simply because of their spatial remoteness. Consequently, the physical exploration of the cosmos offers the only reliable means of fulfilling the yearning for universal truth. In *Niger*, therefore, the author represents the ultimate mission of the explorer as the pursuit of 'the mysteries of life' (*Niger*, p 262). And in a whimsical conversation which takes place between Domina Riddoch and Malcom Maudslay in *The Thirteenth Disciple* he even considers the existence of a Prime Mover standing behind life as a remote possibility, although in keeping with the materialistic character of his vision this figure remains undetachable from the physical realm; indeed, this motivating force can only be attained and apprehended through physical exploration, via the 'Expedition of Consciousness against the dead universe' (*TD*, p 196).

To Leslie Mitchell, then, the spiritual dimension of life is inextricably bound up with the material universe. God exists only as a pagan figure. Mitchell's universe is basically 'mindless', and human life is perceived in distinctly non-miraculous terms.

LIFE AND DEATH

In 'The Land', Mitchell calls himself 'a jingo patriot of planet earth', advancing as his motto the phrase, 'Humanity right or wrong!' (*SH*, p 79). While his unflagging social and political commitment bears out the truth of this self-analysis, however, Mitchell never allowed his philanthropic sentiments to blind him to mankind's comparative insignificance within a universal context. As the primitive poet reminds Gay Hunter, all human life is just 'part of a greater singing' (*GH*, pp 278–9) and, irrespective of his devotion to human progress, Mitchell retained throughout his life an awareness of man's cosmic unimportance.

It was typical of Leslie Mitchell that from his boyhood he should enlist the help of the sciences of archaeology and astronomy in order to increase his understanding of the universe around him, and in his mature writing he remained unwilling to extend beyond the compass of the physical sphere. However, this limitation he imposes upon his vision is a liberation in another sense, so that ultimately his philosophical outlook could be described as one of breadth rather than depth, his view of life inclining towards the secular rather than the religious, with insight being dependent upon scientific rather than spiritual criteria. This is most impressively represented in the synopsis of his autobiography—whose title, Memoirs of a Materialist, is particularly pertinent here. The draft contains the plan for a chapter on the following theme:

> The Shadow on the Wall: An essay on the bounds of the physical world; on exploration as the escape from self; on the new physics; on (the author contends) the essentially mechanistic properties of the relativitist universe.[16]

Because life is apprehended materialistically, therefore, science replaces philosophy as the key to its understanding. The idea of 'the essentially mechanistic properties of the relativitist universe' stands in direct opposition to the gnostic conception of reality as a physical manifestation of the divine, and this again refers right back to Mitchell's early vision described in his school essay book, of Christianity retreating before 'the cold, cool demon, with its undefeatable energy, and heavily entrenched facts—Science'.

Scientific developments thus allowed Mitchell to achieve a deeper understanding of the cosmos as it existed in the present, and in addition he was afforded greater insight into its past evolution. In the projected *History of Mankind*, in fact, he planned to write a prefatory study of the universal context which witnessed the birth of mankind, and inevitably these conditions were to be viewed scientifically, with the author considering the following topics:

(iv) The earth some 9000 million years old. (v) Its place in space and time. (vi) A finite universe. (vii) Theories regarding its origin and extinction. (viii) The origin of the earth. (ix) The planet cools down.

The arrival of terrestrial life is also treated with scientific objectivity, as a minor and rather arbitrary event in this vast evolutionary process, Mitchell referring to:

(x) The apparently mechanical origin of life—an accident in a little by-pass of the chemical process. (xi) Methods of reconstruction. (xii) The geological ages. (xiii) Life seeks the land. (xiv) Consideration of the urges to change: the power of environment, the power of desire.[17]

Following upon all these far-reaching preliminaries, therefore, the second chapter, dealing with 'The Ascent of Man', inevitably comes as an anti-climax, and as a result man's place in the universe is greatly diminished.

Seeing the human race as a product of the wider cycle of evolution, Mitchell apprehends life in a similar, essentially materialistic, manner. In 'News of Battle: Queries for Mr. Whyte', he reduces human experience to the pattern of 'Birth, and life, and death', as he found it in nature, to a formula which is heavily reminiscent of T S Eliot's *reductio ad absurdum* in *Sweeney Agonistes*, in which Sweeney tells Doris:

> Birth, and copulation, and death.
> That's all the facts when you come to brass tacks:
> Birth, and copulation, and death.[18]

Eliot's analogy has a more farcical quality, but the overall impression is basically the same. Unlike Edwin Muir, who in his autobiography professes a belief in the immortality of the human spirit, Mitchell tends to view life in Sweeney's banal terms. He would have been encouraged in this matter-of-fact approach by the farming atmosphere in which he was brought up for, as is seen in the following passage from a fine rural novel of northeast Scotland predating *Sunset Song* by all of twenty years, farming folk characteristically adopt a fatalistic attitude to life, the hero of James Bryce's popular novel learning from one of his elders:

Ay, Jamie; it's a' by like a dream. And oor turn'll come some day; we'll pass awa and be as if we had never been. We're just like the weeds out there that we delve into the ground. They live for a year and we live for fifty or sixty, or it may be eighty year; that's a' the difference: it comes to the same in the end.[19]

In Mitchell's own *Nine Against the Unknown* also, death is realised in sternly physical terms, which consequently lends an air of ironic futility to the lives and achievements of the avaricious explorers such as Magellan and Vitus Bering who are spotlighted in the volume.

This blunt realisation of death as physical termination rather than spiritual elevation may be compared with the sobering vision received by Birkin when he considers Gerald's death in the closing pages of *Women in Love*. A similar stoicism is evident in Mitchell's fiction also. This is most striking in a passage in *Image and Superscription* in which the hero's mind is turned to consideration of this subject by the terrifying prospect of war. Thus, Gershom Jezreel thinks aloud:

Killed? Finished and put by, riven flesh grown black and then shrinking into bones and dust and manure this thing that was himself, that sat here alive, this thing that was "I", hungry for food and air and light and ease and the wonder of dead men's thoughts, books and books and long treks in bush and the sound of the sea. . . . Killed, he might well be killed, never again make love to women as once he had done, with Maruja that day by Laguna de Terminos, never again lie with a woman in kindness and delight (*IS*, p 182).

Approaching the subject of death thus, in terms of the joys and wonders of the life which it brings to an end, Mitchell gives to death a fearful aspect. In fact in *Image and Superscription* and *Nine Against the Unknown*, his vision acquires an austerity redolent of the Absurd philosophy of Malraux, Camus or Beckett.

In *Image and Superscription*, Mitchell's vision of a universe devoid of spiritual meaning lends credibility to Gershom's Camus-like affirmation of the logical human recourse to the supreme nihilistic act of suicide, the hero realising:

Life was no flower, it was mindless, the crawling of a mindless fecundity, changing and passing, changing and passing. Man was a beast who walked the earth, snarling his needs and lowing his fears, and with other beasts he would perish and pass, a ripple on the cosmic mind that itself was mindless. . . .

And a great amazement came on him there that evening in the Hertfordshire woods, that so few of his fellow-men should ever stand agaze on this horror of the Wastes he beheld so plain. It they should, if they should—! It would mean world-madness, world-suicide, to look in the freezing abyss either side of the path that men climbed, poor, blinded beasts. An end altogether of surely the strangest, most grotesque of adventures Life had ever attempted throughout the universe . . . (*IS*, p 193).

Although Gershom comes to discover hope in the future of mankind, the idea of the spiritual neutrality of the cosmos persists in the book, giving the theme a convincing immediacy. Early in the novel, the hero's grandfather declares: 'There was no order at all in the universe, no plan, no threat, no law, nothing but a fight to feed the stomach and plant the seed of the genitals' (*IS*, p 19), and this disquieting vision has something of Sweeney's sense of the ridiculous. Gershom finally discovers purpose in the unspecified plan to advance the human cause, but fails in the more demanding search for universal meaning, with the result that the final tone of optimism appears vague and insubstantial. Thus, the whole human adventure is rendered trivial and aimless in a universal context, Mitchell describing with the help of a potent termite analogy in one particularly memorable passage how:

> It flowered its greenery of spring, this little planet, a skin and a fairy feathering, it blossomed white as with down in the apple-blossom and the cherry-blossom, it darkened to autumn's slow brown, it grew bare and it rose to green again. And amid this lush growing and dying, florescence and fading, a piping of little voices rose unending, unbeginning, a maggot-imagery and a maggot-swarming questioning the white hands of Space . . . (*IS*, p 44).

In *Nine Against the Unkown*, Mitchell's outlook has even more in common with the later philosophy of the Absurd. In the very first chapter, the author presents the lives of the nine explorers seeking the mythical Fortunate Isles as tragic epics, and this leads into the correspondingly bleak coda that 'So in a fashion . . . all human life' is 'a tragic epic' (*NAU*, p 19). This chilling view of human transience finds an echo in the closing chapter, in which Mitchell reproves Nansen for his 'naive vanity', which he defines as, 'a kind of blindness to his own ephemeral quality (as all mankind are ephemeral)' (*NAU*, p 295). In this way, from the particular Mitchell receives a sense of the general, of the inconsequential nature of life as a whole. Ultimately, in fact, this portrait of Nansen in *Nine Against the Unknown* represents his most devastating study of the vulnerability of the human position within a universe lacking both order and purpose.

Nansen's 'naive vanity' is explained away as a momentary lapse, for his attitude is otherwise shown to be exemplary, involving as it does the kind of honesty which Mitchell so admires, described in Nansen's case as, 'the modern Stoic's acceptance of the terror and beauty and ultimate tragedy of all life' (*NAU*, p 310). There are important ecological factors involved in the integrity of Nansen's approach to life, however, for his 'appalling visionings of time and space' (*NAU*, p 295) are largely induced by the austere physical circumstances in which he finds himself—particularly at the North Pole— where life appears in all its harsh simplicity, stripped of all unnecessary diversions. In this desolate environment the explorer, in his own words, discovers 'cold winds to bring you to the edge of consciousness till the human reason stands aghast at its own existence, silences so deep you can hear the Galaxy turn, the edge of the Eternally Unknowable' (*NAU*, p 291). The truth perceived by him in these exceptionally deprived circumstances is correspondingly bleak.

Through Nansen's experience, Mitchell demonstrates the demoralising effect that the realisation of the 'mindlessness' of the universe can have upon mortals bestowed with the power of rational thought, especially when, like

Nansen himself, they are deprived of all the distractions associated with modern life. The loneliness Nansen experiences in the Arctic and elsewhere in his travels thus proves highly instructive, indeed revelatory, presenting him with an image of the whole human predicament. Thus, Mitchell relates of his hero how, looking across the sea from Naples, he came upon an understanding of the universal truth of human life in general:

> He was looking out into that remoteness of the human spirit that is man's terrible heritage, seeing man himself a lonely figure in the wastes of a little planet wheeling about a little sun, without guide or light or surety or safety, uncompanioned by God or devil, hope and fear but the staves that he carves for himself . . . (NAU, p 295).

Five pages after this, traversing Greenland, Nansen receives a similar appreciation of the macrocosm:

> He dragged his sledge untiringly, staring at that splendour upon the sky, staring almost appalled at the great Arctic moons that came and seemed to refuse a setting; close to the earth they hung so that the conviction of the earth as a tiny globe in space amidst strange kin wanderers sunk into the naked consciousness like a frozen knife. Sometimes Nansen found himself humanizing that unearthly terror—or did so in his record long afterwards—into stillness and peace where indeed there was only negation.

Later in the portrait, man is again trivialised in the face of the natural cosmos of which he is a diminutive part:

> He would walk out on the ice alone and stand and look at that great arching of the Galaxy above him and realize again the loneliness of Man, what a little adventure in truth was his, how strange the puny aims and hopes and fears he had in this brief flicker of light betwixt darkness that he called life (NAU, p 309).

Mitchell thus makes studious efforts throughout his work to address the major themes of life and death with scientific detachment, and, scorning the traditional props of religious faith, his vision subsequently attains a bleakness and an austerity which looks forward to the later philosophy of the Absurd.

NATURE

So far, I have concentrated upon the more negative aspects of Mitchell's role of 'blasphemer'. However, his denunciation of the traditional attitudes to God and religion paved the way for a more positive undertaking, involving the development of pragmatic methods of philosophical disquisition. Nature played a decisive part in this exercise.

In its most extreme articulation, Mitchell's materialistic approach to life produced the stark atheistic vision proffered by Nansen in *Nine Against the Unknown*. However, Mitchell tended to be more indulgent when he considered the natural world. Indeed, the specially close relationship that he had with nature from his boyhood seems to have had a salutary effect upon his mature philosophy.

Although he had no illusions concerning the hard life that the crofting farmer led, more than fifteen years after his initial departure from the Mearns Mitchell wrote in 'The Land' of the strong bond that he preserved with his homeland, owning to a fierce sense of pride in his 'peasant rearing' and in the fact 'that the land was so closely and intimately mine (my mother used to hap me in a plaid in harvest-time and leave me in the lea of a stook while she harvested)' (*SH*, p 68). The relationship is presented in even more intimate terms ten pages later:

Autumn of all seasons is when I realize how very Scotch I am, how interwoven with the fibre of my body and personality is this land and its queer, scarce harvests, its hours of reeking sunshine and stifling rain, how much a stranger I am, south, in those seasons of mist and mellow fruitfulness as alien to my Howe as the olive groves of Persia.

Mitchell's early attraction for this natural environment was largely instinctual, and one can imagine him absorbing these sensuous experiences in much the same way as he later portrayed the young Mungo Park in *Niger*:

Mungo had lain on the grass and the heath and the bells of the hills, looked at the twining convolutions of the buttercups, the purple bells of the heather-drops, watching the busy insect-world at its play of life, looked at the blood pulse down the veins in his own arm. He had seen the play and perhaps the majesty of life (*Niger*, pp 18–19).

As his school essay books confirm, Mitchell himself was fully aware of the 'play of life' as it went on around him at Arbuthnott. And it was virtually inevitable in a boy of his intelligence and sensitivity that he should subject these spontaneous experiences to intellectual scrutiny, eventually achieving a sense of 'the majesty of life'. Indeed, in one of his school essays, he arrives at a quasi-Romantic understanding of the life-force represented by the natural macrocosm, of that which Lawrence calls 'the tremendous *non-human* quality of life'.[20] The thirteen-year-old writes in his essay, simply titled 'Power':

What an irresistible feeling of power comes over one—or at least it has with me—when, on a calm, clear night, you gaze up at the millions of glistening worlds and constellations, which form the Milky Way. . . .'Tis then—and then only—that one can realize the full power of the Creator . . . and the truth of the wild dream of the German poet; 'There is no beginning—yea, even as there is no end!'[21]

Mitchell's rural upbringing stimulated his imagination and added a philosophical dimension to his thinking. His immersion in the organic patterns which governed life in the country promoted in him a pragmatism which gave precedence to the accepted knowledge of the physical realm over the search for metaphysical meaning. As a result, Mitchell's outlook has much in common with Lawrence's philosophical approach. John Alcorn defines this outlook as 'naturist', writing, 'The naturist world is a world of physical organism, where biology replaces theology as the source both of psychic health and of moral authority.'[22] Mitchell goes further than this in his mature work, however, for on several occasions he directly associates nature with God.

This association is made most graphically in the study of 'The Land'. In a conceit devised at the close of the essay, the harvest nourished by the Land is itself assigned a mystical power as the natural manifestation of the divine. Mitchell describes, in a semi-devotional style which looks forward to George Mackay Brown's writing, how:

> The corn is so ancient that its fresh harvesting is no more than the killing of an ancient enemy-friend, ritualistic, that you may eat of the flesh of the God, drink of his blood, and be given salvation and life (*SH*, p 81).

Thus the author not only denies the existence of a Christian-type God standing behind 'the mask of the natural' as in the panentheistic vision of Hopkins or Mackay Brown himself but actually supplants it with a natural deity. This substitution is best illustrated in one of Mitchell's many unpublished poems titled 'When God Died', in which the death of the Christian God is contrasted with the healthy continuation of the natural processes (see Appendix B).

Although Mitchell frowned upon gods and religions as such, in 'Religions of Ancient Mexico' he himself indulges in a heavily pagan deification of the natural elements when he tolerantly considers 'simple or homely gods, naturally evolved by barbarous people from observation of the sky at noon and night, the ripening of the maize, the lightning flash and the like phenomena'. Mitchell is lenient towards pagan concepts which have evolved from an external natural context.

Nevertheless, it is in 'The Land' again that this association of God and nature is most clearly made, for towards the end of the essay nature is directly represented as the single ordering force presiding over life in the universe: 'Nature unfolds the puppets and theatre pieces year after year, unvaryingly, and they lose their dust, each year uniquely fresh' (*SH*, pp 78–9). In this scheme, nature is unambiguously apprehended as the dominant power in life.

In this light, then, Chris's belief that 'nothing endured at all, nothing but the land' (*SQ*, p 97), and Rob Gault's conviction that 'the fields mattered and mattered, nothing else at all' (*SH*, p 25) are both recognisable as Mitchell's own. And the pagan bond made with the distrusting pirate by the eponymous hero of *Spartacus*—who presents Mitchell's own viewpoint throughout the novel—also acquires a personal significance in this context: 'The Pirate asked by what God he swore, and then Spartacus swore by the earth and the air (for he knew no other Gods)' (*Spart*, p 230). Like Spartacus, Mitchell spurned the traditional divinities of his own age, seeking to establish a religious approach of a more functional character in their stead.

Even when nature is not directly presented in divine terms, the metaphor frequently conveys a similar sense of reverence. This is particularly well represented by the legend inscribed inside the front cover of Mitchell's army notebook which was later to become the theme for the short story 'Clay' and which the author evidently regarded as a kind of personal philosophical motto, the epigram proclaiming, 'All life that was clay and awoke and strove to return again to its mother's breast.'[23] The maternal metaphor emphasises man's obligation to nature as the very source of life itself.

In keeping with this reverential attitude towards nature at large, human life finally assumes a sense of purpose beyond its material function as a physical organism, a purpose associated with the sublime power attributed to nature as a whole. In its most profound sense, therefore, human birth is represented as a projection of what Lawrence called the 'creative quick'.[24] In *Nine Against the Unknown*, human life is reduced to this natural base when Mitchell refers to all humans being moulded from 'lowly clay' (*NAU*, p 17), and the birth of Mungo Park's father described in *Niger* is directly related to the wider natural order which embraces the farmer and his wife who conceived the child:

Where he came from there is no knowing, except from the soil, up out of its darkness with that horde of men of like kind, the dour even-tempered peasants of Scotland (*Niger*, p 10).

It is as a homogeneous part of this same natural pattern that Mitchell perceives the Scottish peasantry in general when he declares in 'The Land' that, 'Those folk in the byre . . . are The Land in as great a measure' as the tilthe itself (*SH*, p 67).

Just as life emanates from, and is subsequently sustained by, nature so Mitchell represents death as a return to the source, as the act of natural absorption. The idea constantly recurs in his writing and, as I will consider later, it is of central importance in *A Scots Quair*. This is the conception which brings 'Clay' to its close, Rob Gault's daughter Rachel using an appropriately affectionate maternal metaphor to describe her father's final union with his beloved land. This sense of the unity of all life in the natural absolute ultimately provides reassurance, if not actual hope, at the prospect of death.

The theme of universal conformity also dominates the earlier story 'Daybreak', in which the heroine's miraculous recovery from illness is directly attributed to the benevolence of the natural world with which she has always had a peculiar rapport. And the fate of Mungo Park, whose intimacy with nature extended from the peasant legacy he inherited at birth, is realised as a natural act, the hero being engulfed by the universe which held such an ineluctable attraction for him:

But morning found the traveller [i.e., the Niger, in which Mungo and his colleagues have just drowned] in a low dank land; reeds whistled in the strange salt wind that came from the place the sunrise had not yet touched. The waters flowed slow with silt, and broke and spun in long slow eddies through the hot mist. As the day rose they split in a dozen streams and quested west, the Nun, the Brass, New Calibar, Bonny, Opobo and Wari. Mangroves clawed at them with dripping roots. The day-heat rose and passed over the uncertain flow, till remote in the sunset, by a dozen mouths, the waters that rose in the far-off mountains of Liberia passed out to the open sea (*Niger*, p 308).

While this passage gives a certain ironic sense of the futility of human endeavour, the final impression is of human life swallowed up, and perhaps finding some kind of fulfilment, in the natural macrocosm.

Spartacus gives a similar intimation of the spiritual recesses of the natural world. In this novel, death is frequently realised in intensely physical terms —as is only natural in a book dealing with such a bloody period in history— but the physical accomplishment is customarily preceded by a premonition, by a quasi-religious recognition of the spiritual importance of the natural world. Before they actually meet with their respective fates, certain characters experience a kind of supernatural intimation of their impending death, and this heightened state of awareness is induced by the stimulating effect that the natural environment has upon their senses. Crixus is the first to experience this sensation:

> Then on Crixus there came a fine gaiety. And suddenly it seemed to him that the air was sweet and good; though he had never noticed such things before. And in that early-morning light there clung to his eyelids a fine web from the night-time mist; and the wonder of that on his eyelids was strange on his spirit for a moment. Then he called to the bucinator to sound (*Spart*, p 149).

Later in the book, a young tribune has a similar mystical experience, realising suddenly, 'In the air was the smell of the morning's green coming, and somehow, despite his bonds, he felt a strange gladness upon him.' The night before the battle with Crassus beside Lake Lucania, Brennus's brother, cherishing the sensation as 'all the earth sent forth a dry, growing smell that caught at his throat' (*Spart*, p 256), also attains this transcendental awareness. And although Spartacus's own vision is rather less an 'intimation of immortality', in this context his sentimental feelings, when in the final book he contemplates the mountains facing him, have a distinctly prophetic quality.

In the final analysis, however, this intuitive apprehension of the sublime is no more valid in an empirical sense than the traditional theist argument to which Mitchell was so strongly opposed. Setting the philosophical and historical background in *Nine Against the Unknown* the author laments how 'faith'— 'that naive faith that had haunted civilized man since the first Egyptian pondered on the dead beyond Nile Bank'—had come to replace 'knowledge' as the cornerstone of existential enlightenment (*NAU*, p 201). In these terms, Mitchell's own appreciation of the natural absolute, particularly as it is represented in 'Daybreak', in *Spartacus* and in 'The Land', is open to criticism as an untenable proposition which is sustained by 'faith' rather than 'knowledge'. In his most mature work, however, he attempts to justify his philosophical probings by more sound empirical means.

I mentioned earlier how Mitchell drew inspiration from the nineteenth century tradition of scientific rationalism, and he appears to have been particularly heavily influenced by materialist ideology as it was expounded by Huxley and Haeckel, and Marx, Engels and Lenin. Mitchell's mature philosophy, in fact, has much in common with the concept which has come to be known as 'dialectical materialism'.

Marx and Lenin both adapted and extended the Hegelian dialectic for socio-political purposes but, in his *Anti-Duhring* and the unfinished study of *Dialectics of Nature*, Engels applied the doctrine to the universe at large, as a system which discovered sense—but not necessarily meaning—in universal disorder. In Engels's scheme, change itself is the keynote in both human history and in the universe as a whole, and this principle, which is presented as an inevitable product of the eternal conflict of the contradictory elements of which reality is composed, provides hope for the future of society, and of life itself. This state of constant flux, Engels argues, is a dynamic and progressive condition.

Although it is not known if Mitchell was familiar with either the *Anti-Duhring* or *Dialectics of Nature*, his library contained critical books on Hegel's logic,[25] and in *Hanno* he himself promotes the Philosophy of Change as an alternative to the religious search for stability, observing that, 'because men have scarcely attempted the upbuilding of a workable Philosophy of Change, a stable background to life is sought after as a desperate necessity' (*Hanno*, p 77). Mitchell chose not to take the idea any further in this instance, in a book which is after all a study of the science of exploration, but 'the upbuilding of a workable Philosophy of Change' became a major concern for both the political 'reformer' and the religious 'blasphemer' and played a decisive part in his greatest work.

The parallel between Engels's doctrine of 'dialectical materialism' and Mitchell's 'Philosophy of Change' is intensified by the active role that nature plays in both systems. In *Socialism: Utopian and Scientific*, which is something of a companion piece to the *Anti-Duhring*, Engels states specifically that 'Nature is the proof of dialectics',[26] and he goes on to explain in this pamphlet:

Modern materialism embraces the more recent discoveries of natural science according to which Nature also has its history in time, the celestial bodies, like the organic species that, under favourable conditions, people them, being born and perishing.[27]

In this alternating process of growth and decay, Engels discovers the principle which governs all life, and when Mitchell considers the Land, as a paradigm of nature at large, he finds a similar pattern, an image of the universal condition. Place was more important than time in his development of the idea, for it was chiefly from the Land, epitomising the endless cycle of birth, life and death that Mitchell ultimately derived a sense of the eternal.

When the author reduces life to its most basic principles, in *Image and Superscription* and *Nine Against the Unknown*, this produces a grim vision of the Absurdity of the human situation in a meaningless universe. However, when he performs a similar operation in relation to nature, the effect is much less disquieting. Accepting the idea of 'a finite universe', Mitchell found an image of perpetual life in the endless reworkings of nature. And in his greatest work, *A Scots Quair*, he provides a form of utilitarian verification for this affirmation, representing the cycle of birth, life and death as a molecular process, as a constant transformation of the 'spraying of motes' which reality comprises in its lowest form (*SQ*, p 236). A fantastic extension of this is to be found in one of Mitchell's most heavily romantic stories, 'Near Farnboru', in which 'the First Woman', describing the world of the future, relates how scientific progress has helped solve some of the most vexing problems of human existence. The time-traveller hero learns that:

> Life and Death are merely different arrangements of matter, and the extinction that the old animal-humans so dreaded never existed. Now all the life-forms we use for foods are also laboratory products, and the atom-cells of a man who has passed to so-called death are often re-grouped and re-vivified in some new body.[28]

The vision of life as an eternal recycling of matter is again in agreement with Engels's scheme, which exploits nineteenth-century findings in the realm of cellular biology and the conservation and transformation of energy. Like Engels, Mitchell drew upon these scientific developments in his analysis of the universal condition, and as a result his mature philosophy has a worthy empirical validity.

Mitchell's mature vision is both more lyrical and far-reaching than Engels's 'dialectical materialism'. Indeed, his view of life approximates more closely to what Hugh MacDiarmid defines in that profound poem 'Island Funeral' as 'thoroughgoing Materialism'.[29] MacDiarmid, like Mitchell, reduces life to its basic physical essence, and he also finds the idea of the constant reworking of matter a source of strength and hope, declaring that ultimately 'materialism promises something/Hardly to be distinguished from eternal life'.[30] Human life is regarded as one expression of this universal transformation of matter, and consequently, viewed as a part of the eternal process of decay and change, death becomes less forbidding, as a natural return to the material base. Thus, although MacDiarmid's outlook is essentially materialistic in that he confines his attention to the physical realm, in his affirmation of the eternal nature of life he provides a vision of religious import. Mitchell's Philosophy of Change ultimately has a similar status, for, as I will consider later, this finally comes to represent for Chris a vision of 'the only truth that there was' (SQ, p 207). As a rational 'blasphemer', Mitchell defines his mission as the pursuit of 'truth' or 'knowledge' as opposed to 'faith', and the final attainment of 'a workable Philosophy of Change' subsequently emerges as equivalent to religious experience.

FREEDOM

It has become fashionable in recent years to describe Chris's experience at the close of A Scots Quair as existentialist. Douglas Young writes, 'Chris embodies a philosophical position which . . . is non-rational and existentialist',[31] and Patricia J Wilson claims that Chris's final withdrawal from society 'is something of an existential [sic] act, an assertion of freedom'.[32] I feel this is an inappropriate term to use in reference to Mitchell's work in view of the rationale for Chris's final experience, and in view of the logic which informs the author's philosophy as a whole. Existentialism, as it is defined most famously by Sartre in Nausea in 1938, describes an experience which, in accordance with the acceptance of general meaninglessness, is non-rational:

on the other hand, Mitchell's definition of the spiritual state of FREEDOM (as the word is printed at the close of the *Quair*) is sustained by a strictly disciplined process of logic.

The first point to bring into perspective when considering Mitchell's concept of Freedom is that he regarded such spiritual matters as the responsibility of the individual. In *Nine Against the Unknown* he criticises the traditional religious approach by comparing it with the 'rationalistic' attitude adopted by Thales, which involved 'the envisagement of the world and all the terrors of life and death and time through individual eyes and independent reasoning (*NAU*, p 50). Mitchell's own ideal of Freedom signifies an inward state achieved by virtue of independent reasoning and inspired by external conditions, as is the case with Nansen and with Chris Guthrie in particular. In this scheme, therefore, spiritual fulfilment can not be achieved by ritualistic or devotional means, and yet the individual may still achieve a kind of epiphany by coming to terms with the ultimate reality of existence as it is represented in the natural order. This whole philosophical enterprise thus has a great deal in common with the mode of approach which Martin Esslin singles out for praise in the literary movement known as the Theatre of the Absurd, of which he writes:

When it is no longer possible to accept complete closed systems of values and revelations of divine purpose, life must be faced in its ultimate, stark reality. That is why, in the analysis of the dramatists of the Absurd in this book, we have always seen man stripped of the accidental circumstances of social position or historical context, confronted with the basic choices, the basic situations of his existence. . . .[33]

This idea of the 'stripping down' of reality to its fundaments is not a new one, as the Polish critic Jan Kott has shown in his impressive Absurdist interpretation of *King Lear*,[34] but it has been most fully explored by the modern writers whom Esslin considers in his study. The major difference with Mitchell is that whereas the Absurdists, like Beckett or Sartre, view existence in a basically pessimistic way—with political involvement for Sartre coming to represent a very necessary diversion from the unpleasant theme of the meaninglessness of life—for Mitchell this process, taken to its furthest extreme, as in *A Scots Quair*, provides hope and points the way to the ultimate achievement of spiritual fulfilment. While he uses a similar method of enquiry to the Absurdists, Mitchell reaches a very different conclusion. To use a convenient analogy, the Absurdist attitude is basically that of orthodox materialism, in that it involves an acceptance of the bleak prospect that life, reduced to its most fundamental form, affords. Mitchell's philosophical vision, on the other hand, approximates more closely to MacDiarmid's 'thoroughgoing Materialism': Mitchell argues that when reality is reduced to basics, ultimately it promotes a sense of perpetual life, of eternity. The apprehension of this idea is thus an affirmative act and, at its most profound, this experience has an almost religious significance, culminating in the achievement of Freedom.

The attitude of the 'blasphemer', like that of the 'reformer', thus incorporates both destructive and constructive elements. Mitchell attacked traditional religious doctrine, repudiating both the idea of immortality and the theist view of God: he worked out a convincing alternative, heavily dependent upon rationalistic principles and upon a scientific understanding of the material universe. In its most extreme form, this produces a desolate vision of the futility of all life, a vision which looks forward to the philosophy of the Absurd elaborated from the Second World War on through the fifties by writers like Camus and Sartre. However, in Mitchell's case, the bleakness of the vision is alleviated when he takes the process a stage further and discovers in the natural cycle of birth, life and death an image of the eternal. The appreciation of this universal principle is consequently represented as an act of quasi-religious significance, as an enlightenment which ultimately provides spiritual liberation.

THREE

The English Stories

EARLY ATTEMPTS AT FICTION

Believing in what he called 'the major art of the novel',[1] Leslie Mitchell evidently regarded the short story as an inferior literary form; and yet, most probably for reasons of economy, it was in the shorter mode that he first expressed his serious literary aspirations. At the very least, the abbreviated form furnished him with a convenient means of testing his literary powers and investigating the practical mechanics of writing, and thus although the bulk of his work in this field is fairly undistinguished, his shorter fiction merits examination for the light it sheds upon the author's shaping as a writer. The stories deserve consideration for the additional reason that they provide a valuable index to the developing ideas of the 'reformer' and the 'blasphemer' throughout the late twenties and up to his death. Ultimately, Mitchell's interests and priorities in his minor fiction have a considerable bearing upon the themes which dominate his greatest work.

Alexander Gray, who was unswervingly loyal to his former pupil throughout Mitchell's leanest times, played an important part in the protégé's early endeavours to carve out a niche for himself as a fiction writer: from 1926, Mitchell made regular consultations in his correspondence with his old dominie regarding the writer's craft in general, and relating specifically to his own efforts. Although his experiments at fiction from this time have not survived, the author's preoccupations at this early stage in his career seem to have been of a rudimentary order, Mitchell focusing his attention in his earliest letters chiefly upon rather mundane considerations of plot structure and narrative form. In one early fictive précis, he announces that, 'A writer these days who takes over long to introduce action into his story is doomed', adding that, 'He must act or perish.'[2] Accordingly, the accent in his first published short stories is very much upon action.

Mitchell's first two published stories both rely heavily upon the traditional device of the surprise ending, and although both 'Siva Plays the Game' and 'If You Sleep in the Moonlight' are tolerably amusing as 'tales of the unexpected', both remain forgettable as literature. Mitchell's first story, dating from October 1924 and reprinted in *A Scots Hairst*, sets up an intriguing confrontation between romantic and realistic conceptions of the Orient through a plot involving the exploitation by the unscrupulous natives of Siva of an English author with inordinate cravings for romance; and the twist fashioned at the tale's close, in which the western author finds by default the romantic fulfilment he has been seeking, restores the delicate balance between the two perspectives. Thus, Mitchell's fictive debut is fairly complex, with the author creating humour from the ambiguity which arises from the dissolution of the dividing line between romance and reality. The second offering, which appeared four years later, is more orthodox, but no less entertaining. 'If You Sleep in the Moonlight', a psychological thriller, was the opening tale in an anthology of rather second-rate horror stories entitled *Grim Death*.[3] The plot of a jealous husband's frantic uncertainty as to whether the fear that he murdered his wife is founded upon dream or reality may seem lightweight, and yet Mitchell again appears in complete control of his material. The lively pace of the narrative, vividly realistic descriptive work and skilful creation of tension and suspense combine to make the story a success within the admittedly limited scale of its ambitions.

The potential which Mitchell displayed in his first two stories produced more substantial returns in the following two, 'For Ten's Sake' and 'One Man with a Dream'. The former was in fact the piece which, by securing the approval and support of H G Wells and Leonard Huxley, marked Mitchell's real breakthrough as a fiction writer, 'For Ten's Sake' being the first of over twenty stories by him that were to be published in Dr Huxley's *Cornhill Magazine* (which happened by coincidence to be one of the periodicals which Neil Gunn had solicited when he was trying to get his work published in the mid twenties[4]). Mitchell's first *Cornhill* story, also republished in *A Scots Hairst*, shows an improvement in his technique; the biblical quotation and the representation of Christ look forward directly to 'Forsaken'. Even more auspiciously, 'For Ten's Sake' touches upon some of the themes and ideas which provide the backbone to his major works.

Dr Richard Southcote's discovery of ten sufficiently worthy inhabitants who deserve to be spared the wholesale destruction of the depraved city of Mevr dramatises Mitchell's determination to find some goodness in all mankind, and this indicates why later he found the diffusionist view of evolution so appealing. 'For Ten's Sake' has greater significance as an illustration of Mitchell's adult thought, however, for Southcote's development—away from the fanatical Calvinist belief in a God 'waiting round the corner ready to be unpleasant' (*SH*, p 202) to a more reasonable and sympathetic belief in the qualities of pity and mercy personified by Christ—reflects Mitchell's own attitude towards Christian philosophy. As a 'blasphemer', he did not believe in the divinity glorified in the Bible but—as with Bernard Shaw, Upton Sinclair and Jack London before him, and indeed many other socialist writers—his atheism did not prevent him from believing passionately in the historical existence of Christ, and in the relevance of his moral teachings. Christ thus has a much more forceful presence in Mitchell's writing than the traditional Christian-style God has, and this early story is the first work in which he brings Christ to life, as a human inspiration rather than an emanation of the divine.

In 'One Man with a Dream', published in *The Cornhill* four months later, Mitchell turns his attention to radical politics. Although the Egyptian setting deprives the plot—of Rejeb ibn Saud's attempts to found 'the Green Republic of Islam'[5]—of much of the immediacy and topicality that it might have had, the beliefs of the 'reformer' are still strongly in evidence. The compassionate concern which ibn Saud expresses for the welfare of the ordinary folk is clearly the same moral force which fuelled the author's political aggression, and ibn Saud's cosmopolitan ideal of the Brotherhood of Man[6] also has a direct correspondence with the ultimate aim of the 'reformer'. However, the specific conclusions that Mitchell reaches in this story concerning revolutionary method and procedure are less in keeping with the political views he expressed in later life. The Egyptian's outright dismissal of the expedient of violence stands at odds with the author's mature attitude, that violence would be a regrettable but necessary factor in the successful insurrection of the working classes. Nevertheless, while Mitchell was to revise his opinions with regard to the practical details of revolution, 'One Man with a Dream' suggests that his basic aims and principles were firmly entrenched by this time.

   Mitchell's first four fictional fragments thus become increasingly serious in terms of the essential ideas they represent, with his favourite political and religious themes gradually coming more into play. This trend continued in his next project, which involved the characteristically ambitious plan for a story-cycle. This was published in *The Cornhill* as the *Polychromata*, and subsequently collected in one volume as *The Calends of Cairo*.

POLYCHROMATA

The form of the story-cycle could be said to take in such classics as *The Canterbury Tales*, *The Decameron* and *Tales from the Arabian Nights*, but Mitchell with his love of Russian literature most probably drew his initial inspiration for his *Polychromata* from Turgenev's *A Sportsman's Sketches*, the definitive example of the form from the nineteenth century. And the final stimulus to adopt the mode doubtless came from more contemporary sources, for Joyce's *Dubliners* and Sherwood Anderson's *Winesburg, Ohio*, models of their kind, had appeared only the previous decade. However, direct comparison with *Dubliners* and *Winesburg, Ohio* reflects badly on Mitchell's work, for while his *Polychromata* is imbued with an admirable sense of spirit of place—most impressively in the author's graphic account of Elia Constantinidos's early morning wanderings, in the fifth story in the series[7]—the characterisation appears wooden, the narrative mode dated and affected, and the action forced when set against those of Joyce and Anderson.

   The *Polychromata* stories are connected by Mitchell's over-elaborate narrative mode and by the use of Cairo, the 'Polychromata' of the title, as setting, one of the author's objectives being to bring out the significance of this description, to represent 'the scents and smells of her, her days and nights, colours and chance voices'.[8] The plots are uniformly banal, however, all twelve tales relying to some extent upon the conventional theme, unimaginatively realised, of romance between man and woman. The device of the shock ending, prominent in his first stories, also recurs, first, in the cycle in such tales as 'He Who Seeks', in which the hero inexplicably refuses the romantic reconciliation which has been his life's quest when his goal is actually in his grasp; and, second, in 'East is West' which, involving a startling discovery in family genealogy, vaguely anticipates the turnaround in events contrived at the climax of 'Smeddum'. Two-thirds of the *Polychromata* stories, including 'East is West', build up to an optimistic conclusion, while the remaining four—'The Epic', 'Gift of the River', 'Vernal' and 'Daybreak'— thrive upon a carefully created tone of mystery and ambiguity; and yet neither expedient is deployed wholly convincingly. The collection is slightly redeemed by the author's intellectual preoccupations, however, and in these stories, Mitchell begins to tackle the themes which stand solidly behind his greatest work.

The *Polychromata* contains vehement protests against the sexual, religious, racial and social bigotry which Mitchell observed in contemporary life and, in general accordance with the dual properties of the role of both the 'reformer' and the 'blasphemer', his destructive purpose in the stories is allied with a more positive intention to point the way forward from these iniquities.

'The Road' stands as Mitchell's most forceful statement concerning sexual equality, the simple parable of Jane Hatoun's martyrdom in the battle she fought for female rights in the archaic and bigotted moral climate of Egypt providing a moving call for the pursuit of a more even balance between the social status of men and women. Yet Jane Hatoun's message is no idle sermon on the subject of women's liberation for, in a manner typical of Mitchell's writing, her plea is subsumed by a more wide-ranging purpose, that of the general emancipation of all mankind. Thus, Anton Saloney, Mitchell's dragoman raconteur, affirms that Jane 'preached no war on men, but rather the flaming creed that was to purge love of cruelty and abomination for those who set their feet on the Way', and he concludes, 'Somewhere, attainable by a mystic Road, was an amazing, essayable happiness, life free and eager, life in the sunlight beyond the prisons of fear and cruelty'.[9] Jane Hatoun is no narrow-minded feminist, therefore, but a figure 'of heroic mould',[10] very like Dasha, the enlightened heroine in Gladkov's early proto-type for the novel of socialist realism, *Cement*, who stands up for her fellow women but works ultimately for the general benefit of all her comrades irrespective of their gender.

Another *bête noire* of Mitchell's that is vilified in the story-cycle is the stifling Calvinistic approach to religion condemned in the earlier portrait of John Southcote in 'For Ten's Sake'. The sardonically named James Freeman in 'Vernal' is a similar character who also believes in 'the ancient, cruel God of sacrifice and supplication and the bitter codes',[11] and he gets his just deserts at the end of the story when his daughter Norla goes her own way and marries the freethinking Bohemian Alexandr Sergeyvich.

Racial prejudice is most freely denounced in 'East is West', the eighth Polychromata. Here Mitchell decries bigotry which is based on creed and colour: he concentrates upon the romantic happiness found eventually by an aristocratic Englishwoman and an aeronautical engineer of mixed origin who become engaged to be married, despite the protests of her racialist brother. As in 'A Volcano in the Moon' and 'O Mistress Mine!', one of Mitchell's later *Millgate* stories, the author demonstrates through this how harmony can be found among people from markedly different backgrounds: and the sting in the tail of the piece, in which the obstructive relative learns to his horror that he himself is descended from a mulatto, forces the point home with some humour.

The theme of social justice does not figure prominently in the story-cycle, but a mild form of socialism is apparent. The political temper of the *Polychromata* is actually much less astringent than that of *Spartacus* and *A Scots Quair*, and the political references scattered throughout the stories give a fair indication of the author's general attitude throughout the series. Significantly, there are no reference at all to communist theory and revolutionary strategy, and the names of Lenin and Trotsky and Marx and Engels, which came to mean so much to Mitchell, are conspicuous by their absence. Instead, the author promotes a much more diluted form of socialism which is based on more widely accessible aims and ideals. In 'He Who Seeks', for instance, Saloney makes glowing reference to 'the pity of the Christ';[12] in 'The Road', he praises the 'Pre-Raphaelite Brotherhood' for its liberated outlook, particularly with reference to the role of women in society;[13] and in 'A Volcano in the Moon', he commends the German Spartacist, Karl Liebknecht, for his pacifism.[14] Mitchell's political moderatism at this time is captured most succinctly in the complimentary reference he makes, again in 'The Road', to 'Ruskin and Morris and the gentle rebels of those days',[15] which suggests that the author's personal credo had more in common with the utopian sentiments expressed in a work like Morris's *News From Nowhere* than with the more forthright approach advocated by Marx or Lenin.

At isolated points in the story-cycle, Mitchell recognises the need to strike a happy balance between political idealism and cold hard pragmatism, qualities which Spartacus and Ewan possess in abundent measure, and in 'Daybreak', Dawn and Roger Mantell, 'doer and dreamer' respectively,[16] represent the ideal blend produced by a combination of these virtues. Less explicitly, Flore Gellion and Friedrich Freligrath stand for a similar conjunction of idealism and realism in 'A Volcano in the Moon', with Flore's somewhat dreamy proclivity for star-gazing being balanced by her partner's more purposeful interest in constructional engineering. The political ideas operating throughout the *Polychromata* are generally more characteristic of the 'dreamer' than of the pragmatist, however, with Wells's influence being particularly noticeable in the work's cosmopolitan and utopian elements.

The cosmopolitan outlook which Mitchell advocates in his essay on 'Glasgow' in *Scottish Scene* is sustained to a large extent by his violent hatred of fascism with its theories of racial superiority, but in these early stories this attitude is less closely connected with political realities. In 'One Man with a Dream', Rejeb ibn Saud expressed a romantic belief in man's ability to live in peace with his neighbour the world over, and this theme of universal harmony reappears in Jane Hatoun's inspiring vision in 'The Road' and in the unlikely romance which flourishes in 'East is West'—an apt title for a tale dealing with this theme—between the proud Englishwoman and the multi-racial scientist, Simon Mogara. This cosmopolitan approach crops up again as a side-issue in 'It is Written', in which Gillyflower Arnold, an American mineralogist contracted to search for oil in Egypt, directly endorses the idea of a world board of control being set up to encourage economic cooperation among nations and to promote greater international understanding. Mitchell's cosmopolitanism is more directly expressed in 'A Volcano in the Moon', one of the most promising of his early stories, only vitiated, like 'He Who Seeks', by the author's crude efforts to burden the narrative with symbolic meaning. The plot of a rift between two eminent selenologists, which is caused by the outbreak of the First World War and which is healed by the union of their son and daughter in marriage, has the simple structure of Shakespearean comedy and, despite the story's unnecessary symbolic complications, the message of universal cooperation remains meaningful. In 'Gift of the River', Keith Landward's efforts to create a World-Speech have an implicit political purpose, Saloney describing his abiding passion as follows:

> It was his dream to build up a scientific international language—not one of the so-easy elisions and evasions, but a tongue founded on the broad evolutions of human speech, a flexible, synthetic World-Speech that would presently be taught the earth over. . . .[17]

The theory of 'the language of Cosmopolis' which Mitchell expounds in 'Literary Lights', with particular reference to Grassic Gibbon's experimentation, has an obvious parallel with Keith Landward's linguistic ideal, and this correspondence is further emphasised by the fictional character's Scottish identity. In addition, the political motive which, Landward acknowledges, lies behind his scientific research—when he tells his wife zealously that, 'there won't be a frontier or a fort in Europe fifty years after we've finished'[18]—reflects something of Mitchell's own enterprise in the use of language. Saloney's revelation that Landward is one of those crusaders 'who toil for the ultimate brotherhood of men' merely confirms the obvious, that neither Landward nor his creator approaches language as a mere scholar: they are socialists trying to foster universal harmony and equality among men.

The majority of Mitchell's *Polychromata* stories end on an overwhelmingly optimistic note, and Wells's influence is evident in this aspect of the story-cycle also. The vision of utopia features in 'The Road', 'A Volcano in the Moon', 'The Life and Death of Elia Constantinidos', 'Vernal' and 'It is Written'. This vision is generally sustained by the force of romantic idealism rather than by any realistic belief in its accessibility. The golden road to freedom which Jane Hatoun envisages is described as a 'mystic' phenomenon, and this is fairly representative of the idealised quality of the political perspective proffered throughout the story-cycle. In addition, the unreservedly optimistic endings grafted on to 'The Life and Death of Elia Constantinidos', 'It is Written' and 'The Passage of the Dawn' fail to expunge the very deep sense of suffering and despair established in the preceding pages. This parallels the central flaw of the early novels. In the stories Mitchell attempts to exorcise his desolate preference for 'the stark deserts of atheism'[19] by creating an exaggerated sense of hope in the glorious future he sees awaiting mankind. *Spartacus* and *A Scots Quair* have an intellectual clarity—which is lacking in the earlier fiction—because Mitchell takes both the secular and spiritual themes further in these books, and because he distinguishes more sharply between the secular and the spiritual, epitomised by Ewan's final discrimination between the search for God and the search for Freedom. In *The Thirteenth Disciple* and *Image and Superscription*, Mitchell goes so far as to suggest that belief in man is comparable with the discovery of faith in God, and the three novels in which this is most pronounced all have their genesis in stories from the *Polychromata*.

Despite certain minor differences, 'The Life and Death of Elia Constantinidos' and *Image and Superscription* follow the same narrative pattern, Elia and Gershom Jezreel each undertaking a quest for hope and meaning in the darkness of modern life, represented powerfully in both works in the joint images of sexual corruption and war. As in the novel, the hope which Elia eventually finds amidst this social and spiritual destitution is of a highly symbolic kind, with his dying vision of 'the People of the Sun' proving an ineffective means of superscribing or eliminating the original Image. Saloney's conclusion is of little more practical relevance in resisting the desolate view of existence provided in the early portions of the story, the glib optimism of his interpretation of the action looking forward to the unrestrained and largely unsustained idealism of the imaginative romances.

The similarities between 'It is Written' and *The Lost Trumpet* are even more striking. Both works use the same plot—the archaeological search for a sacred relic whose discovery promises to be more than just historically important. In the novel the object of the dig is the trumpet with which Joshua is said in the Old Testament to have destroyed the walls of Jericho, while Godfrey Steyn's search in the story is for something even more desirable, 'a Lost Testament, in the handwriting of our Saviour Himself'.[20] Both quests are successful in so far as the ancient trumpet and the lost parchment are eventually run to ground, and both works boast a similar twist in that the significance of the discovery lies not so much with the miraculous properties of the treasures themselves as with the effect that the whole experience has upon the seekers. In both works, the archaeologists seek much the same reward from the exercise—the rediscovery of some kind of faith within the stifling social and spiritual atmosphere of modern life—and in both the talisman is found but crumbles to dust. The trumpet is blown once restoring hope to those who hear it, while the parchment dissolves to dust before its message can be deciphered. However, the act of discovery itself promotes understanding in the participants, providing them with the vital sense of direction which hitherto they lacked. *The Lost Trumpet* and 'It is Written' also initially address the same profound theme of the existence of God and, although Mitchell brings the theme to an unsatisfactory conclusion in both works, the theological problem is especially well set out in the story.

In his introduction to 'It is Written', Saloney observes how traditional religious values are being eroded in modern society. The Islamic creed is pronounced dead, and he takes this to be symptomatic of the general trend in society at large. While he is confident in his prognosis, however, understandably he is less sure of the answer to the question this begs, as to how the void left will subsequently be filled. Four years after this time, in his essay on 'Religion', Mitchell asked himself the same question and predicted,

'One sees rise ultimately . . . in place of Religion—Nothing', explaining that 'one does not seek to replace a fever by an attack of jaundice' (*SH*, p 171); he then went on to describe the happy state of freedom to which men would consequently be introduced. However, it is not strictly true that the demise of religion will leave a complete vacuum, for Mitchell carries on in the essay to consider the moral and spiritual recovery which this liberation would initiate, and he then speculates how this in turn will leave men free to realise their collective destiny in a free and just society, and ultimately to pursue their personal spiritual happiness. *A Scots Quair* is the only work in which Mitchell fully develops this theme to the point where he arrives at an alternative understanding of the spiritual fulfilment—the Freedom in Ewan's terminology—available in modern times. In many of his other works he remains content to achieve the revised understanding of God as some kind of secular aim in life, and 'It is Written' is one of the first works in which he attempted this philosophical revision. Thus, assuming that the traditional religions are indeed dying out, Saloney sees this as a change for the better which promises to banish the more esoteric elements from man's thinking and bring him closer to God, and narrator considering wistfully that 'perhaps there comes the era of God Himself, creedless and testamentless, without priest or shrine, triumphant slowly amidst the darkness'.[21]

The early portions of 'It is Written', which are dominated by the theological discussion between Saloney and Godfrey Steyn and, later on, Gillyflower Arnold, are by far the most interesting part of the work. While Saloney remains fairly non-committal on the subject of the existence of God, Gillyflower, the scientific rationalist, argues vociferously against Steyn who clings to the idea in his passionate desire to find stability and meaning. Gillyflower asks, 'What good has belief in gods ever done?', and 'Isn't our job in this age plain enough—to bring order and decency into human life for the first time and bring adventure back?'.[22] Her own philosophical stance is not completely secure, for she lacks a sense of purpose and direction in her life.

Predictably, the ending of the story is a let-down, as Mitchell's resolution of the two contrasting viewpoints provides no real solution to the crucial theological points which are raised in the course of the narrative. Steyn and Gillyflower agree to settle for the restricted definition of God as personifying the forces which have worked against evil throughout human history, and finally they resolve to devote themselves to this struggle. Ewan's quest for the communist millennium in *Grey Granite* has a compellingly practical appeal, but the understanding of God which Steyn and Gillyflower achieve is more weakly realised, Mitchell refusing to become involved in the precise details of their new mission. Thus, Saloney finally concludes limply that 'perhaps indeed scripts and gods, faiths and fears—they matter nothing if the Message that is written endures'.[23] When the story was republished in *The Calends of Cairo*, Mitchell judiciously left out this bathetic ending, for the work's thematic shortcomings, in which the profound theological questions of the search for spiritual meaning and the role of human suffering are simply left hanging in the air, are made manifest in such an inept conclusion.

The final Polychromata, 'The Passage of the Dawn', also prefigures one of Mitchell's novels, namely *The Thirteenth Disciple*, in theme and execution.

The plot is virtually the same in both works, the author describing in the story how John Gault, like Malcom Maudslay in the novel, sacrifices everything including eventually his own life to explore a remote and inhospitable area of the globe in search of a mystical and elusive ideal, defined in the novel as 'the City of the Sun', and termed 'the Passage of the Dawn' in the story. In the shorter work, as in the novel, the arcane symbolic ending conflicts with the realistic flavour of the preceding narrative, and this detracts critically from the unity of the piece.

In the first half of 'The Passage of the Dawn', John Gault has a strong similarity with Ewan in *Grey Granite* in that Gault is extremely rational and self-assured, being described by Saloney as 'cruel and crude, restless of outlook, tenacious of purpose, without honour and without faith—yet stirred by the gleam occasional of a new vision and a new selflessness',[24] Saloney directly associates this new purposefulness with the demise of the old gods and creeds, affirming that 'there is no courage like to that of their [modern] generation—the generation to which the gods are foolishness and the codes and restraints but maunderings of dull dotards', and adding, 'They cry for life without veils or reticences, and face it without veils themselves.'[25] This is roughly equivalent to the utilitarian approach which Ewan and Chris, in their separate ways, advocate in the trilogy: the emphasis now rests upon philosophical truth, and the article of faith, such a crucial component in traditional religious ideology, comes to represent an increasingly redundant feature within a society based upon rationalistic principles.

Having condemned the traditional attitude out of hand, however, Mitchell shies away from the harsh prospect that he is then afforded, of 'the stark deserts of atheism', and consequently 'The Passage of the Dawn' ends, like 'It is Written', with a shameful compromise. Whereas in the earlier story Mitchell tried to fill the spiritual void represented by a godless universe by exaggerating the importance of the discovery of secular mission, in the final story he uses highly symbolic and romantic techniques to suggest that some form of spiritual fulfilment may still be available to humanity. However, whereas Chris's final act of union with the Land is the logical conclusion of the trilogy, Gault's experience is explained much less lucidly. In fact, where finally Chris's experience is justified in context, the optimistic conclusion which Saloney draws from John Gault's fate is based upon nothing more than a romantic leap of faith. The manner of Gault's death at the hands of hostile bandits is fairly mundane, especially in comparison with Chris's lyrical withdrawal from life, and even Malcom Maudslay, killed by wild beasts, receives a vision of his goal before he dies. Gault himself departs the scene more quietly, and it is left to Saloney to invest his experience with a greater significance. He exclaims at the close:

> The Passage of the Dawn! All his life he had sought for it—and who does not share that search? Somewhere, we dream, between the twilights of love and hate, ease and unease, there is the morning. Somewhere, beyond the mountain-walls, there is wonder and the morning.[26]

An impression emerges in this passage of a sublime spiritual dimension standing behind life, but this is only vaguely asserted without being either brought out into the open or justified within the action of the story. Mitchell himself evidently realised his error in making this belated and half-hearted attempt to give the work deep symbolic meaning, for in *The Calends of Cairo* the final two sentences are emended slightly, with the voice being changed from the first person plural to the third person singular and the tense being switched from the present to the past. By doing this, the author makes Saloney's conclusion seem much more in keeping with the events described, the responsibility having thus been shifted from man in general to Gault himself, the narrator now observing:

> Somewhere, he dreamt, beyond the twilights of love and hate, ease and unease, there was the morning. Somewhere, beyond the mountain-walls, there was wonder and the morning.[27]

Mitchell shows greater assurance in his handling of the question of the spiritual significance of life in 'Gift of the River' and 'Daybreak'. Here again the theme is approached in an unduly oblique way without being fully substantiated. Nevertheless, the important role played by nature in both these stories gives a fascinating foresight of the mature philosophical vision of the 'blasphemer' conceived in *A Scots Quair*.

'Gift of the River' is one of Mitchell's more obscure mystery stories. In it, Joan Landward dies of consumption, but the River Nile with which she had a mystical intimacy comes to represent a benign life-force with supernatural properties, for the mysterious young woman whom Keith Landward later rescues from the river-floods is identified as a reincarnation of his late wife. Mitchell's main intention in this tale, it must be said, is merely to mystify the reader by presenting him with a paranormal situation for which there is no rational explanation and, in his introduction to the narrative, Saloney actually begs leave of his listener to 'tease you for moral'.[28] There is of course no logical explanation for these fantastic events, but Joan Landward's strange affinity with the Nile looks forward, albeit indirectly, to the intimacy which Chris experiences with the Land. Where Joan Landward's story merely gives a hint of the sublime, however, Chris receives insight and enlightenment and eventually consciously apprehends the pattern to which all life conforms.

Mitchell is less guarded in his celebration of the natural world in 'Daybreak', working through a similar plot towards a passionate affirmation of faith in the life-force that he sees at work in nature. The human and natural spheres are welded together from the outset through Dawn's passionate identification with the hills among which she grew up in Scotland, and through the luscious passage describing the events which take place when Roger returns to Scotland to make their wedding arrangements. This passage, with its sensuous fusion of the human and the natural, is especially redolent of *The Rainbow*, Saloney giving a vibrantly rich evocation of the 'earth-magic' which is the young lovers' charmed pre-nuptual experience.[29]

The influence that the environment wields upon human affairs is elaborated further in the remaining portion of the story, when the miscarriage which Dawn suffers in the harsh and unnatural setting of London recommends a move to the more temperate climate of Cairo. There the change proves therapeutic and, fortified by the sensation of spring as it steals over the city, Roger reacts stoically to Saloney's unhappy life-story, reassuring him:

> That is life . . . . And it seems blind chance and aimlessness. . . . But there's some-thing behind it greater than a dark malignancy. Though that malignancy is real enough.[30]

Here again, therefore, Mitchell seems about to perform a leap of faith comparable with that which is effected in 'It is Written' and 'The Passage of the Dawn'. Asked by Saloney to expand this optimistic affirmation, Roger's reply is as woolly as the idealistic endings appended to these other pieces, the speaker basing his faith upon the idea of 'something equally nameless and untheological', which, 'has led us up through the dark Defile of history, has turned in many guises to help again and again the stragglers and the lost in their hour of utmost despair'.[31] Indeed, his conclusion, that, 'It will lead us to the sunrise yet', seems uncomfortably close to the chimerical idealism exuded at the close of 'The Passage of the Dawn'.

The climactic events in 'Daybreak' are designed to bear out the confidence which Roger Mantell and Saloney expressed earlier, that 'there's something behind it [life] greater than a dark malignancy'. However, whereas Mitchell indulges in some sleight of hand in 'It is written' when he attempts to put the theme of faith in man on a par with the theme of faith in God, in this story the central ideas progress in a more straightforward manner and produce a more balanced conclusion.

The tragic prospect afforded by Dawn's determination to carry her second pregnancy through to its conclusion despite the warnings that it could cost her her life shocks both Saloney and Roger, and from this both men attain a bleak vision of the futility of all life, Saloney recalling how 'it seemed to me then, as I think to Roger himself, that the dream of his history was false, that alone and unfriended man wandered amidst the cold immensities of space and time'.[32] This desolate vision stands at the heart of Mitchell's early work, and it reappears sharply in his study of Nansen in *Nine Against the Unknown*. Occasionally, the author himself seems loath to accept this harsh view of life, however, and *The Thirteenth Disciple* and *Image and Superscription* reflect his wish to find something positive to believe in, even something of purely secular importance. 'It is Written' and 'The Life and Death of Elia Constantinidos' both involve this abrupt diversion of interest away from the more distressing spiritual questions towards more promising subjects, and the idealistic symbolism in 'The Passage of the Dawn' shows how far Mitchell was willing to go in order to maintain the illusion of hope.

Mitchell's approach in 'Daybreak' is more honest and purposeful. Dawn's miraculous recovery from her death-bed is little more convincing than is the suggestion of Joan Landward's reincarnation in 'Gift of the River', but at least the philosophical explanation for the event is directly stated, Saloney refuting the formal medical explanation for Dawn's sudden revival by attributing it to dimly perceptible supernatural forces. Thus, moved by these marvellous happenings, in his conclusion Saloney contradicts the stark atheistic pronouncement that he made earlier in his narrative and makes instead a conventional pantheistic affirmation of divine meaning as it is made manifest in the workings of nature, finally overruling the medical verdict in the closing sentence of the piece:

> Yet until prevail the years that make all things dim will it seem to Roger and me that once, in an hour of desperate need, we were granted glimpse of the kindlier, nameless thing that verily shines and abides behind all the blind ways and destinies of Nature.[33]

Looking forward, therefore, *A Scots Quair* thus involves the dynamic fusion of the two philosophical propositions which originally appeared independently in Mitchell's work, the vision of universal meaning being most positively asserted in 'Daybreak', and the justification for this vision being formulated over a year later in 'Near Farnboru'.

STRAY PIECES

The last *Polychromata* story was published in *The Cornhill* in June 1930, and it was over a year before Mitchell's work began to appear again in its pages. In the interim he was kept busy with his historical and archaeological studies and with the writing of his second novel. As a result he wrote only two short stories in this time, 'Near Farnboru' itself—the apocalyptic fantasy which is strongly reminiscent of Wells's 1899 novel *When the Sleeper Wakes*, and which is only remarkable for the isolated paragraph in which the author reaches an approximation of the concept of 'thoroughgoing Materialism'— and 'Roads to Freedom'.

Two months after *The Millgate* had reprinted 'Siva Plays the Game' in April 1931, as the first of five Mitchell stories which appeared in the magazine, it published an original, 'Roads to Freedom'. While the straightforward narrative approach adopted in this piece makes a welcome relief from Saloney's tortuous yarns, Mitchell delves back beyond his *Polychromata* to his early tale of suspense, 'If You Sleep in the Moonlight', for the necessary inspiration in action and method. The *Millgate* piece does, however, have a slightly more pointed theme that its predecessor, and its strictly designed plot, as a slight moral tale of virtue rewarded, harks back to the Augustan novelists, and to Fielding in particular. The escaped convict deserves to win his freedom primarily because he has been unjustly condemned in the first place, nobly chosing to take the blame for a crime committed by his wife. He also earns the freedom that he gains at the end of the story by turning down two opportunities which come his way to make good his escape, on the grounds that innocent parties would be injured. Finally, justice is done when the fugitive wilfully breaks cover because he, like Hardy's Jude, cannot bear to watch a rabbit struggling in a snare; and in the final twist to the tale he is directly rewarded for his compassion, in risking his own freedom in order to set the animal free. Thus, the emphasis in 'Roads to Freedom' is primarily upon its value as entertainment, although the moral propriety of the tale indirectly endorses the qualities of pity the compassion.

PERSIAN DAWNS, EGYPTIAN NIGHTS

The components of Mitchell's second collection of English stories are not organically united in the same way as the *Polychromata*. Indeed, the authorial acknowledgement placed at the beginning of *Persian Dawns, Egyptian Nights* which states that 'These two story-cycles have appeared in the *Cornhill Magazine*' glosses over the truth of the matter, that the tales contained in the collection are actually of diverse origin. The *Persian Dawns* half of the book consists of a story-cycle which, like the *Polychromata*, had been serialised in *The Cornhill*, although the final story in the sequence, 'Dawn in Alarlu', only surfaced in the periodical three months after the book had appeared. The *Egyptian Nights* sequence is made up of more disparate elements, for only two of the six stories are taken from the pages of *The Cornhill*, and these, 'Revolt' and 'Dieneke's Dream', were originally published under different titles, 'One Man with a Dream', which I dealt with earlier, and 'Thermopylae' respectively. Two of the remaining contributions, 'Camelia Comes to Cairo' and 'The Children of Ceres', are originals, and 'Siwa Plays the Game' is Mitchell's first published story expanded to almost twice its length, while 'Amber in Cold Sea' is a reprint of the *Millgate* work called 'The Refugees'.

Despite these motley beginnings, *Persian Dawns, Egyptian Nights* is a remarkably cohesive volume, and Mitchell registered his personal satisfaction with the final product by comparing it favourably with *Sunset Song*, which had been published to great acclaim three months earlier, the author remonstrating with Helen Cruickshank in November 1932 that '*Persian Dawns, Egyptian Nights* is, you know, much better stuff (technically) than *Sunset Song*. But nobody seems to think so, except myself.'[34] It is not surprising that this opinion should have found so little support, for *Sunset Song* provides much more tangible proof of Mitchell's powers as a writer. However, the author deserved to draw some satisfaction from the knowledge that in his second collection of stories, he managed to create an appreciable impression of order from the heterogeneous constituents.

The two story-cycles contained in *Persian Dawns, Egyptian Nights* are closely related to the *Polychromata* in both theme and technique, and several of the characters from the earlier collection reappear in the *Egyptian Nights* series. In addition, similar subjects are considered throughout the volume as a whole and, although Mitchell exercises uncharacteristic caution in his approach to political and philosophical issues, the radical bent of the 'reformer' and the distinctive vision of the 'blasphemer', which dominate his most enduring work, can both be seen taking shape.

The *Egyptian Nights* section is actually a direct continuation of the *Polychromata*, again set in modern-day Cairo, being narrated by Sergei Lubow, a surrogate Saloney whose narrative style is only marginally less stilted than his predecessor's, and involving essentially the same *dramatis personae* as appeared in the first volume. The *Egyptian Nights* stories are, if anything, more dispensable overall than the *Polychromata* ones. 'Siwa Plays the Game', as a slightly more sophisticated rendering of 'Siva Plays the Game', remains of little interest. 'The Refugees', or 'Amber in Cold Sea' as it is called in the book, is a rather pointless romantic 'fairly-tale'[35] in the style of 'He Who Seeks' involving a similar quest for a lost lover, the plot being designed simply to tease the reader for meaning. 'Camelia Comes to Cairo' and 'The Children of Ceres' are also trite works, but the former is of interest as a companion piece to 'Smeddum' in that the twist manufactured at the climax, when Dr Adrian's and Camelia's agreement to retire to bed provides a well deserved slap in the face for the puritanical Kate Adrian, looks forward to the surprise sprung by Meg Menzies at the end of the Scots story. Mitchell's courage seems to fail him in the English work, for he declines to push the moral challenge embodied in this risqué element right through and opts instead to cover himself by disclosing that Adrian and Camelia are, in fact, respectably married. In Meg Menzies's case, the dénouement epitomises her whole uncompromising attitude to life, and consequently 'Camelia Comes to Cairo' appears ill-conceived and weakly carried out in comparison.

Of the six pieces which comprise the *Egyptian Nights* cycle, only 'Revolt', which I considered earlier under its *Cornhill* title of 'One Man with a Dream', and 'Dieneke's Dream', originally called 'Thermopylae', have a direct bearing upon either Mitchell's mature thought or upon his major work. The latter appeared in *The Cornhill* two and a half years after 'One Man with a Dream', and thus, as both stories are projections of the beliefs of the 'reformer', comparison of the two tales highlights the artistic and ideological advances that Mitchell made in that time.

There are shades of *Spartacus* in Mitchell's use of historical legend for political purposes in the later story, but whereas *Spartacus* purports to be some kind of imaginative historical reconstruction, 'Thermopylae' takes the form of an updating of the ancient historical episode of the heroic stand made by the Spartans against the armed mass of the Persian army at Thermopylae. Like *Spartacus*, 'Thermopylae' also has a strong political undercurrent, and its radical temper is much closer to the stern revolutionary perspective which holds sway in *Spartacus* and *A Scots Quair* than to the comparatively innocuous vision of utopia which figures in 'One Man with a Dream' and elsewhere in his weaker fiction.

At this time, Mitchell's shorter fiction was still heavily dependent upon romantic action, but 'Thermopylae' is one of the few of his English stories in which this aspect remains of incidental importance to the overall effect. 'Thermopylae' shows clearly the author's increasingly radical political opinions, and significantly the fictive mode to which it is most closely related is that of socialist realism.

In 'Thermopylae' Mitchell considers the themes of freedom and heroism within the context of a political dispute which takes place in Cairo between a band of Greek immigrants, who stand up for their rights against the profiteering landowners, and the unsympathetic city authorities. Rhizos's mysterious race-memory tenuously associates the Greeks with the heroic band of Spartans who defied the mighty Persian army, 'holding liberty and Thermopylae against the hosts of Asia',[36] and although this is not a wholly satisfactory way to draw the connection, undeniably the heroic act of resistance performed by Rhizos and the Greeks benefits from the parallel. This gambit emphasises the story's status as socialist realism, for one of the major purposes of the genre, as it is represented most forcefully by Gladkov in his description of the workers' struggle to reopen the abandoned factory in *Cement*, is to illustrate the heroic qualities displayed by the working people in the course of their battle for social justice. Gladkov, Gorky, Silone and, to a slightly lesser extent, Sholokhov all do this in their novels, and 'Thermopylae' is the first work by Mitchell in which he attempts to put his knowledge of such works as *Cement* and Gorky's *Mother* to practical use. In fact, Mitchell's description of the Greeks' efforts to remove the mound of waste from their allotment could have been penned by Gladkov or Gorky; Mitchell writes:

They did it. It turned in the telling of later years into an epic of struggle, a thing of heroism and great feats, intermingled with shouted laughter. The fatigue and horror and weariness the years came to cover with the tapestry of legend: how Londos, stripped to a breech-clout, dug and excavated and filled every one of the sacks and baskets for four days on end, the while the others bore them on their two-mile journey—Londos, gigantic, unsleeping, pausing now and then to drink the coffee brought him, and vomit up that coffee at the next nest of dreadful stenches and even more dreadful refuse his shovel uncovered; how the gentle Trikoupi bore loads without ceasing, day or night, till he was found walking in his sleep, a babbling automaton; how the women, laughed at and pelted by the Cairenes, bore load for load with the men. . . .[37]

Mitchell's highly tuned proletarian sympathies, which extended right back to his youth, are manifested in stories like 'One Man with a Dream'. However, the pacifism and romantic idealism of the earlier piece give way to more pragmatic principles in 'Thermopylae'. The two characteristics of pity and courage which were exemplified in the martyrdom of Rejeb ibn Saud remain of critical importance in Mitchell's stance of 'reformer', but these are now accompanied by sterner qualities. Dedication to the common cause now involves a willingness to take up arms if so desired, and Rhizos, on whom the responsibilities of generalship devolve, is certainly more 'doer' than 'dreamer'; he emerges as the quintessential Leninist leader who is not only compassionate but brave, resourceful and, most importantly perhaps, utterly dedicated into the bargain. Thus, it is appropriate that he should give the most eloquent summation of the principles which lie behind the heroic action of the Greeks. His affirmation to Zara that, 'I'd rather mime in the dark than crawl like a coward in the sunlight'[38] is ultimately one of the few really memorable phrases coined in the English stories.

The progression away from the romantic utopianism of 'One Man with a Dream' to the more down-to-earth approach of the socialist realist is also reflected in the scope of the vision which embraces the particular as well as the universal, and 'Thermopylae' actually provides a tolerably sharp picture of a workers' commune as it edges steadily closer to the ideal of a fully integrated, self-sufficient community:

Yet out of its profits the little community succeeded in banking scarcely a piastre. Replacing the saving instinct of generations a new habit had grown upon the weavers—the enrichment and embellishment of Little Perfume. Its gardens grew famous throughout the Warrens. They even planted trees—quick-growing Australian trees procured by Rhizos Trikoupi when he learnt of those plants in botany lessons. A great shed, built of mudbricks, airy and cool and flat-roofed, gradually rose to being in the centre of the one-time rubbish depository. This was the communal loom-shed. Round it, one by one, were built the houses of the weavers—twelve houses with much space and garden-room. Those houses at night were lighted no longer by candles, but by electricity. The long-tapped well brought water to each. . . .[39]

While the political sentiments expressed in 'Thermopylae' may still be basically utopian—for 'Little Perfume' belongs more to the world of the ideal that to reality—the political theme is all the more compelling for the imaginative way in which the ideal is represented. Indeed, the model commune of 'Little Perfume' is very much a New Lanark or a New Harmony, being based upon a methodical plan worthy of someone like Robert Owen.

Of all the stories included in *Persian Dawns, Egyptian Nights,* 'Thermopylae' alone gives a direct foretaste of the themes and techniques which characterise Mitchell's finest work. In purely literal terms, however, the *Persian Dawns* cycle is slightly more satisfying and consistent than the second sequence.

Apart from the fact that the six *Persian Dawns* stories are set in ancient Persia rather than contemporary Egypt, this cycle has an unhealthy resemblance to both the *Polychromata* and the *Egyptian Nights* series. Mitchell again settles upon the form of a first person narrative in order to encourage involvement in the action, although here the narrative actually takes the form of a collaboration between the thirteenth century chronicle, 'those fabulous pseudo-histories leavened with ingenuous moralisings' written by the Nestorian Bishop, Neesan Nerses,[40] and the modern 'raider in history' who acts anonymously as literary mediator and translator.[41] The *Persian Dawns* series is intended to have a kaleidoscopic appeal similar to that of the *Polychromata*, and indeed Bishop Nerses's chronicle, mixing 'record of Alarlu's life and Mongol morals, Nestorian rites and denunciations of the Roman Church, beggars' tales and Persian legends',[42] is actually described as his 'Polychronicon',[43] which obviously echoes Saloney's term. Neesan Nerses's narrative style has the same ponderous strangeness, attributed to its antiquity, as both Saloney's and Sergei Lubow's stories, and although tales such as 'A Footnote to History' and 'Dawn in Alarlu' provide greater insight into the social and cultural life of the ancient Persian world in which they are set, in the long run the *Persian Dawns* tales are no more memorable than Mitchell's other English pieces.

The *Persian Dawns* cycle breaks very little new ground. 'A Footnote to History' constitutes a trite 'tragi-comedy',[44] focusing upon the unlikely friendship which develops between the Bishop's son, who is a Christian, and a Mongol warrior, who is a pagan. The rather cloying account of the two soldiers 'following and misjudging each other in a passionate obstinacy of love'[45] remains of negligible interest, either as art or entertainment. 'The Lost Constituent' is slightly more amusing, as a heavily Marlovian tale of the 'quest of the life-essence' carried out by a heroic Persian warrior.[46] Berkhu, like

Faustus, is dissatisfied with his common lot as a human being, and he resorts to sorcery in an endeavour to find the elusive secret of eternal youth. However, the closing portions of the story are embarrassingly inept: a promising plot is allowed to degenerate into a banal symbolic endorsement of the quality of love, as it is represented by the *deus ex machina* of Berku's miraculously rejuvenated Caucasian slave. 'The Lost Constituent' thus marks an unwelcome return to the inane symbolism which vitiates early works like 'Vernal' and 'The Epic'.

'The Last Ogre' is a simple 'beauty and the beast'-style adventure story in which Nerses's headstrong daughter Amima lands at the mercy of the last representative of a pre-human species, 'uncomprehending, forgotten, discarded in God's vast purposes as yet might be their own conquerors in the deeps of unborn days'.[47] A similar anthropological theme is pursued in *Three Go Back*, in which the time-travellers come face to face with the neanderthalers who, along with the golden hunters, were believed by the diffusionists to have inhabited the world in primitive times. The story is perhaps less sophisticated than the novel, and yet Mitchell achieves an added poignancy in the way he draws the sober moral at the end of the tale, the narrator correcting the conventional image of neanderthal man as a brute, and adopting a more enlightened viewpoint in his summing up.

In 'The Floods of Spring', Mitchell returns again to his vision of utopia, and the more romantic elements of this vision can be attributed to the increasingly obtrusive role which diffusionist dogma was beginning to play in his writing at this time. Zeia and Romi, the messianic representatives of the diffusionist standpoint spreading the anarchistic gospel of 'no-rule' among the Christian villagers of Bashu,[48] criticise civilised values and generally advocate a return to a more natural form of existence. Although their message appears heretical to the more devout members of the village, Nerses recognises the legitimacy of their arguments, and the story ends on a characteristically idealistic note, with Romi's affirmation that, 'some time our dream will come again, no dream, for us and all the world' being borne out by the symbolic 'promise of the sunrise' and by their final triumph over the Euphrates' floods.[49] 'The Floods of Spring' thus seems little removed from the aimless romantic idealism of such stories as 'It is Written' and 'The Passage of the Dawn'; however, the vision which brings it to a close has a more specific political significance as a symbol of revolutionary ardour. The Bishop looking skywards in response to the promptings of one of the villagers discovers that:

> The morning had hesitated still in the sky, strangely. Then, slowly out of darkness, that grey shape like a clenched hand grew to clarity again. From its midst a long red beam of sunlight traversed the sky, quivered, hesitated, acquired hilt and guard, became a sword, and twice, gigantic, arc'ed across the sky.[50]

It would be foolish to read too much into this device, especially considering the comparatively innocuous tone of the rest of the story, and I would not, for instance, compare this image directly with the symbol of the clenched fist which Fionn MacColla identifies as the mark of political fanaticism.[51] It is worth noting, however, that 'The Floods of Spring' was originally published in *The Cornhill* in November 1931, and that 'Thermopylae', which shows undeniable signs of influence by the school of socialist realism, appeared in the very next edition of the magazine. This suggests that Mitchell was not only politically aware when he was writing 'The Floods of Spring', but that he was actually contemplating introducing a radical political dimension into his art. More tellingly, the glorious celestial image of the sword occurs elsewhere in his work in a context which has a pronounced political character, his own 'hymn' to Lenin which ends:

> How long? The years are sun-motes in your sight:
> *'It comes.'* And still by daylight and by night
> Hangs sky-obscuring, making faint the light,
> The shadow of a sword.[52]

In the light of this evidence, it seems reasonable to assume that the vision described at the climax of 'The Floods of Spring' has a covert significance as a symbol representing the radical measures which Mitchell deemed to be necessary for the ultimate fulfilment of his political objectives.

'Cartaphilus' is a complex mystery story which employs the familiar device of the surprise ending, Baisan Evid himself turning out to be the apocryphal figure of Cartaphilus, who is described as, 'the Jew who had mocked the Passion of Christ, and because of that mocking still wandered the world unresting and undying; Cartaphilus the Denier; Cartaphilus the forsaken of God and men'.[53] With Evid transmuting into Cartaphilus, it transpires that the mysterious figure whom he had taken for the wandering Jew is in fact Christ himself, and this portrayal of Christ as an outcast from society clearly anticipates 'Forsaken', which makes a condemnation of contemporary urban society by realising Christ as a lonely misunderstood figure lost in a modern Scottish city. In 'Cartaphilus' Christ is also represented as the personification of the quality of compassion, and as in the Scots story, Christian ethics are ascribed a latent political purpose, offering the key to the 'salvation of earth's agonies'.[54] The world represented in 'Cartaphilus' is a world of pain and senseless suffering and, like Godfrey Steyn in 'It is Written', Evid desperately strives to believe that there is something greater than this, something that will offer some kind of justification or solution. In 'It is Written', Steyn and Gillyflower Arnold acquire a titular and unspecified sense of purpose, but in 'Cartaphilus', Evid's hopes have a direct political character as an embodiment of Mitchell's twin ideals of freedom and equality, Evid asking himself impatiently during his quest, 'Why then did the Christ delay that Second Coming of His that was *to crumble away prison and palace alike* like the wrack of a dream?' [my italics].[55]

While 'Cartaphilus' takes over where 'It is Written' leaves off in the previous story-cycle, 'Dawn in Alarlu' plays much the same role in the *Persian Dawns* cycle as that which 'The Passage of the Dawn' plays in the *Polychromata*, bringing the series to an optimistic conclusion. 'Dawn in Alarlu' is, however, a more interesting piece of work than the rather bland Saloney story, for it develops the theme, touched upon in 'The Floods of

Spring', of the inadequacy of traditional ascetic discipline as a means of attaining spiritual fulfilment in the modern world. Although the story lacks the authority of A Scots Quair, there are certain similarities between Nerses, as he prepares to meet his fate, and Chris as she faces up to the prospect of death at the end of the trilogy. While Nerses fails to attain the state of absolute spiritual liberation which is Chris's reward, his endorsement of Eskandar's sensuous attitude, which he finally prefers to Eidon's contrastingly ascetic approach, does give a foretaste of the later principle of Freedom as it is defined in the trilogy.

The choice facing Nerses is an expression of the Cartesian duality of man, as constituting both body and soul. Given warning that he is nearing his death, the Bishop considers how best to prepare for this, and the choice is externalised in the persons of Eidon and Eskandar. Inspired by Eskandar's rebellious indulgence in the physical and sensuous aspects of life—which harks back to Browning's intemperate monk in 'Fra Lippo Lippi'—Nerses finally decides to meet his fate in the world for which he has such an affection rather than shut himself away in a monastery in order to make his peace with God. In making this choice, Nerses is condoning Eskandar's revision of the biblical epigram with which Eidon taunts him, the original rhetorical question, 'What shall it profit a man though he gain the whole world and lose his own soul?' being twisted and flung back in Eidon's face as Eskandar asks, 'What shall it profit a man if he gain his own soul and lose the whole world?'.[56] As a 'blasphemer', Mitchell consistently condemned the view that spiritual fulfilment is attendant upon religious observance and, while it does not go nearly so far as A Scots Quair in outlining a positive alternative, 'Dawn in Alarlu' at least points the way forward to the mature vision.

MASTERPIECE OF THRILLS

Mitchell's most elusive stories are without question the seven contributions published in Masterpiece of Thrills, an extremely rare anthology produced as a free gift by The Daily Express in London. Although Geoffrey Wagner included details of the volume in his original bibliography of Mitchell's work,[57] neither Ian Munro nor Douglas Young makes any reference to the volume in their books on Mitchell. I could not find any British library that could lay claim to owning this item, and even The Daily Express itself was unable to trace the book for me. Indeed, so far as I am aware, the only institution which has a copy in its possession is the Library of the University of Louisville, Kentucky, in the United States.[58] I am therefore indebted to Dr Isobel Murray of the English Department at the University of Aberdeen for giving me access to her personal copy of the book.

Of Mitchell's seven stories, one, 'Kametis and Evelpis', is credited jointly to J Leslie Mitchell and Fytton Armstrong, while half the remainder are attributed to Gibbon. Three appeared elsewhere: 'First and Last Woman', here accredited to Grassic Gibbon for unknown reasons, is the Mitchell story 'Near Farnboru' published in Reynolds's Illustrated News in 1931; 'The Road to Freedom' is the same tale which appeared in The Millgate in 1931 as 'Roads to Freedom'; and 'Lost Tribes' is none other than 'Lost Tribe', which appeared in *The Millgate* in January 1934.

I have already discussed 'The Road to Freedom' and 'First and Last Woman' in their earlier incarnations, and, with one exception, the five other Mitchell offerings from this collection are equally undistinguished. 'Lost Tribes' is a whimsical Rider Haggard type adventure yarn in which an explorer turns down the chance to elope with a beautiful Central American princess on racial grounds, only to discover that she is of even purer lineage than he himself. 'Kametis and Evelpis', another adventure story, only more redolent of Conan Doyle's *The Lost World* than of Rider Haggard's romances, also pays lip-service to Mitchell's interest in exploration. Again, it is rather far-fetched, and despite the author's cautious and muted endorsement of libertarian politics and the slight incidental interest provided by the reappearance of Andreas van Koupa, the poet from *Stained Radiance*, overall it remains unimportant. Mitchell turns from the world of exploration to that of archaeological investigation with little more success in 'A Stele from Atlantis', this being a trite tale involving the mysterious discovery of a crime of passion inexplicably recorded in its execution by an ancient Ionian device resembling a record player; and 'Busman's Holiday' is an even more bizarre suspense story in which a gang of car thieves is brought to justice by a captive who turns out to be a man in drag.

'The Woman of Leadenhall Street' is the only Mitchell contribution in this collection which has any lasting appeal, and even then it can be accounted only a minor work. The tale is well told, however, as the author explores with sensitivity the credulous and naive mentality of one of man's primitive ancestors. In addition, the symbolic dimension introduced to the narrative through the agency of the emblem of the 'Shining Stone' deftly forges a connection between the sacrificial rites of ancient times and the ills of modern civilisation, thus giving the story a representative status which is wholly absent in Mitchell's other contributions to *Masterpiece of Thrills*. Indeed, symbolic techniques are seldom used to such good effect in Mitchell's work as they are in this short fragment.

Although the majority of Mitchell's English stories are inconsequential as literature, they provide a valuable index to his political and philosophical ideas as they evolved over the years, with the increasing militancy of the 'reformer' and the developing assurance of the 'blasphemer' gradually becoming more prominent. In addition, the three *Polychromata* works which spawned full-blown novels indicate that Mitchell directly regarded the shorter mode as a testing ground for the mature art of his major fiction.

FOUR

The Scots Stories

'GREENDEN'

Although the work published under the pseudonym of Grassic Gibbon is Mitchell's most memorable, it is easy to overestimate the importance of this fact. Indeed, the Scottish stories explore the same basic themes as the English ones, and the most striking differences between the Mitchell and Gibbon products are essentially technical.

The shorter Grassic Gibbon fiction was clearly written by Mitchell as an attempt to cash in on the spectacular success that he had won in 1932 with the publication of *Sunset Song*. 'Greenden' was published in *The Scots Magazine* in December 1932, only three months after *Sunset Song* had made its original appearance, and although the characterisation, setting and narrative technique of the story all have their origins in the innovative approach of the first Gibbon novel, the plot has its genesis in a crude synopsis by Mitchell of a more conventional mystery story called 'The Lost Whaler', the action of which was summarised as follows:

> The young, dour captain marries the fresh, simple girl who has never left the land. They set out for the Arctic. No whales. The captain refuses to turn about. The girl grows very silent. Whales.
>
> They turn south. The captain hears his wife below singing 'There is a green hill far away'. He goes down to her. She is mad.[1]

The nautical action is dropped and the tragedy deepened in the Scots tale, but this synopsis remains recognisable as the prototype for 'Greenden', for it contains the same song motif and roughly similar characterisation, and the same basic theme of the dangers of human alienation from the sublime influence of nature is central to both works.

Of all the Gibbon stories, 'Greenden' has most in common with Mitchell's shorter English fiction, both in its melodramatic action and in its suggestive thematic approach which is reminiscent of Saloney's predilection for teasing the reader. The theme of 'Greenden' itself looks back to pieces like 'Gift of the River' and 'Daybreak', for it also concerns the relationship between man and nature, although this is a considerably more complex issue in the Scots tale. In the English stories, Mitchell employs mainly romantic techniques to promote his theme and, although 'Greenden' has much in common with these, Mitchell uses the same realistic literary techniques in the shorter work as those he had used three months earlier in *Sunset Song*. The story in general, and the theme in particular, benefit enormously from being so strongly rooted in reality, and the magic of 'Greenden' lies in its subtle fusion of realism and romance, in the way in which it remains so firmly grounded in reality and yet retains a greater symbolic power.

The complex interaction between realism and symbolism has proved something of a stumbling block for critics, who have tended to describe the work in terms which serve to simplify the story beyond all recognition. This is a criticism I would make of Douglas Young's definition of the piece in question as 'a Diffusionist parable',[2] and D M Budge uses the same simplistic phrase in his introduction to the schools edition of the Grassic Gibbon essays and stories.[3] I feel, however, that the tensions created in the work and the author's oblique approach contribute greatly to the overall effect, and that consequently those critics who attempt either to ignore or resolve these tensions are doing the work a disservice.

Two of the most important elements of this story probably came from Mitchell's own experience in the Mearns. Whilst the farm described in 'Greenden' does not seem to have been based upon any actual location, the name came readily to hand, for one of the crofts, now derelict, lying off the Reisk road less than a mile from the Mitchells' 'sma' holding' of Bloomfield is called Greenden. In addition, it is most likely that the idea for the fictional suicide came from real life, as two particularly notorious cases occurred in Arbuthnott during the early years of this century when Leslie Mitchell was still living at Bloomfield.[4]

The characterisation in 'Greenden' maintains an impressive balance between the black and the white, with the kindliness of the grocer Alec Webster atoning for the scurrilous behaviour of the Murdochs of the Mains, and the disloyalty of George Simpson being counterbalanced by his wife's innocent trustfulness. Mitchell also employs the same narrative mode first introduced in *Sunset Song*, incorporating frequent shifts in point of view and involving a similar representative 'folk-voice' which thrives upon hearsay and, ignoring truth, revels in malicious gossip. As in *Sunset Song*, this narrative mode is the source of much humour as well as some biting satire: it also has an ulterior motive in the story, in that it adds to the brooding, claustrophobic atmosphere which gradually builds up throughout the piece.

The tone of the story underlines the theme, as the irrepressible humour of the opening stanzas gradually gives way to a more sombre tone which culminates in the pathos evoked by the tragic events detailed at the close. Mrs Simpson's experience is tragic, although not in any classical sense of the term, for her death is not morally edifying; and its significance cannot be fully explained in rational terms.

'Greenden' is not just the simple tale of marital neglect and environmental alienation that a crude plot summary would suggest. For although George Simpson is the one who takes to the country way of life, and although his wife herself later confesses to Alec Webster, 'I've tried not to show it . . . but the trees—they hate me, the fields' (*SH*, p 37), paradoxically she is the only character who is sensitive to the freshness of the experience of the natural world. Having newly arrived at Greenden, she tells Alec Webster that 'the country's lovely to live in' (*SH*, p 70), and this romantic notion—basically that of the incomer—receives practical confirmation later on as she recognises the irresistible 'earth-magic' of the country, conveyed even in such a slight phenomenon as the rustle of the trees. In one way, therefore, her upbringing in the town has made Ellen Simpson more responsive to the natural world with which the indigenous country dwellers like the Murdochs and even the otherwise sympathetic Alec Webster have lost contact: familiarity for them has indeed bred contempt. Ultimately, Ellen's intimacy with nature is concentrated upon the opening through which she can see the sunlight playing upon the hills:

> . . . it was from the kitchen door alone of Greenden that the swathe of the trees and the broom was broken and through the hollow that was left in the gloaming the sun struck light on the Grampian slopes, long miles away and across the Mearns, shining immediate, yet distant and blue, their green earth-hazed in the heatherbells (*SH*, p 35).

The immediate surroundings of Greenden are of a markedly different character, however, and Mitchell subtly plays off the idealised image of the green hills, with their 'quiet faces' (*SH*, p 39), against the hostile environment of the 'green den', the farm in which they are 'smothered away from the world' (*SH*, p 36). The oppressive atmosphere associated with Greenden—for which Joan Lindsay's fine novella *Picnic at Hanging Rock* provides a modern analogue in the mysterious ambience of its remote location—is not merely a projection of Mrs Simpson's disillusionment with the reality of country life, for others sense this peculiar quality in the vicinity of the farm. Thus, two-thirds of the way through the story, the anonymous narrator feels a curious sense of fear when he is returning from a visit to Greenden:

> . . . going up home through the dark you'd be filled with fancies daft as a carrying woman, as though the trees moved and the broom was whispering, and some beast with quiet breath came padding in your tracks; and you'd look, and 'twas only a whin that you'd passed. And you'd heave a great breath, outside of the Den, up in the light of the evening sun, though the Den below was already in shadow (*SH*, p 35).

Ellen Simpson's strange behaviour in response to this peculiarly oppressive environment is not unprecedented either, for when Alec Webster first discovers her derangement he is immediately reminded of old Grant, her predecessor at Greenden, who 'also had whispered and whispered like that' (*SH*, p 37). Just as in *Picnic at Hanging Rock*, the key to 'Greenden' lies in the external agencies involved in the action rather than in the personal psychology of Simpson's wife.

The central issue in 'The Lost Whaler' is the girl's separation from her native environment, and there is a similar theme in 'Greenden', for the appearance of Murdoch's barn finally cuts Ellen Simpson off from sight of the green hills which are all that have sustained her in her isolation. On a personal level, there is latent irony in that her husband's friends the Murdochs should be the ones to precipitate her fate by separating her from the source of sanity. And in a fashion this critical environmental change is a symbolic reflection of the action, with the swelling structure of the barn coming to represent the husband's increasing negligence and profligacy. Ultimately, however, the story has a greater significance beyond the personal sphere.

The most prominent contrast established in the narrative is that between the 'green den', which is a repressive, stifling domicile, and the inspirational 'green hill'. These give a sense of the ambivalent influence of the natural world, at once kind and cruel, serene and severe, and it is against this dichromatic backdrop that the human tragedy is played out. In this case, the tragedy revolves around the wife's self-sacrifice for her husband, and is reinforced by the words of the hymn 'There is a green hill far away' which originally convinced Ellen that they should remove to the health-restoring environment of the country; the act gains added poignancy from its tacit association with Christ's sacrifice, Simpson's wife exclaiming in her hysteria towards the end of the story, 'George—he's safe now, he's safe, God died, but I needn't, He saved him, not I' (SH, p 37). Contrary to her belief here, however, Ellen is later driven to take her life by the eclipsing of the light shining on the hills, and the impact of the story as a whole rests largely upon the interpretation of this event. There is undoubtedly a sense that she is, in a Christ-like way, assuming the responsibility for the sins of her husband, and indeed for the community as a whole; certainly, in her innocence, she stands apart from the maliciousness and bitterness of the rural community. There is also a sense that she herself has been permanently contaminated by city life and that, despite her avowed empathy with her rural environment, she is in some way eternally smirched, and hence the sinister natural forces operating in the Den are relentlessly set against her. Indeed, the final impression the story gives is that she has succumbed to forces infinitely greater than herself—both the forces of civilisation from which she strives unsuccessfully to escape and which in the shape of Murdoch's barn finally shut out the life-giving light shining on the hills beyond, and the elemental forces which consequently drive her to despair and suicide.

It seems morally reprehensible that George Simpson, who has so neglected his spouse, should survive while his wife, whose innocent and childlike qualities are stressed throughout the story, should forfeit her life, and yet this deepens the tragic effect of the piece in a Hardyesque fashion. In the closing paragraph, however, Alec Webster, travelling for the doctor, appreciates the benevolence of the hills from which Simpson's wife became estranged, 'the green hills that stood to peer with quiet faces in the blow of the wind from the sunset's place' (SH, p 39), and to a certain extent, again in a manner reminiscent of Hardy's major novels, this alleviates the human tragedy.

Although I would dispute Douglas Young's claim that 'Greenden' constitutes anything as explicit as a 'Diffusionist parable', I would agree that the work has a lasting power that extends beyond the merely literal. The simple story of a woman driven to madness and suicide ultimately touches upon the mysteries and iniquities of the human condition itself by providing a fleeting impression of man as a vulnerable creature at the mercy of vastly superior forces. The vision is thus basically tragic—in the modern philosophical sense of the term—and yet it is not devoid of hope for at the end of the story the green hills continue to turn 'quiet faces' upon the human scene, even if the people themselves, excepting Alec Webster, are oblivious to their benign presence.

It is, however, virtually impossible to do full justice to 'Greenden' by process of elucidation because much of the action is left unexplained as Mitchell strives to achieve a certain effect rather than communicate any specific idea. Ultimately, like the finest of MacDiarmid's lyrics in *Sangshaw* and *Penny Wheep*, the story is greater than the sum of its parts and, in view of its inner tensions, it cannot be simplified without being deprived of much of its power. 'Greenden' does not 'tease', but it does depend heavily upon delicate measures of suggestion and understatement. Its beauty and appeal, unlike the other stories, cannot be easily pinned down, for it represents a potent mixture of disparate elements, of realism and symbolism, comedy and tragedy. Such a bold experiment could have proved disastrous but, in the final analysis, the story works extremely well.

'SMEDDUM'

The next Gibbon piece to appear is a very different proposition from 'Greenden'. 'Smeddum' is arguably the most popular Gibbon story, which is not really surprising, for it is the most humorous and possibly also the most straightforward. However, the lack of complexity belies the hard work which went into the piece's creation and, as with 'Greenden', the plot of 'Smeddum' can be perceived in another early synopsis by Mitchell, this time for a story entitled 'Gypsy', which runs as follows:

> The fisher-girl wishes to marry the gypsy. Her parents refuse to have anything to do with the matter. Parents discover couple together in embarrassing circumstances. Girl hints that they'd be compelled to marry.
> Father and lover go out of room. Mother and daughter talk. Mother hints that her daughter is daughter to a gypsy also. Advises daughter to marry *her* lover. Daughter and lover discuss matter afterwards. Daughter laughs over stratagem—there is no necessity for them to marry.[5]

Such a crude summary perhaps seems an unlikely forerunner for such a justly celebrated work as 'Smeddum', and yet the elements of domestic upheaval, marital intrigue and moral challenge undeniably anticipate the superb twists conceived in the Scots story. Of course, it is quite a jump from this embryo to the final version of the tale as it was published in *The Scots Magazine*, and a notebook containing plans drawn up in pencil by Mitchell for *Cloud Howe* (under the working title of 'The Morning Star') and *Grey Granite* also contains two drafts for 'Smeddum', originally called 'The Old Woman', and later simply 'Freedom'.[6] Although the old woman's original family of fourteen children was later pruned to nine, both these drafts are identifiable as prototypes in characterisation and plot, and—in 'Freedom'—also in theme.

Mitchell was especially fond of the surprise ending, and stories like 'He Who Seeks', 'East is West' and 'Camelia Comes to Cairo' all exploit this particular device. 'Smeddum' is a peerless example of a story written in this format.

'Smeddum' takes the simplest story form, that of the character study. Meg

Menzies is a marvellous creation, a superb embodiment of the quality of 'smeddum', and Gibbon's distinctive narrative mode creates both humour and pathos fron the portrait. Meg's fearsomeness as the matriarch who terrorises family and community alike is compromised by her blind spot for Will's weaknesses, especially his lazinesss and his fondness for whisky. Despite this apparent oversight, Meg implements a rigidly strict code of justice in which both those who transgress against her offspring, such as the teacher and the doctor, and the children who, like Jock, are themselves the transgressors, are punished accordingly. Indeed, it is when Meg is forcing Jock to do the honourable thing by Ag Grant that the story title is given its first tentative explanation, Meg telling her errant son that, 'It needs smeddum to be either right coarse or right kind' (SH, p 8). As the superb dénouement proves later, Meg herself matches up perfectly to this definition, her apparent coarseness being counterbalanced by the generosity of spirit which she shows in her various dealings on her family's behalf.

Apart from Will, Kathie is the only character who seems to escape Meg's iron rule, and Mitchell drops several clues throughout the story which prepare the way for the climactic revelation that Meg and Kath are truly 'like mother, like daughter', two of a kind. Early on, the anonymous rustic narrator interprets the unusual relationship between Meg and Will as an endorsement of the institution of marriage, commenting with comic disingenuousness, 'it was well that there was a thing like marriage, folk held together and couldn't get apart; else a black look-out it well would be for the fusionless creature of Tocherty toun' (SH, p 6). However, in discussion with the minister at Ag's wedding, Meg is strangely unforthcoming on the subject of matrimony. Throughout the narrative, Mitchell also carefully emphasises the resemblance between Meg and Kathie, who stands apart as 'a limner that alone tongued her mother' (SH, p 9). Her self-assurance is obviously inherited from her mother, and in addition she has a certain physical resemblance, being described as 'tall, like Meg, and with red hair as well' (SH, p 10).

In the light of these subtle promptings, therefore, Meg's observation that Kath 'takes after myself' (SH, p 14) has a sharp ring of truth, although of course it is not yet known just how diligently Kath is following in her mother's footsteps. Meg's ultimate confession of her adultery—or revelation, for she gives no impression of guilt—provides a glorious ending to the story, confirming the similarity between mother and daughter and turning the tables upon the hypocritical members of the family who wish to see Kath brought to heel. The comedy with regard to Meg herself is that both the factual manner in which she discloses her secret and the actual essence of the disclosure itself are so true to character. Kathie, like her mother, is independent and carefree and utterly careless of conventional moral standards, and this, as Meg explains abruptly to her startled family, is the living definition of 'smeddum':

> She's fit to be free and to make her own choice the same as myself and the same kind of choice. There was none of the rest of you fit to do that, you'd to marry or burn, so I married you quick. But Kath and me could afford to find out. It all depends if you've smeddum or not (SH, p 14).

Meg thus fully vindicates herself for the 'reign of terror' which she perpetrated earlier, for it transpires that the stern line she took with the weaker members of her family was adopted for their own good. Meg is not just a strict disciplinarian by nature, for her attitude towards her family is discretionary, but she is astute enough to realise when strict measures are required in order to help the weaker members. Far from being a tyrant, she is a strong character who turns out to have had the kindness to stick with her nominal husband when she had no legal obligation to do so, and when he in fact was not deserving of her support: she also turns out to have had the motherly concern that her children should fulfil themselves to the best of their capabilities, and the intelligence to recognise whether it is best for her to adopt an active or a passive role in their development. Thus, Jock and Ag, lacking 'smeddum', are thrust into marriage. Kathie, however, possesses 'smeddum', and therefore like her mother, she does not require the formal security afforded by marital ties and, again like Meg, she has the courage and assurance to seek some greater form of fulfilment.

Mitchell's accomplishments in 'Smeddum' justify the three other titles which he considered at one time or another for the story. As a character study of tremendous vitality, 'The Old Woman' would seem most appropriate, but 'Freedom' is most representative of the challenge which Meg Menzies makes to established social *mores*. And it is apt that the earliest surviving draft of the story should centre upon the figure of a gypsy, as the moral challenge which Meg Menzies represents in her flouting of traditional standards bears some resemblance to the Rebelaisian sense of anarchy and freedom evoked in Burns's 'The Jolly Beggars'. Overall, however, 'Smeddum' is the most satisfactory title for the piece, for this expressive and ultimately untranslatable Scots word captures both Meg's distinctive mettle and the greater theme of 'Freedom'.

The author's anarchist principles are involved in 'Smeddum', although they are more muted in this work than in stories like 'The Passage of the Dawn' and 'The Floods of Spring'. Legal ties are necessary only for the weak, as is the case with Ag and Jock, while their mother's robust sense of freedom and independence, her 'smeddum', places her beyond such considerations. In this way, Meg Menzies is a humorous personification of Mitchell's anarchist ideal of self-sufficiency and self-determination. Yet although she asserts her individuality this is not an indictment of her social sympathies and her concern for others. On the contrary, being so sure of herself, Meg sees more clearly what is in the best interests of others.

In the final analysis, it is not for its comparatively lightweight theme that 'Smeddum' is best remembered, but for the superb manner of its literary execution. The story has many graces, from the compellingly vigorous narrative to the controlled simplicity of the plot which ushers the reader inexorably on from the powerful opening paragraph through to the superb dénouement engineered at the tale's close. 'Smeddum' may not be one of Mitchell's most profound works, but it is certainly one of his most impressive.

'CLAY'

The last Gibbon piece published in *The Scots Magazine* is Mitchell's finest
story overall, for it marries the artistry of 'Smeddum' with a thematic
profundity unparalleled elsewhere in his shorter fiction. This story seems to
have been more spontaneously conceived than 'Greenden' and 'Smeddum',
both of which are indebted in some measure to themes and techniques
evolved in earlier work. The most important component of 'Clay', however,
the theme expounded in the closing paragraphs, is obviously a distillation of
Mitchell's own deepest philosophical beliefs, and in fact the epigram which is
the focal point of the work is derived from the inscription written by the
author inside the front cover of his army notebook, 'All life that was clay and
awoke and strove to return again to its mother's breast.'[7] This theme thus
borders upon territory covered more fully in *A Scots Quair*, and the literary
techniques employed in the story are also derived from this source.

Although the rural background is graphically realised in 'Smeddum' 'Clay'
is steeped even more deeply in the routines and rituals of farming life, as is
appropriate in such a study of a compulsive farmer. As he does consistently
throughout *Sunset Song*, Mitchell succeeds admirably in creating a vivid
sense of beauty in his depiction of rural life in the story, and he does so
without romanticising it. In 'Clay', this particular talent is seen to best effect
in the evocative representation of Rob Galt's early morning start at the
ploughing:

> And then, while the dark still lay on the land, and through the low mist that slept on
> the fields not a bird was cheeping and not a thing showing but the waving lanterns
> in the Segget wynds, he'd harness his horses and lead out the first, its hooves
> striking fire from the stones of the close, and cry to the second, and it would come
> after, and the two of them drink at the trough while Rob would button up his collar
> against the sharp drive of the frozen dew as the north wind woke. Then he'd jump
> on the back of the meikle roan, Jim, and go swaying and jangling down by the
> hedge, in the dark, the world on the morning's edge, wet, the smell of the parks in
> his face, the squelch of the horses soft in the clay (*SH*, p 19).

In this half paragraph, Mitchell captures beautifully the stern lyricism of
the life of the land. Gibbon's versatile narrative mode also gives adequate
scope for the creation of impressive onomatopoeic effects, such as the verbal
and syntactic imitation of the rhythm of ploughing shown in the following
sentence:

> Then he'd spit on his hands and cry *Wissh, Jim!* no longer ill-natured, but high-out
> and pleased, and swink the plough into the red, soaked land; and the horses would
> strain and snort and move canny and the clay wheel back in the coulter's trace, Rob
> swaying slow in the rear of the plough, one foot in the drill and one on the rig (*SH*,
> p 19).

Despite the arresting power of Mitchell's descriptive work, however, 'Clay'
amounts to far more than just a realistic portrait of farming life in the
Mearns. As in 'Greenden', the animistic techniques which Mitchell uses to

bring Rob Galt's 'fiere' vividly to life are intimately related to the philosophical vision standing at the heart of the story. The vitality with which Rob's land is described, repeatedly being accorded human characteristics, adds credibility to the central proposition, articulated elsewhere by Mitchell in stories like 'Gift of the River' and 'Daybreak', that nature is a benign force, and that ultimately, as the 'earth mother', it represents the basis of all life.

'Clay' has the same basic tonal movement as 'Greenden', the hilarity of the opening gradually giving way to the poignancy of the ending. The logical development of the plot, however, corresponds more closely with the tight structure of 'Smeddum', but whereas the effect of the latter depends largely upon the twist fashioned at the climax, 'Clay' progresses towards the final conclusion in a more steadfast manner.

Although Rob Galt's experience does not have the significance of Chris's return to the Land in *A Scots Quair*, there is a similar air of inevitability, indeed, of propriety, in the way he gravitates towards the ancient grave which opens up invitingly in the clay soil of Pittaulds.

The farmer's graduation from the carefree worker introduced at the start of the story through to the monomaniac for whom 'the fields mattered and mattered, nothing else at all' (*SH*, p 25), is accomplished smoothly, in distinct stages. Rob's relationship with his family is the main yardstick by which this growing obsession with the fields of Pittaulds is gauged. To begin with, even the thrawn narrator praises Rob as 'a fine, frank childe that was kindness itself' (*SH*, p 17). Before he gains the lease of Pittaulds, he displays a seemingly unquenchable appetite for sheer hard work, but this does not interfere with his happy home life in the early stages: the kindness that he lavishes upon his wife and child at this time is excessive, the narrator noting dourly that he 'spoiled them both' (*SH*, p 18). Having settled in Pittaulds, however, Rob becomes more crabbit in general, and as he becomes increasingly preoccupied with the farm, so he also becomes increasingly prone to neglect his duties, both as father and husband. As her father's dedication to the life of the soil turns into an actual addiction to the clay fields of Pittaulds, therefore, Rachel soon discovers that the only way she can get through to him is by helping out with the farming chores. She gains little reward for her services, and when an opportunity arises for Rob to demonstrate his love and show his gratitude to her by sponsoring her further education at college, such is his devotion to his work that he never gives the idea a second thought, but continues instead to reinvest his profits in the farm.

As in 'Smeddum', the secondary characters, who happen again to be the protagonist's immediate relatives, play an important role in the later stages of the story. Rob's alienation from his family reaches a nadir when, in his eternal 'trauchle' with the coarse land of Pittaulds, he abandons his wife, who is terminally ill with cancer. This set of priorities is beautifully captured in the tragi-comic episode in which the farmer obeys his daughter and looks in on his wife as she lies on her sick bed, only to deprive the act of all its poignancy by using the opportunity to file a report on the current state of the harvest.

At this point in the story Rob's status as a sympathetic character comes under severe threat, and his subsequent detachment at his wife's funeral borders upon the criminal. However, Rachel now consolidates her position as the second most important character in the story, for it is primarily through her final inability to hate Rob, 'hard though she tried' (*SH*, p 25), that Mitchell retains his reader's sympathy for his protagonist.

Rachel serves a dual function in 'Clay' for, as both promising academic and sympathetic onlooker she is admirably qualified to articulate the theme at the end of the story. Rob's death is reported with deliberate economy, although not before he himself has indicated the representative nature of his experience by acknowledging kinship with the farmer of ancient times whose grave is unearthed in his fields. Like the crofters in *Sunset Song*, however, his responsibility is merely to act, and he does this by responding spontaneously to life. He is incapable of capturing the essence of his experience in words, and thus Rachel, sensitive to the 'whistle of the whins' and the 'whisper' of the fields (*SH*, p 27), is left to draw meaning from her father's life at the end of the work, in precisely the same way as Robert Colquohoun acts as eloquent legislator for the dead crofters of Kinraddie at the end of *Sunset Song*. Rachel's summation is not rhetorical like Robert's but indirectly channelled through her consciousness, yet the similarity remains clear.

The thematic parallel between 'Clay' and *Sunset Song* is even more striking, however, for in both works Mitchell elucidates his ingrained sense of the elusive quality which he had described nearly three years earlier in 'Daybreak' as 'the earth-magic'. In *A Scots Quair* as a whole and in 'Clay', Mitchell explores this quality more deeply, with the result that these works are substantially more powerful artistically and intellectually.

The three years which separate 'Daybreak' and 'Clay' in Mitchell's bibliography are reflected in the aesthetic and also the ideological properties of the stories. 'Daybreak' is a highly romantic piece, not just with regard to its action, for it is both vague and assertive in its thematic approach, the author making no effort whatsoever to provide proof for the central idea that nature represents a benevolent life-force. In 'Clay' Mitchell pursues the same basic theme, but he attempts to provide some objective form of philosophical justification to sustain his sentiments. Indeed, the vision embodied in 'Clay' is itself of a much higher order than the essentially romantic affirmation made in 'Daybreak', for it has much in common with *A Scots Quair*, in which the author follows a line of thought which ultimately reduces life to its most fundamental level, although without depriving it of meaning.

The attractively simple symbolic development in the story helps to lend credibility to the theme. To begin with, the substance represented in the title merely describes the poor quality of the land which Rob Galt has to contend with at Pittaulds, but it acquires a greater significance at the end of the piece where Rachel, fired by her meditation upon Rob's life and death, achieves an apprehension of sublime meaning. Like Chris's last vision, Rachel's also creates a sense of stability from the fusion of the two contradictory forces of life and death. Chris eventually finds security in the prospect of eternal Change, and similarly Rachel sees clay as the material embodiment of this eternal fluctuation between life and death. The lowly substance thus comes to signify the ultimate truth of existence: life emerges from it and death returns to it—as Rachel realises:

All life—just clay that awoke and strove to return again to its mother's breast (*SH*, p 27).

As with Chris's, so Rachel's vision also has a stark sense of finality, and yet as the intimacy of the maternal metaphor suggests, this does not produce despair. In both 'Greenden' and 'Clay', nature is invested with a sublime power. In 'Greenden' it contributes to the human tragedy, forcing Simpson's wife to fatal realisation of her isolation and alienation. Nature is granted a more positive power in 'Clay', ending the story on a triumphant note. Rob Galt's end, like Chris's, provides an inspiring sense of spiritual fulfilment, of ease and tranquility, as he sinks into the earth, 'where sleep and death and the earth were one' (*SH*, p 27). At its most exalted 'Clay' thus gives a brief but vivid glimpse of salvation.

Although 'Clay', like *A Scots Quair*, is both humorous and lyrical, it also has a philosophical depth and power which bely its abbreviated form. On this account it must be acclaimed as the finest of the Gibbon stories.

'SIM'

The fourth Scots offering is the most readily expendable of the five Grassic Gibbon stories, but this is more a tribute to the quality of the others than an indictment of the piece itself. Like 'Smeddum' and 'Clay', 'Sim' also takes the simple form of a character study; indeed it is a kind of companion piece to 'Clay' as a psychological study of a farmer who is thirled to his work. Yet Sim Wilson has little in common with Rob Galt apart from his farming vocation, for, whatever their ultimate effect upon his wife and daughter, Rob's actions are instinctive and unpremeditated, as the land of Pittaulds comes to dominate his very being. Sim, on the other hand, is a much less sympathetic character who is motivated by materialistic, or at least acquisitive, principles, and he merely exploits the land of Haughgreen for his own purposes. As a simple moral homily against the vice of avarice, 'Sim' is obviously a less profound work than 'Clay', but the moral is beautifully pointed.

The structure of 'Sim' is simple. Sim Wilson works relentlessly from objective to objective, gradually making his way from destitution in Segget to become the definitive self-made man. He has no one grand aim in view at the outset but, deriving no lasting satisfaction from the fulfilment of each particular ambition, one achievement merely leads on to another. The plot thus unfolds in distinct stages charting the protagonist's progress at school, then at work at Upperhill and Haughgreen, and finally at home with his wife and children. Devaluing this impressive record of Sim's achievements, however, Mitchell periodically iterates, either through Sim's own mouth or through his critics' sardonic responses to his accomplishments, the fearfully impoverished code of life by which his protagonist lives.

Sim is isolated from his companions from the very start by his questioning attitude to life. Whereas his schoolmates and then his workmates rest content to swim with the tide and accept what life has to offer, Sim stands apart from this general trend, showing a precocious sense of independence and self-assurance while still a boy. Indeed, when he is only five years old, he proves strong enough to resist the designs of the aunt who adopts him *in loco parentis* when his mother does a 'moonlight flit', and his forthright response to the headmaster's prediction that he will 'gang a hard gait through the world' has something of the character of a personal manifesto, the schoolboy replying bluntly,—'Maybe; but I'll gang it myself. And I'll know what I'm getting ere I gang it at all' (*SH*, p 41).

Throughout his life, therefore, Sim is not content to follow the path which has been mapped out for him, and whereas the other farm workers prove happy with their lot, he is more calculating, grudging the effort he is asked to expend as a 'fee'd loon' performing thankless and monotonous tasks for someone else's benefit in order merely to earn his brose. However, Sim proves to be 'swack' as well as 'sweir' for, once he is given a personal incentive, then he is roused quite spectacularly from his indolence. His life thus follows an alternating pattern in which long periods of inactivity are punctuated by bouts of fierce industry: for once he has set a target, whether it be to win a prize at school or to marry the girl of his dreams, Sim becomes dedicated to the realisation of his goal.

Mitchell's protagonist explains his actions throughout the course of the story. At Upperhill, this apparent schizophrenia in his character is succinctly explained when he boasts to the bothy-billies, 'Show me a thing that is worth my trauchle, and I'll work you all off the face of the earth!' (*SH*, p 41), and this challenge is repeated four pages later when the Upperhill foreman recalls Sim's credo, 'Trauchle the day just to trauchle the morn! But show me a thing that is worth my chave and I'll work you all off the face of the earth!'

Sim's final come-uppance at the end of the story has strong overtones of the stern climax of *The House with the Green Shutters*—a book which Mitchell owned—in the way in which retribution is visited upon the protagonist through the agency of his own family. It is also highly appropriate that the mongoloid Jean should be the one to promote disclosure of her father's final shame by pointing to Jess's embarrassing condition, for she has suffered particularly severely from her father's fickleness. The ending of the story thus provides the moral censure by demonstrating how the protagonist's folly, his unrestricted personal ambition, rebounds upon him. The correct attitude to life has already been established within the narrative in the comparatively moderate and unassuming attitude shown by Sim's compeers in general, and by the Upperhill foreman in particular. In his reasonable approach he is the antithesis of Sim, and it is fitting that he should not only embody the correct stance, but that he should also give it verbal definition. He it is who puts the theme of material ambition into perspective when, lost in consideration of Sim's restless discontentment, he has a vision of human life in general, concluding that, 'there were some that had aye to be looking ahead, and others looked back, and it made little odds, looked you east, looked you west, you'd to work or to die' (*SH*, p 47). This fatalistic attitude is re-established soon after when the anonymous narrator adopts a more critical attitude to Sim, but arrives at the same conclusion, that life is a 'riddle' and 'not a race to be run with a prize at the end' (*SH*, p 49).

Although 'Sim' like 'Smeddum' is comparatively unadventurous both artistically and ideologically, it also has a descriptive authenticity, a memorable vigour of action and image and a structural cohesion which are seldom evident in Mitchell's English stories, and which are in fact seldom bettered by other writers in the genre.

'FORSAKEN'

'Forsaken' is an anomaly among the Grassic Gibbon short stories, in that it is the only one of the five which takes as its setting the Scottish city as opposed to the Scottish countryside. It also stands apart from the Cairo stories, as the author tries in it to give some impression of the spirit of the people as well as the character of their environment. In marked contrast with 'Sim', Mitchell is attempting to break new ground in this story, endeavouring to give a realistic impression of life in a modern Scottish city, and this is something he had not yet attempted in any other work. Thus, whereas the four other Gibbon pieces are in some ways adjuncts of, or accessories to, *Sunset Song*, similarly 'Forsaken', which first appeared in *Scottish Scene* in June 1934, may be regarded as the precursor of *Grey Granite*.

The most noticeable difference between 'Forsaken' and the other Gibbon stories is idiomatic. Gone is the lilting balladic prose style first unveiled in *Sunset Song*, to be replaced by a harsh urban dialect much more heavily dependent upon the use of slang phrases and colloquialisms. The flexible narrative technique employed in previous Gibbon work is emulated in 'Forsaken', however, despite the fact that the narrator who appears throughout the rural fiction giving an impression of omniscience has no urban counterpart. Nonetheless, Mitchell does show the same willingness to flit from one consciousness to another, and although this device has a more disconcerting effect in this piece, it is essentially the same as the narrative technique which is used throughout *Grey Granite*.

Although 'Forsaken' is a pioneering work, both within Mitchell's own canon and within the wider context of modern Scottish fiction as a whole, as is commonly the case with his work some of the most striking elements of the piece can be traced to their source in earlier stories or fragments. 'Forsaken' has its roots in earlier work by both Mitchell and Gibbon.

'Forsaken' is a potent blend of heavily realistic techniques and fantastic action. The literary techniques, as I have suggested, are predominantly original to this particular story, but the central plot, in which Christ is resurrected in modern times, has antecedents in previous work by Mitchell. The historical figure of Christ evidently had a powerful identity for Mitchell. *Stained Radiance* contains a brief but vivid evocation of the crucifixion, and Christ also plays a particularly important role in the action of 'For Ten's Sake' and 'Cartaphilus'. Indeed, the central plot of this latter work, whereby Christ—described more than once as having been 'forsaken' by mankind[8]—is represented as an outcast, anticipates the plot of the Scots story. And by 1934, the image of the persecuted Jew expelled from modern society would have had a peculiar topicality, for antisemitic attitudes were very much in the ascendancy in fascist countries. 'Thermopylae' has a less direct bearing upon 'Forsaken' than 'Cartaphilus' but it is important as indirect forerunner of the Scots fragment, involving the same stratagem of updating historical legend, the rewriting of a famous historical episode within a modern context.

However, the strongest foretaste of 'Forsaken' comes from *Cloud Howe*, which appeared the year before the story. In the second section of the book, when Chris and Robert are arguing good naturedly about religion, Robert attempts to make a point about the unique character of the Scottish people by imagining how they would react to Christ if he were alive in modern times. Chris's bitter-sweet interpretation of this fantasy contains the germ of 'Forsaken', as she speculates how the Scots folk 'would feed Christ hungry and attend to His hurts with no thought of reward their attendance might bring', and she adds knowingly, 'Kind, they're so kind. . . . And the lies they would tell about how He came be those hurts of his—' (*SQ*, p 258). The essence of 'Forsaken' exists in this extract, for the story represents the imaginative fulfilment of the fantasy conceived in this passage, the moral of which was most likely suggested by the episode in The Gospel According to Matthew known as 'The great judgement', in which Christ describes the 'sheep' who show pity upon him inheriting 'the kingdom prepared for you from the foundation of the world'.[9] Just as the extract from *Cloud Howe* has a comic-serious flavour, so also is the situation exploited for humorous effect in 'Forsaken', without reducing the story's impact.

Very like 'Clay', 'Forsaken' initially captures the reader's attention by humorous means, focusing here upon the bewilderment produced on both sides when the city urchins encounter the strangely garbed foreigner. As happens in the earlier story also, the levity gradually subsides as the serious theme develops throughout the narrative. And yet paradoxically, whereas 'Clay' concerns the lofty theme of spiritual fulfilment, 'Forsaken', for all its fantastic techniques and its biblical significance, considers more concrete matters of social and political import. Indeed, the position which 'Forsaken' occupies in the Grassic Gibbon bibliography—falling in between *Cloud Howe* and *Grey Granite*—is reflective of its political tenor.

Throughout his writing, Mitchell invokes the human qualities of Christ as a figure of profound moral and political importance, as opposed to 'the Son of God'. In 'Forsaken' therefore, Christ is represented in a heavily realistic manner in order to stress this particular quality: the fact that he speaks the same language as the Gordon family and strikes up such a friendly relationship with them enhances his character as a human being, and it is significant that he himself does not understand his apparently miraculous resurrection. In fact, he is entirely oblivious to the mythical status which his life-story has subsequently acquired, and this is exemplified by the ignorance he betrays three quarters of the way through the text concerning the name by which he has come to be known, when he asks his hosts to their abject embarrassment, 'Who is Christ?' (*SH*, p 59).

The Christ portrayed in 'Forsaken' thus corresponds with the idealistic image perceived by Robert in the early stages of his ministry in Segget, in which Christ appears as a simple champion of the people. The biblical influence does not stop in the story with the manifestation of Christ, for the individual members of the working class family which accepts him into their midst are identified as contemporary incarnations of biblical characters— Martha, Peter, Mary Magdalene and Saul. More serious than Christ's failure to recognise his own name, therefore, is the inability of the modern family to identify their guest. This does not reflect any drastic change in the character of ordinary people, because the Gordons are living proof of Christ's own recognition of 'the filth and the foolishness in folk, but the kindly glimmer of the spirit as well' (SH, p 52).

The historical continuity of character also runs hand in hand with a basic continuity in human values and ideals, represented in the equation which Mitchell draws between Christian ethics and communist principles, the proletarian sense of comradeship being directly compared with the Christian affirmation of universal brotherhood. Christ thus looks back upon his life as a struggle fought with 'the New Men' to bring about the universal change of heart, which will eventually establish the 'Kingdom of God' on earth (SH, pp 58-9). Peter, like Robert Colquohoun, identifies this programme with his own political cause, arguing that the Christian religion and the principles of communism are one and the same. However, just as Robert's Christian Socialism proves inadequate to effect the desired changes in Cloud Howe, so Peter's own attitude appears impractical and sadly out of date. The human character and basic human values have not changed, but social conditions have and, as Will explains, there is now no room for compassion:

That's been tried and found useless over long, Comrade. Waiting the change of heart, I mean. It's not the heart we want to change, but the system. Skunks with quite normal hearts can work miraculous change for the good of men. People who have themselves changed hearts are generally crucified—like Christ (SH, p 59).

Will's political pragmatism and his yearning for a foolproof means of realising his political objectives have a direct correspondence with Ewan Tavendale's search for a creed that will 'cut like a knife'. Will, like Ewan, represents the Leninist conception of leadership, being brave, intelligent and also utterly determined. Appropriately, therefore, he is the one who points out the deficiencies of the Christian faith, expounding the political significance of Christ's experience—as seen from his radical perspective—for his guest's benefit:

So that was the way of it, you see, this Prophet childe started with the notion that men's hearts would first need changing, to make them love one another, care for the State—he called it the Kingdom of God in his lingo. And what happened was that he himself was crucified after leading an army against Jerusalem; syne, hardly was he dead than his followers started making a god of him, quite the old kind of God, started toning down all he'd taught to make it fit in with the structure of the Roman state. They became priests and princes in the service of the temples dedicated to the dead Jesus, whom they'd made a God. . . . And, mind you, that change of heart must have happened often enough to folk when they heard of the sayings of this Jesus. Thousands and thousands changed—but there was no cohesion—no holding together, they put off the Kingdom of God till Eternity: and were tortured and murdered in Jesus' name (SH, p 60).

This remarkable passage demands to be quoted in full, because it explains the political reorientation, and the revised conception of God that is created in *Cloud Howe* and *Grey Granite*. God, as Ewan comes to understand, is only of relevance to mankind as an embodiment of a moral code or a political standard, and any spiritual considerations are a potential distraction from the main issues, as the challenging political banners are replaced by what Christ himself calls 'the flaunting flag of God' (*SH*, p 60). Will also foreshadows Ewan's political understanding in the belief he expresses in the need for a concrete and rigid plan of campaign in their efforts to reform society, in the knowledge that love is no longer enough: and Mitchell puts a questionmark against the radical communist mandate at the end of the story when Christ, very like Chris in the trilogy, finds that he is unable to sympathise with this depersonalised credo.

As in *Grey Granite*, Mitchell is cautious in his endorsement of communism as a programme for human improvement. However, in the climax of the story, communism is presented as the only alternative to utter dejection and despair. Christ finally disclaims kinship with the modern counterparts of Martha, Peter and Saul, but for different reasons. Martha he disowns because of her 'facing fear and pain without hope' (*SH*, p 62), and Peter is also denied for his loss of faith, for, he 'was not the Peter of that other time, weak and leal and kind he had been, but more of the kindness now, little of the love, forsaken of the trust and uttermost belief'; and he concludes, 'No thing in him now you could ever touch except with a cry of despair' (*SH*, pp 61–2). Will, the hard-line secretary of the Communist branch, is a different proposition, Christ apprehending:

> Saul with the bitter face and creed, a leader once for that army you led up the heights to El Kuds, never for that love you had led it with. Looking into his heart with that ancient power you saw the white, stainless soul that was there, but love had gone from it, faith and trust, hope even, only resolve remained. Nothing there but resolve, nothing else that survived the awful torment your name had become . . . (*SH*, p 62).

Will is thus a less sympathetic character than Ewan, but this does not diminish the political impact of the story, for Mitchell uses the same sober method of promoting the communist effort in both works, not by glorifying it, but by representing it as the only practical alternative in the modern world.

Mitchell's closing gambit is irresistible. For the irony of Peter and Will's failure to decipher Christ's final cry of anguish proves an extremely poignant endorsement of the theme. Christ's cry is both a reflection and an indictment of the modern crisis of faith which has been so forcefully projected in the story. And by intensifying the overall sense of despair, Mitchell encourages the reader to focus more sharply upon the one positive alternative outlined in the work—the austere ideology of communism.

The final Grassic Gibbon story is a sophisticated piece of work which anticipates *Grey Granite* in theme and technique, and yet Mitchell's flamboyance is justified in the contribution that it makes to the tale's impact. On the evidence of this story, the author's literary powers were continuing to expand, just as the political philosophy of the 'reformer' was developing. As 'Forsaken' testifies, these two qualities together form a quite formidable force.

A conspectus of Mitchell's minor fiction sheds light directly and indirectly upon the novels, and the same basic paradox can be seen at play in them, whereby Mitchell's confinement to a purely Scottish context, without having any explicit cultural or political significance, has an intellectually liberating effect. In addition, 'Clay' and 'Forsaken' have a direct correspondence with *A Scots Quair*, although they represent the culmination of themes and techniques evolved in earlier stories. However, 'Clay' finally stands out as Mitchell's finest achievement within the short story, and it does so for much the same reason that *A Scots Quair* is his finest novel, as the most complete embodiment of his deepest philosophical beliefs.

FIVE

The English Novels

THE EARLY NOVELS

Mitchell had little patience for the time-consuming task of revising his novels. His widow told me that, rather than rewrite something he was dissatisfied with, frequently her husband would vent his exasperation by destroying his whole manuscript in the kitchen stove. Mrs Mitchell feared that this was the sorry end which greeted the manuscript of the first novel in Gibbon's projected Covenanters trilogy, but thankfully most of his major work avoided this fate, as the impulsive practice appeared comparatively late in his life. Indeed, Mitchell put quite uncharacteristic effort into his first major works of fiction.

Stained Radiance evidently received special care and attention in its composition, for Mitchell's first reference to the completed draft of this first novel appears in a letter written to the Grays in January 1928,[1] and apparently the book went through several drafts before its publication in September 1930.[2] The deliberate manner of conception had an ambivalent effect, in that most of the faults of the work are typical ones for a first novel—the narrative frequently falls prey to verbose cleverness and is riddled with gratuitous literary references, while the plot seems over-complex. In a nutshell, *Stained Radiance* is too consciously 'literary'. Mitchell himself voiced reservations as to the stylistic merits of the book when, forwarding a complimentary copy to his old dominie, he asked Mr Gray to remember, that, 'It's the Leslie Mitchell of 1928, not of 1930.'[3] Despite these shortcomings, however, the book is charged with the most deeply held ideas from which ultimately the themes embodied in *A Scots Quair* evolved, ideas which Mitchell later tended to suppress in his writing when he became preoccupied with promoting the doctrines of diffusionism. It is as well to remember that *Stained Radiance*, as a product of 'the Leslie Mitchell of 1928', is an immature work, but equally, the book's artistic weaknesses are substantially redeemed by its thematic integrity. Two months after he had written so apologetically about the novel's style, the author expressed considerable pride in his 'Fictionist's Prelude', its subtitle, as an honest attempt to 'try to portray life as you see it'.[4]

The profession of honesty is reflected in Mitchell's frequently ironic form of realism, and this ultimately gives the book a disconcerting bleakness redolent of the later literature of the Absurd, and, more precisely, of the 'nouveau roman', defined by Alain Robbe-Grillet as a work concerned with demonstrating the fundamental problems of human existence, as opposed to providing actual enlightenment.[5] *Stained Radiance* certainly offers no easy solutions to the most pressing existential problems, but it does confront these problems with honesty and courage.

There are many interesting parallels between Mitchell's first novel and *A Scots Quair*. Thea Mayven's home in Scotland, for instance, boasts the same name as Chris's final haven, the croft of Cairndhu (*SR*, p 120) and, like Chris, the earlier heroine also evinces the pride Mitchell himself felt in his 'heritage of the earth' (*SR*, p 18). In addition, the doctrinaire Communist Storman, with his 'inhuman, selfless cruelty' (*SR*, p 54), is cast very much in the mould of the unflinchingly purposeful politically mature Ewan of *Grey Granite*, and while the tension which the Englishman subsequently experiences between his political ideals and his personal romantic desires looks back to Rejeb ibn Saud's predicament in 'One Man with a Dream', it also foreshadows the conflict of loyalties which threatens and finally destroys the romantic bond between Ewan and Ellen Johns. The sardonic portrait of the Labour leader Meaken in the early novel also anticipates the satirical figure of Bailie Brown in *Grey Granite*, while the battle which takes place between the police and the unemployed who gather at Waterloo Station to see Meaken off on his trip to South Africa is a prototype of the riot described in 'Epidote' in *Grey Granite* where the unemployed marchers of Duncairn clash with the forces of law and order. The resemblance between the two incidents is strengthened by Koupa's recommendation that the mob should arm itself with beer bottles (*SR*, p 82), which looks forward to Ewan's inspiration in *Grey Granite* (*SQ*, p 396). Again, Koupa's embezzlement of the party funds fifty pages further on recalls Selden's crime in *Grey Granite*, while Storman's secretion of pepper upon his person in case of involvement in physical combat (*SR*, p 178) foreshadows the crime in the Scots novel for which Ewan is unjustly convicted and imprisoned.

Ultimately, however, *Stained Radiance* has an interest beyond that of mere influence, for although it lacks the artistic poise and the philosophical assurance of the later volume, the early novel has a thematic scope and coherence which make it worthy of consideration on its own merits.

The inscription of *Stained Radiance* which gives the book its title comes from Shelley's long poem, 'Adonais':

> Life, like a dome of many-coloured glass,
> Stains the white radiance of eternity.

'Adonais' is one of Shelley's most profound works, dealing with fundamental questions of human existence, with the question of the nature of reality and the prospect of death. In its later stages, the poem develops an inspiring contrast between the trials and misfortunes borne in ordinary life with the final promise of immortality, of eternal life gained after death through union with the universal whole. In the context of the poem, Shelley's image is a spiritually comforting one, holding out hope in the prospect of life after death. However, by lifting the two middle lines out of context, Mitchell exaggerates the bleakness of the vision, concentrating upon the image of the 'stain' of life rather than 'the white radiance of Eternity'. This emphasis is also reflected in the social and philosophical themes of the novel, both of which are informed with a desolate sense of futility. By this time, Mitchell's social conscience was fairly well developed but, in this first novel, the voice of social protest is countered by a contrasting sense of disillusionment with contemporary political parties. Consideration of the more profound themes of life proves equally disturbing.

The three major themes which Mitchell pursues in this novel are all familiar ones to his work in general, the author examining the role of the artist in modern society, and conducting a search for both political and philosophical truth, a search which is markedly less successful here than in the trilogy.

The literary means which Mitchell employs to explore these themes in *Stained Radiance* are, barring the occasional stylistic lapses, simple and effective. Basically, the book focuses upon the fortunes of two young couples, John Garland and Thea Mayven and James Storman and Norah Casement, as they make their way through life in the London of the post-First World War depression, a life with which Mitchell himself, then living in a tenement in Hammersmith, had become all too well acquainted. The domestic fortunes of the two couples follow a similar course, culminating in both cases in the simultaneous discovery of unwanted pregnancies. Up to this point, Garland and Storman have been at opposite ideological extremes. Garland originally appears in a rather obvious self-parody of Mitchell himself as an ironic novelist with a deep-rooted cynicism and a clinical scientific detachment from society. In another conscious parallel with the author, due to intensely felt financial pressures, he is forced to tolerate life in the Air Force and, again probably in agreement with Mitchell himself at this time, his understandable unhappiness with this situation merely heightens his cynical feelings:

> He believed nothing and everything. He did not believe in himself. He watched the passing pageant of life with ironic humour, yet constantly found himself plunging into that pageant, grabbing a banner, insisting in joining in the song. And always, sooner or later, because he was conscious of singing out of tune, because he saw the ludicrousness of the banner and his fellow-marchers, he deserted (*SR*, p 25).

Storman is introduced in direct contrast to Garland with his sardonic detachment from creeds and causes, as a singleminded and unscrupulous Communist with a blinkered devotion to the one political cause:

> Keen, calm, a mathematician, he was a mystic and religious, with Communism his religion. He looked at the world with the blind, clear eyes of faith (*SR*, p 20).

Being of such radically different temperaments and miens, the insecure sceptic Garland and the austere Communist Storman react differently to the similar domestic crises which occur in their lives, although in both cases the personal trauma has a humanising influence in the long term. This is seen in Storman's appreciation of the destitution in contemporary London as an emotive social issue rather than one of purely academic politico-economic interest, and this revelation comes upon him in a passage appropriately imbued with a moral vigour strongly reminiscent of Jack London's most passionate socialist diatribes; Storman tells his partner:

My God, Norah! I never realized it before—the abyss of poverty. . . . Communism's done nothing. . . . I've schooled myself to be cruel and unwavering—for what? There's a greater cruelty—the Cruelty of the Streets, senseless, unemotional as that of an octopus. There is something worse than the beast in man—an evil older than Life itself (*SR*, p 195).

From this point on, Storman becomes increasingly withdrawn into himself and at the meeting of the South Wales Anarcho-communist group he finally renounces the formal symbols and cliches, the 'revolutionary bunkum, proletarian pap' (*SR*, p 239), of Marxist-Leninist ideology which the Welsh miners desperately cling to in their plight. His apparent change of heart is confirmed by the uncharacteristic kindness he shows to the bourgeois Garland—with whom he now recognises a common humanity—in defiance of communist policy. Finally, he registers his political disillusionment in a formal letter of resignation from the Party in which he proclaims, 'I have finished with politics and parties', and signifies his withdrawal to an individualistic position:

I can no longer believe in the saving of the world through the sinking of individuality in a common cause. Mob salvation is a proven lie. I can no longer believe that the common good is greater than the good of the individual. There is no common good (*SR*, p 276).

When Storman finally disappears from the scene he is almost entirely taken up with his own welfare, but his renunciation of his former political ideals is not as final as it seems, for after withdrawing to the personal security offered by his family and by respectable bourgeois employment as Kyland's manager, he still retains his belief in man's common destiny, even though this is now centred upon his son. Thus, he realises towards the end of the book:

Now he knew that which his letter of resignation had lacked. Mention of his son. The days of mass-enthusiasms, mass-achievements, were indeed over for ever. Yet, through the individuals, here and there, by hands and means unguessed, might yet be laid the first, unguessable foundations of the City of the Sun. . . .

His son would carry him on, would, in the years to come, presently bear out into the world a torch to add to that light that has so often flickered and seemed to fail, yet is inextinguishable—the Light that men call by many names, by the names of Freedom and Knowledge, of Anarchy, and of God (*SR*, pp 278–9).

Although Storman retreats from his extreme political role as militant Communist to a more self-interested position promoting the idea of the freedom of the individual he still cherishes a belief in a social utopia, in the ultimate attainment of 'the City of the Sun'. He remains unsure as to the practical means of achieving this goal and personally excludes himself from the official political efforts geared towards its ultimate achievement, yet the actual goal itself remains as attractive as before.

Garland's experience follows a very different course. Early in the novel, he is characterised by a singular lack of faith in any ideological programme, whether secular or religious, and the basic insularity of his outlook is captured in his early assertion that his romance with Thea is his 'only reality in Life' (*SR*, p 112). At this stage he is open-minded and sensitive to the diversity of experience which life can offer, to which he responds alternately with wonder and despair; and the position from which at first he views life is the detached and neutral position of the scientist. From the beginning, however, the neutrality of his standpoint is tainted by a sense of his own comparative insignificance. Mitchell writes of him early on in the book:

> Love, life, planets, stars, death, fate, the worm that dieth not, and words like widdershins and swastika intrigued him. He was interested in them as a scientist—with the wish for knowledge and with no ulterior hope of gain from that knowledge. Sometimes, as a result, a loneliness and a horror of himself and his incessant, ruinous curiosity would come upon him (*SR*, p 25).

At this point Garland is a curious blend of the romantic and the ironist. For where on the one hand he can appreciate Robert Louis Stevenson's most sentimental verse, this is balanced by his inescapable conviction of the futility of life itself. Fortified by his unhappiness with his personal situation when he is 'conscripted' into the Air Force by financial pressures, Garland's ironic self becomes more dominant, as is demonstrated vividly by his periodic outbursts against either man himself, whom he describes as 'the ugliest of all the animals' (*SR*, p 39), or later, against 'the rottenness called Life' (*SR*, p 160).

Even before domestic turmoil casts a shadow upon Garland's life, these sporadic outbursts have attained a desolate coherence worthy of an ironic novelist. This is evident in the graphic representation of urban society as a whore (*SR*, pp 41–2), which contrasts with Mitchell's pastoral personification of the coming of summer in *Sunset Song* as a wholesome peasant girl 'marching up each morning with unbraided hair' (*SQ*, p 141). Embarking ship, bound for military service in Egypt, Garland's pessimism seems all-embracing when he owns to 'an insane hate—hate of the place, Life, Thea, himself' (*SR*, p 184).

In addition to his dyspeptic attitude to life as a whole, Garland also has an intensely cynical approach to religion, preferring 'the cold air and frozen spaces of atheism' to the warmth and comfort offered by the Christian faith (*SR*, p 229), and these articles all combine to convince him of the essential Absurdity of human life—frequently portrayed in an insect metaphor common in Mitchell's writing—in a universe devoid of spiritual meaning. The two central notions of the minuteness of man and the vastness of his universe combine in the Absurd conception of life on earth, visualised as the 'unending tweeter' of 'the insects on their mud-ball', and human existence is subsequently denuded of all sense of purpose and meaning in an extension of the insect metaphor which represents the basic human experience as, 'creeping from the slime to a fluttering of wings against a twilit sky, to a freezing extinction on a falling night or the brief, agonized enscorchment of the candle flame' (*SR*, p 88).

Even before his wife's tribulations, therefore, Garland's outlook is deeply pessimistic, However, Thea's needless suffering and her near death from a miscarriage which occurs when she is in poor health, exacerbated in turn by the hostility shown towards her by society at large, all conspire to wring a change in Garland himself. These traumatic events arouse bitter indignation in him which is manifested in his jaundiced and perverted apprehension of God as a devil who, with all the clinical coolness of a scientist in a laboratory, consciously introduces death and disease to the human realm for no other reason than to contemplate the pain and suffering which ensue (*SR*, p 265).

Following Thea's unconvincingly miraculous recovery, which is close to the banalities of plot in stories such as 'Gift of the River' and 'Daybreak', for a time Garland retreats into a romantic shell, but he continues to rage, with 'a welling of blood-red indignation against the whole outer world' (*SR*, pp 279–80). Yet as his anger subsides to more reasonable proportions, his resentment eventually finds a more satisfactory outlet in the aims and policies of communism, which results in the reversal of roles contrived at the close of the book, with Storman leaving the Anarcho–communist Party to become Kyland's manager (*SR*, p 277), the very post which Garland vacates on the day Storman takes his place in order to assume Storman's old position as secretary of the Anarcho–communist Party (*SR*, p 282). Thus, where Storman's bitter personal experience moves him to consider his personal concerns rather than the plight of the working classes at large, in Garland's case the personal crisis prises him out of himself to an awareness of the more worthy claims of mankind as a whole. Garland's final statement of intent is thus directly opposed to Storman's individualistic manifesto. Garland makes a passionate affirmation of faith in 'some brotherhood of the shamed and tortured' as a practical political force (*SR*, p 283).

This reversal of roles produces an ironic sense of inconclusiveness as to whether individual or communal values should take precedence. Through the mutually contradictory experiences of Garland and Storman, Mitchell demonstrates the inherent worthiness of any attempt to make 'the City of the Sun' a social reality, although he also indicates that no effort towards this noble end is guaranteed to succeed. In contrast to the cautiously optimistic political theme elucidated in *A Scots Quair* and the confidence exuded in *Spartacus* with regard to the possibility of a successful proletarian revolution, the political question in *Stained Radiance* remains largely inconclusive, particularly over the basic choice between anarchism and communism.

Andreas van Koupa represents a third mode of experience in *Stained Radiance* which does little to dispel the overall sense of political uncertainty. Originally, he is the visionary whose political ideals are sustained by his romantic poetic sensibility as much as by any profound sense of moral purpose, and this marks him out as an influential figure who can even sway the obdurate Storman by merely 'visioning', by singing 'an epic saga—of a doctrinaire's dream that shod itself in blood and iron and climbed through wreckage and destruction to Purpose, pitiless, selfless, and sane' (*SR*, p 63).

Mitchell's interest in Koupa is not so much in his political opinions themselves as in the relationship he represents between politics and art. Ultimately, the portrait intimates their fundamental incompatibility. Thus, where Garland to all intents and purposes gives up his self-indulgent aspirations as a novelist in favour of his political activities, Koupa graduates from an apparently sincere role as practising Communist through a less sincere phase in which he is given to much false proselytisation, and finally he completely sacrifices his political principles in order to secure the degree of physical comfort which he feels to be necessary to his work as an artist. To Koupa, artistic endeavour is the single most important activity in life, and all else, including politics, is consequently of secondary importance. In his opinion, the artist must be absolutely free from all other obligations, and interestingly he thus casts himself as the bourgeois writer secure in his ivory tower, rather than as the proletarian ambassador which Mitchell later saw himself to be. Koupa resolves:

> I will put by the dreams of Spartacus and Christ. Things are so. All strivings—they are but the spatterings of the insect in the wayside pool—the insect that hopes to alter the tides. I will keep me secure in the places to which I climb, fenced round with the politics and prejudices of the little bourgeois swine. I shall burn the torch of art behind their shelter, not see it blown to dust and ashes on proletecult barricades. God mine, Art cries for security, for shelter. Have I not earned the so-little share of those now? (*SR*, p 192).

As with the political question in the book, Mitchell's main concern is neither to praise nor condemn Koupa for the choice he makes, but merely to highlight the problems facing the artist in modern society. Nevertheless, it is interesting to reflect here that in *A Scots Quair* Mitchell effects a successful resolution of the two artistic viewpoints, drawing heavily upon the techniques practised in the Marxist school of socialist realism, but finally transcending the formal artistic demands which it imposes by dint of his own literary and philosophical prowess.

The portrait of Koupa in *Stained Radiance* shows that Mitchell was well aware of the main choice facing the artists in modern times. More important, however, is Koupa's philosophical development. Midway through the novel, he receives an alcohol-assisted intimation of spiritual meaning:

> . . . everywhere life swung in rhythm of purpose. Beyond the jungles and the ghouls, secretly or openly, the Life-Force in every planet wrought and selected and toiled with its instrument reason and its goal immortality. Triumphant over itself, matter in motion conquered matter is stagnation, matter whorling in steady rhythm became matter in purpose and conquered matter in mere instinctive motion, matter in purpose intricated its whorlings till it was matter in reason.
>
> The scientific Pentateuch. Reason, God, everywhere—in life, in death, in birth (*SR*, p 152).

Here again, Mitchell comes close to the conception of God which Chris works out more systematically in the trilogy. But the author still seems to be feeling his way in the first novel, for this passage is tentative and restrained. Nevertheless, Koupa's basic faith in the existence of 'Reason, God, everywhere—in life, in death, in birth', is directly opposed to Garland's atheism, and this contradiction disposes the reader to expect the philosophical theme of the book to end on a similar note of uncertainty to the political theme. However, the more profound aspect of the novel ends decisively with Koupa's conversion to Garland's ironic viewpoint and, as in Nansen's case in *Nine Against the Unknown*, the Absurd vision is conditioned by external circumstances and attained ultimately at the expense of his own peace of mind. Mitchell writes of the poet as he contemplates the Milky Way:

> A sudden fear, a desolation, held his soul. Not for the first time had he visioned the end of the world and of life, but never as he did on this night, in the stark silence. An awful loneliness horrified him. . . . For *that* his days and nights. For that all the countless days and nights of humanity, the changings of the innumerable seasons, the burgeonings of the vernal Aprils, autumns with hands red from the winepress. For that the dream and the desire.
> Life! a misarrangement of the electrons, a phantasy against the still splendour of the eternal whorls. . . .

Mitchell goes on to expound the philosophical significance of the book's title, with Koupa acclaiming the Shelley of 'Adonais' as a fellow sufferer in his anguish who he feels was forced subsequently by the crushing burden of his knowledge of 'that terror of the skies' to turn his attention to lighter matters. To Koupa also, wilful avoidance of this chilling cosmic prospect finally appears imperative for his whole future welfare. Mitchell writes of his distressed poet:

> He covered his eyes in a kind of agony. What purpose, what meaning, what hope—the Dome aflame in the wastes of time and space?—Aflare with millennium on millennium, generation after generation since that first amoeba in the Arctic seas. . . . Sceptic, believer, fanatic, fool—they whoomed and shrivelled like calcined flies in the furnace-Dome of Life.
> God mine, forget it as did Shelley. Thou livest. Life is yours, comfort, the padded belly. You are clad in purple and fine raiment. You may build you wall on wall till you shut out the radiance for ever, and in the end pass as a mindless beast through the suttee yourself, with the debt of your blood paid out in replenishing faggots . . .
> (*SR*, pp 287–8).

This stark vision of the painful reality that the universe represents to the man who rejects the philosophical reassurance offered by all creeds and codes foreshadows Robert Colquohoun's terrifying apprehension of 'the fleshless grin of the skull and the eyeless sockets at the back of life' (*SQ*, p 212). Yet in the English novel Mitchell does not even attempt to rise above the horror of Koupa's vision, as he attempts to subvert Robert's perception of the 'grotesque' in the trilogy. That Koupa's final pessimistic vision is sanctioned by Mitchell himself is suggested by the way in which Garland's ironic viewpoint expressed throughout the novel leads up steadily to this climactic scene, and by the fact that Mitchell placed this episode at the volume's close, categorically refusing to alter it upon the request of a publisher interested in the book. And, even though he was desperate to secure a publishing contract for his manuscript at this time, to his credit Mitchell held out against the pressure to rewrite. Eventually he found a company willing to print his novel in its original form.[6]

Mitchell's protest at the social deprivation of modern life and his almost obsessive concentration on the spiritual barrenness of existence marks *Stained Radiance* out as one of his most deeply personal works, fully vindicating the honest aim he attached to it in hindsight as an attempt, 'to portray life as you see it'. Mitchell expresses his own motives behind his novel within the text, Garland the ironic novelist stating:

> What's wrong with the other moderns is the lack of purpose in their infernal books. They believe themselves up-to-date, Neo-Georgian, yet in novel-writing they're a generation behind the times. They're obsessed by the Galsworthy-Bennett tradition. They don't realize that the novel of portrait and manners is a dead dog which nowadays attracts only a casual interest. . . . The world is sick of mere matings and baitings, bickerings and successes and failures in novels. It's grown up, has the world, and knows our characters for mere sawdust puppets. 'We'll accept the puppets—if they're projections of yourself', it cries. 'Live through them. Make them tell us *your* thoughts, *your* vision of life, *your* hopes, *your* hates, *your* beliefs. Never mind them acting in character—damn their sawdust little characters—it's you we want, if you're worth the having . . . (*SR*, pp 87–8).

In this way Mitchell expresses his own intention to represent his personal thoughts and beliefs directly in his fiction. Garland's observation of recent changes in literary attitudes illustrates another important aspect of Mitchell's approach as a writer of fiction, for he himself evidently believed it was imperative that the modern author should constantly extend his art in order to stay a step ahead of his reader. This notion may be held at least partly responsible for the originality of *A Scots Quair*; and this belief also finds a practical response on three separate occasions in *Stained Radiance* when Mitchell practises what Garland preaches, making experimental departures from the formal narrative of the book.

The first of these consciously experimental passages occurs a third of the way through the text, where fleetingly Mitchell explores the possibilities of a symbolic kind of writing through Koupa's highly poetic interpretation of the Christian icon of the Virgin Mary cradling the infant Jesus:

> She, the Virgin, holding in her arms so gingerly that which she had mothered and the Unknown had fathered—holding in her arms that which she feared and would never comprehend—symbolized so much. Matter holding Mind. Or Humanity Faith. Or Death Life (*SR*, p 92).

The exercise is justified in context as a credible line of thought for Koupa, with his artistic intensity, to pursue, but Mitchell apparently did not feel the experiment to be wholly successful, and consequently this in the only example of so ostentatious a form of symbolism in the book.

Later in the novel, Mitchell makes a more sustained and successful attempt at literary innovation when, in the guise of his fictional author John Garland, he inserts a startling allegorical passage within the normal course of the narrative which describes, by focusing upon the particular case of Thea Mayven, the 'Odyssey' of the evolution of human consciousness. There are shades of Joyce in Mitchell's adaptation of the modes of ancient epic for his modernistic purposes, and perhaps the faint echo of *Ulysses*—which Mitchell read—represents a deliberate attempt by him to stress the experimental nature of the passage. And although the extract itself occasionally borders upon the pretentious and the self-indulgent, overall the experiment successfully enlarges the scope of the novel by adding a psychological dimension to its range of experience.

Mitchell's final experiment in this novel appears over a hundred pages later in another obtrusive passage, this time entitled simply 'Subchapter Retrospective' (*SR*, p 230). The passage recreates the historical episode of Christ's crucifixion in heavily realistic terms which, typically, serve to devalue the mythological religious significance attached to the event. Of the three attempts at experimentation in this novel, this in my estimation is the most successful, as it has the simplicity which is characteristic of the finest conceits. Mitchell himself also seems to have recognised the possibilities of this passage, for the later Gibbon story 'Forsaken' follows its lead, the New Testament portrayal of Christ again being demystified through the simple literary expedient of bringing him to life as a human being. Both episodes contain the same quotation from the Hebrew of Christ's impassioned cry, '*Eloi Eloi Lama Sabachthani?*' and, although 'Forsaken' is more sophisticated than the passage in *Stained Radiance*, it clearly owes much to the earlier episode.

Stained Radiance has many crude qualities and stylistic vagaries— particularly the Bertie Wooster-style clipped dialogue—which survive the passage of time rather uneasily. However, the book is substantially redeemed by the author's willingness to experiment with the mode of presentation, and by the honesty with which he reflects that which, in a letter written several years earlier, he designated 'the muddle of life'.[7] The book contains too many stylistic flaws to save it from being accounted a failure, but it must be adjudged an honourable failure in view of the enduring power of its greatest virtues, its innovatory literary techniques and its philosophical integrity. Both of these features actually seem curiously in tune with modern literary trends, and Mitchell's vision of the Absurdity of life has an especially strong affinity with the work of Camus and Beckett. Not until *A Scots Quair* did Mitchell put so much of his own mind and personality into his fiction, and he seldom confronted the major problems of human life with the same diligence and courage as he displayed in his first novel.

In one of our conversations, Mrs Mitchell staunchly supported *Stained Radiance* as a fairly true rendering of their experiences in London in the twenties. Indeed Mitchell's first novel is in many ways the most honest as well as the most 'modern' book that he wrote. Despite this, it remains largely neglected by reader, critic and publisher alike. At the time of its original publication the novel met with a directly hostile reaction, being banned in the Irish Free State and Australia,[8] and causing a similar furore in Britain, as the author himself recounted incredulously to Mr Gray:

> The amount of stupefied indignation 'Stained Radiance' seems to have raised! Mrs Gray disapproves, my mother is shocked, my sister-in-law is coldly polite, the 'Daily Sketch' has a hysteric fit over my 'brutality'—and Boots bans the book from their

shelves as 'indecent'. Most papers refuse to review it at all, and the booksellers are scared to display it complete with its shocking cover. . . .[9]

Mitchell himself was probably not too downhearted at the hostile manner in which his first major fiction work was received, as he was experienced enough by this time to realise that bad publicity was better than no publicity at all in the world of books. Indeed, one can even imagine him taking a perverse kind of pleasure in the notoriety he gained from this novel, for he had expressed a similar desire when he confided to the Grays upon the publication of Hanno, his first book, 'I hope it stirs up a most gorgeous row.'[10]

Despite the hidden benefits of its controversial nature, however, Mitchell evidently heeded the warning made by his publisher prior to the release of Stained Radiance, that 'irony is a futile weapon for any English writer to use',[11] for in his second novel he makes obvious efforts to tone down the ironic element. But in terms of its basic outlook The Thirteenth Disciple is not really any more reassuring than it heavily ironic predecessor.

Mitchell's second novel is even more strongly autobiographical than Stained Radiance, and the description of Malcom Maudslay's upbringing in northeast Scotland is taken largely from the author's own experience. Indeed, in the 'Synopsis of MEMOIRS OF A MATERIALIST', the writer intimates that in the autobiographical account of his early days he intends to follow the line of approach established in The Thirteenth Disciple. Mitchell also readily confesses in a letter written to Mr and Mrs Gray that Malcom's native village of Leekan is firmly based upon his homeland, the author writing a couple of months before the publication of his second novel that:

> The particular locality has such a close resemblance to Arbuthnott and the Howe o' the Mearns generally that I was forced to insert a few entirely fictitious topographical details—in case some enraged Reisker or other fauna sued me for libel.[12]

The plots of the first two novels are interrelated, Thea Mayven hailing from the same remote area of the Northeast as Malcom himself and the Leekan valley to which she returns in the earlier novel being the same fictitious district in which Malcom Maudslay is born. In fact, The Thirteenth Disciple makes direct reference to Thea's father as 'Mayven of Cairndhu' (TD, p 183), and, conversely, the Maudslay farm of Chapel o' Seddel which is Malcom's birthplace in the second novel is originally introduced in Stained Radiance (SR, p 127). The action of the two books also overlaps, for the same episode in which Malcom and Domina watch the minister disinterring an ancient Stone Age grave on Pittendreich's hill rates a mention in both texts (SR, p 123; TD, p 199).

Despite these literal points of contact between Mitchell's first two novels, the books seem to differ in both tone and theme, and perhaps the greatest single perceptible development between the two works concerns the author's informed recourse to diffusionist theory in The Thirteenth Disciple, following his formal acceptance of its historical arguments around the turn of they year. However, as I regard diffusionism in itself to be of superficial importance to Mitchell's personal philosophy, I feel the outlook enshrined in this second novel differs little from the bleak ironic perspective of the first. The approach in the second novel is admittedly different, and yet I think the fundamental outlook remains the same.

The form of *The Thirteenth Disciple* differs greatly from that of the earlier novel, as the almost claustrophobic constrictions imposed upon setting in *Stained Radiance* give way in the later work to a liberating quality of the picaresque, the scene changing with invigorating frequency from Leekan, to Glasgow, to France, to England, to America. The purpose of the book is largely the same as that of the earlier one, however, taking the form of a personal attempt by the author to make sense of life through fiction. Thus, although Mitchell here directly identifies himself with Malcom where previously the autobiographical elements were distributed among the three figures of Garland, Storman and Koupa, the pattern of the book is much the same, as a 'confessional' quest for stability and meaning in 'the muddle of life'.

As has been observed by Douglas Young,[13] the significance of the title of this second novel is best explained by reference to one of Mitchell's stories which had appeared in May of the previous year in *The Cornhill*. In the opening section of 'It is Written', Saloney makes passing reference to 'the Thirteenth Disciple', whom he describes as 'the infidel who feared and doubted and disbelieved'.[14] This disposition to 'disbelieve', to fly in the face of convention and make the effort to work everything out at first hand, was supported and practised by Mitchell himself: in point of fact, this is the very essence of his achievement as a 'blasphemer'. In the novel called *The Thirteenth Disciple*, then, Malcom is less a heretic in the normal sense of the word than a sensitive, angst-ridden freethinker who, like Garland and Storman earlier and, like Chris later, embarks upon a personal quest for some kind of truth in life. However, although Mitchell invests Malcom's fate with the most glorious symbolic significance at the end of the book, realistically his mission has had only limited success. Like Oliver Gault in 'The Passage of the Dawn', Malcom finds the goal he has been seeking, yet he is finally denied the penetrating insight which Chris wins at the end of the trilogy. Mitchell had yet to discover for himself the philosophical faith which leavens his greatest work, and therefore his second novel comes to an unsatisfactory climax, involving the use of empty symbolism and the disclosure of a superficial and largely misplaced sense of optimism.

Marred by this discrepancy, then, Mitchell's second novel cannot be judged a success, and the contrasting uniformity and coherence of the consistently ironic first novel sets it above the sequel. The real Mitchell at this time was evidently still the anguished and pessimistic ironist who as early as 1921 had written to his future wife that he was 'the kind of desperate person who always makes the world uncomfortable for himself'.[15] It is pertinent, therefore, that ten years later, Malcom, who is direct authorial representative throughout *The Thirteenth Disciple*, should be described by Domina in exactly the same terms, as 'the kind of desperate person who's always made the world uncomfortable for himself' (*TD*, p 238). This suggests that Mitchell himself still felt the deep-seated sense of insecurity that he had owned to all those years before.

The Thirteenth Disciple is formally divided into two books, the first of which, 'Ante-Natal', concentrating upon the 'dark corridor' that Malcom journeys through,[16] inspires the finest writing of the volume overall. And again, as is the case with the whole of the earlier novel, the writing is of a deeply philosophic nature, ultimately articulating the same disturbingly bleak vision which dominates in *Stained Radiance*.

The first portion of the second novel follows Malcom's unsuccessful efforts to find purpose in life. He experiences at close quarters the full horror of urban squalor in Glasgow and of the pain and suffering of the First World War which takes the life of John Metaxa, the one friend and confidant he has left after his first wife's death. This disturbing series of events combines with his personal predilection to 'rejoice at the discomfiture of the Deity' (*TD*, p 38), to produce a philosophical stance bordering upon the nihilistic and incorporating absolute disbelief in politics and art as well as God. From the mild Morrissian socialism he believes in during his youth, Malcom eventually comes to the conclusion, under the influence of Meierkhold, an old Russian exile and fellow member of their radical Left Group, that 'perhaps there is no more socialism left', fearing that, 'We have followed something wrongly, and our dream is smirched' (*TD*, p 99). Like Garland, Malcom too loses faith in literature, which he comes to speak of as 'that poor cracked mirror of life' (*TD*, p 81). More important than all this, however, he loses faith in himself, and suffers a crisis of identity when he finds he is unable to answer the basic question as to who the 'essential Malcom Maudsley' is (*TD*, p 101).

Subsequently, the theories of Berkeley give Malcom a krypto-scientific basis for his pessimistic view of life, persuading him that human beings are 'Only a temporary grouping of atoms endowed with a conceit called personality' (*TD*, p 137), and indeed by this time his despair has already driven him to make an unsuccessful attempt to take his own life. Mitchell's exposition of the logic behind Malcom's suicide attempt constitutes one of the most strikingly 'modern' passages in all his books and the justification he offers for taking such a drastic step looks forward directly to Albert Camus, one of the leading proponents of Absurd philosophy, who in *The Myth of Sisyphus* considers similar, if more deeply thought out, reasons for suicide. As with Garland and Koupa and later with Mitchell's intrepid hero Nansen, the human gift of reason proves a philosophical burden, offering Malcom knowledge of 'the untheological insanity of the universe", which leaves him 'too sane to live' (*TD*, p 117). Distressing personal experience is undoubtedly instrumental in Malcom's decision to kill himself, but in this way Mitchell endows the exercise with an objective philosophical significance beyond the merely personal.

Two-thirds of the way through the novel, Malcom remains a disbeliever, and although by this time he has lowered his sights from the universe at large to man's small civilised domain, he is still haunted by the sense of the futility of life, and, mentally scarred by the dreadful scenes he witnessed in the trenches in France, he asks Domina incredulously, 'God, what thinking can answer that, what God or faith justify that horror?' (*TD*, p 190). The difference in this novel is that, in contrast with Garland, Storman and Koupa, Malcom's search for a purpose is pre-eminently successful, and in the second book, 'Birth Pangs', he discovers in diffusionism a cause which he believes to be capable ultimately of saving mankind from the fate which civilisation is preparing for it.

In 'Ante-Natal', diffusionist theories do appear in the narrative, but in a largely unobtrusive fashion. The early explanation of the arrival of agricultural practices in Scotland, for instance, is directly diffusionist (TD, p 23), as is the general condemnation of civilised values (TD, p 47). At this early stage in the book, however, these references to diffusionist ideology are kept firmly in check and are not allowed to interfere with the major theme of 'the untheological insanity of the universe'. Upon occasion, in fact, the despair engendered by the central diffusionist vision of mankind enslaved by the alien phenomenon of civilisation contributes significantly to the general bleakness of the picture. And two-thirds of the way through the text, Malcom himself indicates the comparatively limited importance of this dogma when he criticises the diffusionists for 'not following out their conclusions to the logical extreme and attacking contemporary religion, morals, ethics, politics' (TD, p 223).

Increasingly towards the end of the novel, however, Mitchell abandons his earlier philosophical objectivity and endows the work of the diffusionists with a ridiculously exaggerated significance, eventually presenting the study of the inscrutable Maya glyphs as a step towards the discovery of 'the key to all the secrets of life and death and time' (TD, p 222). Naturally, he neglects to give this whimsy any more practical explanation, which suggests that he himself realised that in this instance he had overstepped the mark.

Douglas Young calls Malcom's experience 'an archetypal journey through darkness to light',[17] but the quest is an unsatisfactory one. For the darkness of the corridor through which Malcom travels is intensely realised, but the symbolic light he apprehends in his final vision of 'the City of the Sun' is dim and pellucid, for as in 'The Passage of the Dawn', the author provides insufficient explanation for his vision. Here Mitchell is undoubtedly inclining towards Storman's view of the responsibility of the individual for his personal destiny, and Malcom's glorious end, described in advance as 'perishing remotely and romantically in the dark places of the earth' (TD, p 56), does much to sustain the view that politically Mitchell was at this time more interested in some form of anarchism than in communism. However, I find it hard to accept Dr Young's later observation that Malcom's death is 'existentialist',[18] even taking into account the wealth of meaning this single term covers, primarily because, unlike Chris's end in the trilogy, the act bears no direct relation to real experience: Malcom's death is representational, whereas Chris's is very real. Mitchell overplays his hand badly in this symbolic episode, for although Malcom's death discloses a purpose, a purpose bound up with diffusionist doctrine, the profound cosmic sense of 'the untheological insanity of the universe', simply suspended earlier on in the book, carries over to the end, overwhelming the vague and superficial optimism extended in such a contrived ending.

Thus, Mitchell's courage seems to fail him in The Thirteenth Disciple, with the result that he ends up sidestepping the main issue considered in the earlier part of the book without winning free of its pessimistic influence. The author finally proves unfaithful to himself, betraying the promise that he offered earlier in the book, in which he explored the same profound themes that he had investigated in his first novel. The thematic split in *The Thirteenth Disciple* weakens the book fatally, and the unsophisticated proselytisation on behalf of the diffusionist approach to history which brings it to a close introduces an unfortunate but inescapable element of bathos to the whole. Like its predecessor, Mitchell's second novel is very much an apprentice work, but in addition to the inevitable signs of artistic immaturity *The Thirteenth Disciple* betrays a more damaging sense of thematic confusion.

Over two years elapsed between the publication of *The Thirteenth Disciple* and *Image and Superscription*, and in this time Mitchell had five other major works published, including *Sunset Song*. However, the chronological distance separating his second novel and *Image and Superscription* cannot hide the strong similarities between the two works. Indeed, it transpires that both were actually planned about the same time, for Mitchell originally meant *Image and Superscription* to be his second novel, and his publisher intended to bring it out early in 1931. Instead, of course, January 1931 saw the appearance of *The Thirteenth Disciple*, complete with several of the components included in the original draft for *Image and Superscription*. Writing to the Grays towards the end of 1930, Mitchell revealed that '*Image and Superscription*, my second novel which is to appear in the spring, opens in Scotland, where the principal character spends his childhood', which is true of *The Thirteenth Disciple*, but not of the later book, whose protagonist spends his formative years in Chatham. Also, the humorous anecdote with which Mr Gray furnished the author, of 'the fishing village near Slains which sank the Santa Catarina with its smell',[19] the pungent odour being that of the cured fish, is used in the second novel (*TD*, p 22), and not, as Mitchell intended at this stage, in *Image and Superscription*. Just as there is a crossover in the plots of these novels, so the books are closely related in structure and theme.

Where the earlier novel follows Malcom Maudslay on his 'adventure through the dark corridor' towards the heavily symbolic vision of 'the City of the Sun', *Image and Superscription* also takes the form of a quest for meaning and enlightenment, Gershom Jezreel travelling through the Image-ridden darkness of modern life towards the hope represented by the equally heavily symbolic 'road to Lorillard'. In both books the optimism created at the close is directly, and rather heavy-handedly, associated with the theories of the diffusionists.

I argued earlier that the sense of despair articulated in the earlier parts of *The Thirteenth Disciple* and the optimism manifested later in the diffusionist conception of human evolution are incongruous and eventually give the book an unfortunate sense of divisiveness and uncertainty. In *Image and Superscription*, diffusionist metaphysic is more efficiently integrated within the whole fabric of the novel, especially at a symbolic level, with the device of the steady decay of Jezreel's Tower throughout the course of the book providing a particularly potent expression of faith in the ultimate passing of civilisation with all its moral, social and religious disorders. Again, however, the optimistic ending grafted on to the work fails to dislodge the overwhelmingly bleak vision of the essential Absurdity of the human condition which dominates the major part of the novel.

Although Malcom Maudslay mystically fulfilled his personal destiny, his experience was unable to wipe out the deeper sense of 'the untheological insanity of the universe'. Likewise, Gershom's personal discovery of a sense of mission is largely ineffective in view of the more convincing 'horror of the Wastes' articulated earlier. The secular theme of the book—that man remains a noble creature, in spite of the incidence of acts of the utmost brutality and the extremest cruelty—is convincingly enough represented through Gershom's gradual recovery from the most bitter personal experience, from the repressive and tyrannical upbringing he receives at the hands of his fanatically religious father to the graphically realised horrors of the war in France. Yet this whole area of human experience is subordinated to the realm of the 'greater singing', which Mitchell considers with contrasting pessimism. Like Elia Constantinidos in the *Cornhill* story, Gershom finally discovers faith in man, but any deeper kind of spiritual faith eludes him. In fact, *Image and Superscription* gives a vivid and sustained impression of spiritual inconsequentiality, and despite the typically hollow optimism projected in the closing pages this brackets the book firmly with Mitchell's severely ironic debut, and with the thinly masked irony of its successor.

Mitchell's condemnation of the religious approach of Gershom's father and of the Lutherans whom Gershom encounters in America towards the end of the novel is made primarily on the grounds that their strict religious observation prevents them, and those who fall under their influence, from appreciating the finer things in life. However, the moral admonishment is in league with a philosophical objection which Mitchell raises to the theist stance itself. In fact a strong atheistic streak runs through the whole work. When still a child, for example, Gershom recalls, 'I'd disbelief even then in my father's god who pried and sneaked' (*IS*, p 12), and, reacting violently against his father's fanaticism, he subsequently discovers 'the ease of unrepentant atheism', as professed by his grandfather (*IS*, p 20). George Shaw's outlook is thus at the other pole from Gershom's father's severe and inflexible code. Shaw proclaims:

> There was no order at all in the universe, no plan, no threat, no law, nothing but a fight to feed the stomach and plant the seed of the genitals (*IS*, p 19).

Within this non-rational universe, human life acquires a quality of the ridiculous, and consequently Mitchell represents man in familiar terms which deprive him of the sense of power and importance that he customarily attaches to himself. Gershom himself is rendered insignificant by being described as 'a young animal of the dominant species on a little planet of a second-rate sun' (*IS*, p 43), and on the following page the whole of human evolution is presented as an exiguous process in the vastness of the universe, as 'a maggot-swarming questioning the white hands of Space'.

Once Gershom is taken in hand by his kindly uncle who introduces him to the world of archaeological excavation upon the ruins of the ancient Mayan civilisation in America, these profound cosmic and theological considerations dealt with earlier in the book give way to the more limited implications of the diffusionist theories. This latest concern is described by the protagonist as a 'mission to pry in the why and where another civilization had vanished from the earth' (*IS*, p 62) and, although this is obviously by no means a petty topic, bearing a strong relation as it does to the major concerns of our own civilisation, this is a considerably less momentous theme than the profound universal questions which had been explored earlier. Mitchell himself also seems less stimulated in this portion of the book, for the exposition of the diffusionist viewpoint is stereotyped and pedestrian, and the romantic elements which pervade this section of the novel are often cloying and unconvincing.

As in *Stained Radiance* and *The Thirteenth Disciple*, traumatic personal experience is the catalyst which promotes deeper insight into the incomprehensible ways of the universe. In Ester's case, the horrific scene she witnesses in America, whose brutality Mitchell is at pains to excuse on the grounds that it is taken from real life,[20] involves the gruesome lynching and disembowelling of a pregnant negress. Her subsequent condemnation of the barbarity of civilisation understandably reaches nihilistic heights, Mitchell describing how:

> . . . she had looked and looked at the thing, filling her eyes with it, impressing it deep in her mind that never again might she believe with a full and glad heart in truth or beauty or the crying loveliness of dawns on the bluegrass, or poetry or painting or peace, or the love of God or the fellowship of men (*IS*, p 180).

On the following page, the protagonist himself experiences a similar crisis of faith, and his conviction of man's cruelty instilled in him in the trenches in France produces a deeper understanding of the 'mindlessness' of the universe which allows these things to happen, Gershom considering, 'the sea that cared nothing, that was neither cruel nor uncruel, insensate, remote, mother of men and mother of life, unknowing, uncaring the horror of this Thing that had crawled to being from the moving slimes of the ancient shores'.

Gerhom's vision here is less jaundiced than the allusion in *Stained Radiance* to the city as the whore who conceived and nurtured mankind (*SR*, pp 41–2), but this vision has a cosmic desolation strongly reminiscent of Hardy, and it is noteworthy that around this time Malcom Maudslay was confessing that, 'queerly, he liked Hardy' (*TD*, p 37). The universe may not be directly malevolent towards humanity, then, but like Hardy's 'immanent will' it is condemned by its cold indifference to human welfare.

As in the first two novels, the unhappy experience of military life is the final personal trauma which eventually provides insight into the greater Absurdity of existence itself, and the accent in Gershom's bleak vision is again upon the 'negation' of the universe of which mankind is a diminutive part. Gershom learns:

> Life was no flower, it was mindless, the crawling of a mindless fecundity, changing and passing, changing and passing. Man was a beast who walked the earth, snarling

his needs and lowing his fears, and with other beasts he would perish and pass, a ripple on the cosmic mind that itself was mindless . . . (IS, p 193).

Mitchell himself came upon a more optimistic belief in human destiny through the lesson taught by the diffusionists, and yet only in his trilogy does he manage to come to terms fully with the intimidating expanses of the universe which surrounds him. In this early work, the very idea of the spiritual 'negation' of the universe at large, of 'the cosmic mind that itself was mindless', is enough to make Gershom promote the act of suicide as the most rational human response in the circumstances, Mitchell's protagonist deciding:

It would mean world-madness, world-suicide, to look in the freezing abyss either side of the path that men climbed, poor, blinded beasts. An end altogether of surely the strangest, most grotesque of adventures Life had ever attempted throughout the universe. . . .

Again, the theme mooted here looks forward to Albert Camus's profound consideration of suicide as a rational philosophical act, formulated nine years later in The Myth of Sisyphus. Where Malcom Maudslay realised the 'insanity' of the universe and consequently pronounced himself 'too sane in live', Gershom's less austere affirmation that the universe is merely 'mindless' rather than directly 'insane' is more convincingly objective, and his subsequent advocacy of the recourse to suicide thus seems even more reasonable than Malcom's.

In the following section, Mitchell describes the pain and suffering in the trenches with disturbing frankness, and the angst which Gershom experienced earlier, and which he then explained so lucidly, understandably acquires a neurotic quality bordering upon the hysterical in this harrowing context of death and destruction. The 'Image' of the corpse hanging on barbed wire which Gershom perceives on the battlefield, and which he regards as further evidence of the madness of the world, promotes a less diffident view of a universe directly hostile to mankind. Contemplating the corpse, he concludes that, 'It was the Image, dead and uncrowned and quiet, snarling, a beast no longer, murdered by God and the cosmos, pitiful, fearful and purposeless' (IS, p 202).

This represents Gershom's pessimistic view of life at its utmost extreme, and yet although Image and Superscription ends on an optimistic note, with Gershom and Ester resolving to 'go in through the bush and find Lorillard at last' (IS, p 287), finally this promise is even less firmly based upon reality than Malcom's vision of 'the City of the Sun' which brings The Thirteenth Disciple to a close. At least Malcom's experience has a vague political significance, tentatively representing the freedom of the individual in a heavily romanticised anarchist pose which contrasts with his earlier attempts to realise his destiny in mass political movements. Gershom and Ester learn from diffusionist dogma that man's cause is a deserving one, and that the fight against the oppression and injustice of civilised society is worthwhile. However, their resolve appears fairly meaningless, lacking even the most imprecisely formulated plan of action.

As he did previously in *The Thirteenth Disciple*, Mitchell shies away from the major existential themes which he develops, with substantial success, in the early portions of the novel. Instead, he latches on to diffusionist doctrine which provides a shallow form of hope in human progress. Whether or not his confidence in man's future was well founded, the deliberate lengths he went to in order to establish this optimistic outlook cannot hide the deeper-seated sense of insecurity that he evinced earlier when he considered the universe at large. As a result, it is hard to avoid feeling that in clutching at the faint promise embodied in the diffusionist theories, Mitchell, very like Koupa in the first novel, is consciously eschewing those wider-ranging themes which had become almost too painful to consider. In *Image and Superscription* as in *The Thirteenth Disciple* Mitchell finds a sense of purpose and discloses some kind of faith in human nature, but he remains as actively opposed to the idea of spiritual meaning as Garland and Koupa in the first novel. To use his own metaphor, the Image represented in the book has a more enduring power than the rather feeble attempt he makes at Superscription.

Overall, Mitchell's early novels may be of limited artistic value, but they are as fresh and interesting ideologically as they are stylistically dated. The vaguely radical political stance adopted in the first two books, both of which waver uncertainly between a pragmatic form of socialism and a more sentimental anarchistic assertion of the freedom of the individual corresponds with the political position commonly advocated in 'Free West' countries today, which tend to promote a bland interest in basic human rights while simultaneously distrusting all totalitarian systems, of left and right wings alike. Certainly Malcom Maudslay's affirmation of the freedom of the individual would strike a happier chord in most sectors of British society today than the more militant ideas expressed by Ewan in the later sections of *Grey Granite*.

Mitchell's approach to the 'greater singing' of the universe in these books is even more strikingly contemporary and, in my estimation, also more convincing than his treatment of the political theme, discrediting the short-sighted advice Mitchell received from his publisher to suppress in later works the unattractive ironic tone sustained throughout his first novel. All three of these early works are shot through with an intense philosophical realism which invigorates with its honesty as it unsettles with its austerity. Throughout the whole of the first novel and for most of the two others, Mitchell articulates a thoroughly convincing sense of the basic meaninglessness of life. The keen sense of despair which this produces pre-empts the contrived 'happy' ending—which in any case, as the chapter resumé suggests, is heavily ironic—of *Stained Radiance*, undermines the idealistic climax achieved in *The Thirteenth Disciple* and renders the effort to 'superscribe' the Image of the third book ineffectual. The didactic passages promoting the diffusionist viewpoint which occur in the later books are thus spurious in relation to the intensely moving and profound 'confessional' portions which come from a much deeper part of Mitchell's being. As Garland remarks in *Stained Radiance*, the author's own thoughts and beliefs are paramount in the modern novel, and on the whole Mitchell's early novels fulfil this requirement quite admirably.

THE IMAGINATIVE ROMANCES

Mitchell's school essays testify that his interest in the imaginative romance stemmed from his boyhood, when he eagerly devoured the work of Stevenson, Ballantyne, Fennimore-Cooper, Wells and Rider Haggard, and later he also confessed to having consumed with similar relish but less discrimination the less illustrious offerings of the kind published in that ubiquitous Scottish newspaper *The People's Journal*.[21] However, the form of the romance released in the style of his writing a more flippant aspect of his personality, and consequently the preoccupations of both the 'reformer' and the 'blasphemer' only feature obliquely in the three books he produced of this type.

My first criticism of Mitchell for turning to imaginative romance is that at its most mundane it constitutes a relatively minor art form. It would be wrong to dismiss this genre *per se* as lacking in the high seriousness which characterises great art, and indeed such books as David Lindsay's metaphysical allegory *A Voyage to Arcturus* and, more recently, Alasdair Gray's avant-garde *mélange Lanark* both vouch for the artistic capabilities of the form of the imaginative romance. However, the more stereotyped conception of this mode from which Mitchell took his lead is much less inspiring than Lindsay's and Gray's innovatory extensions of the genre, and ultimately Mitchell's own efforts in the field do not merit the same attention as his other novels.

The second objection I would raise to Mitchell having resorted to this genre is that his gifts were patently not suited to the form of the imaginative romance but to the more intense 'confessional' mode which gave him virtually unlimited scope to exercise his true *métier* for exploring the more profound themes of life. Although the romantic and utopian elements of the form are particularly well suited to the purpose of extolling the diffusionist standpoint, these elements seemed to discourage more penetrating investigation of the deeper themes of reality explored elsewhere in Mitchell's fiction, themes which would have seemed out of place in such an apparently lightweight context. In fact, Mrs Mitchell herself, normally the most active and loyal advocate for her husband's writing, dismissed this cluster of novels as 'pot-boilers' written more with an eye to financial gain than to artistic acclaim.

Pursuing a policy of 'quantity rather than quality', Mitchell seemed capable of churning out romances *ad nauseam*, for numerous drafts and fragments of books of this kind exist in the body of work left extant at his death, including 'Domina', a planned follow-up to *The Thirteenth Disciple*, 'New Novel: Egyptian Scene', and notes for a further work called 'Lost Tribes', which finally emerged in truncated form as a short story.[22] The three published romances are artistically and ideologically inferior to the early novels, the flaws apparent in the optimistic endings of *The Thirteenth Disciple* and *Image and Superscription* being fully attenuated throughout the later works. Very like Malcom Maudslay and Gershom Jezreel, the later protagonists gain insight into mankind's historical evolution and receive an auxiliary vision of the goal they wish to work towards, and yet, like Wells in

The World Set Free and *In the Days of the Comet*, Mitchell finally fails to offer any practical suggestions as to how this goal may be achieved. In the end, as in *The Thirteenth Disciple* and *Image and Superscription*, the sense of purpose manifested in the imaginative romances appears delusive and simplistic, the author's glib endeavours in these books to 'tame metaphysic by fiction'—as Frank Kermode has described Lawrence's practice[23]—being much less convincing in general than the approach he had adopted previously.

As a marketable commodity, *Three Go Back* fully vindicated Mitchell in his switch to the romantic mode, for the novel was translated into German in January 1932, into Danish in June, and into Swedish in August of that year, and when the Bobbs Merrill Company published the book in the United States, it was made a premier recommendation of the Book of the Month club. In financial and promotional terms, then, *Three Go Back* was by far Mitchell's most successful work to date. However, its sucess is regrettable in that it encouraged the author to stick with the romantic mode in the future rather than return to a form which would afford fuller play to his personal thoughts and beliefs.

Critical opinion is divided over *Three Go Back*. Whereas Douglas Young and Douglas Gifford dismiss it as one of his poorest works,[24] Ian Campbell defends both the form and content of the novel against such criticism, advancing the claim that this was 'one of Mitchell's own favourites'.[25] However, I can find no evidence to suggest that the author viewed this particular novel with anything other than the pride he was accustomed to bestow upon all his work. He did defend the book against Cuthbert Graham's mild expression of dissatisfaction, contending in a letter written to George MacDonald the month after its publication that, 'he hasn't the least comprehension of *Three Go Back*: it's merely propaganda of good science and common sense and he takes it for romantic dithering!',[26] but this is a typical and unremarkable response by Mitchell, who was always quick to defend his work when it was criticised.

The dedication at the start of the volume itself is more illuminating, for here the author confesses candidly, 'I wrote this novel as a holiday from more serious things', and his subsequent acknowledgement that Atlantis, the setting for much of the action, is a mythical location, indicates the romantic form this vacation will take. In viewing the book as a 'holiday' rather than merely a departure, then, the author prepares the reader to expect a more flippant piece of work than his preceding volumes, and this is indeed substantiated by the text which follows. I accept this profession of flippancy as explanation for the very obvious decline in thematic quality from the early novels. Certainly in *Three Go Back*, the author steers clear of the searching issues considered at length in the earlier works. While this book is better coordinated and has greater uniformity of purpose over the piece than its predecessors, it is let down badly by its lack of intellectual ambition.

As with his previous novels, the text of *Three Go Back* is peppered with literary references, and these reflect the differences between the works in question. The earlier penchant for the more lugubrious extracts from Swinburne and the 'cosmic' Shelley of 'Adonais' now gives way to a preference for the more idealistic portions of Romantic poetry, especially that of the 'Ulysses' Tennyson, and of the Shelley whom Koupa visualised at the end of *Stained Radiance* deserting the major themes of life which had become too painful for him to countenance and seeking forgetfulness by confining himself to more mundane secular concerns. Mitchell's own change of approach is marked by this movement away from the more challenging work of Shelley which provided the title and the *raison d'être* for his first novel, to the lighter utopian Shelley of 'Hellas' and 'The Triumph of Life', both of which provide quotations for this novel. The transition between the two books, as represented in the respective views they offer of this poet, is a descent from the realm of the universal to the human sphere, from the sublime to the secular.

Three Go Back takes the familiar form of a quest for purpose in life, and again the protagonists discover a sense of resolve without gaining any substantial insight into the ways of the world. The three main figures are pitched back into the Golden Age of the distant past by a fantastic cosmic accident, but there is nothing arbitrary about the conclusions Mitchell draws from this situation; indeed, the greater emphasis set throughout upon the promulgation of diffusionist doctrine as opposed to its actual explication marks the book out as the 'propaganda' that the author described it as to George MacDonald. The fictive means by which Mitchell represents the diffusionist viewpoint are fairly convincing, with lively plot, credible characterisation and realistic descriptive work, central features of the literature of shipwreck and displacement from *Gulliver's Travels* and *Robinson Crusoe* to *Lord of the Flies*, combining to make the opening book satisfying enough as what Clair herself calls 'a Stone Age idyll' (*TGB*, p 89). This section of the book also contrives to give a satisfying sense of natural harmony without completely eradicating the disturbing and truthful conviction, fleetingly expressed, of the Absurdity of the human condition, for example, when Clair contemplates the stars in the night sky with a clinical Hardyesque detachment, perceiving them to be 'Unchanged . . . and remote and cold as ever' (*TGB*, p 92). From the time when Mitchell originally introduces his simple nomadic paragons on page 100, however, the propagandist takes over and, as the tendency to preach increases, gradually the book falls away. Sinclair the pacifist becomes authorial mouthpiece, and the novelist uses him monotonously and tendentiously to define the greater implications of the action and put human evolution into its proper diffusionist perspective.

Even more unforgiveable is the author's failure to give the historical theory any acceptable practical significance. The faith expressed in the enduring goodness of human nature does underpin a vague socialist belief in mankind's ability to survive and overcome the worst perversions of modern civilisation, as is suggested by the inspiring vision Clair receives among the hunters sleeping in their cave, a vision of the constant regeneration of 'the Christs and Father Damiens, the Brunos and the Shelleys, the comradeship and compassion of the slave-pit and the trench' (*TGB*, p 162). In the main, however, the sense of resolve that Clair and Sinclair achieve at the end of the book is unconvincing, in that their mission, glorified as 'the fight for sanity', revolves around the unsubstantiated promise to 'light a torch and never let it die' (*TGB*, pp 253–4). This resolve is partly sustained by a radical political commitment to the fight for social justice, set directly against the 'lie about the everlastingness of rich and poor' (*TGB*, p 252), but for the most part the faith both Clair and Sinclair acquire in the ultimate achievement of the perfect society is based upon less secure foundations. Not content with merely going back to the past through fiction to demonstrate his belief in human goodness, unrealistically Mitchell pins his faith in the fantastic hope of some kind of physical return to this simple prelapsarian mode of existence, Clair looking forward from her privileged vantage point in the idyllic past to a time when, 'The hunter will come again in the world we left' (*TGB*, p 232); and in the very last chapter of the book, titled 'I shall rise again', the resurrection which she and Sinclair hope for is that 'the hunters come back to the world again' (*TGB*, p 248). The author offers no clues as to how the radical transformation in the very essence of society is to be exacted, so that neither the protagonists' final avowal to 'preach Atlantis till our dying day' (*TGB*, p 252), nor their pledge to 'Remember the road to Sunrise Pass' (*TGB*, p 254) do much to establish the accessibility of their main objective. If ever Hugh MacDiarmid's scathing criticism of Mitchell for his 'Tir-nan-og complex' were justified,[27] it is in the unsatisfactory ending of *Three Go Back*.

As propaganda, *Three Go Back* would win few converts. The ideal mode of life embodied in the past Golden Age is transformed into a goal for the future only by the exigency of unconvincing romantic expedients, and Mitchell is guilty of performing an unexplained leap of faith in the completely unsullied picture he projects of the glorious future awaiting mankind, founded upon a fanciful belief that 'all the world could begin again' (*TGB*, p 138), and that, 'We can re-make the world' (*TGB*, p 176). Although the leading lights of the diffusionist school were predictably pleased with it, the novel is less the 'good science' that Mitchell described it as and more the 'romantic dithering' that, over-reacting to Cuthbert Graham's mild criticisms, he felt it was being denounced as. The author's primary concern in the novel is to promote diffusionist ideology but, relying more heavily upon empty symbolism and romantic idealism rather than rational discourse and imaginative representation, his propaganda falls flat.

The relative unworthiness of *Three Go Back* in comparison with Mitchell's earlier novels is thrown into greater relief by the unwillingness he shows in the book to leave the security of the human sphere and consider the more profound aspects of the 'greater singing' which he had approached so boldly and earnestly in the early novels. In contrast with the inordinate attention paid to the diffusionist argument, the more exalted themes of life appear only in the most subdued form, mainly via the author's delineation of, in John Alcorn's succinct term, a 'naturist' world.

Adopting the modes and values of the primitive hunters, Clair comes to a conscious understanding of the basic 'fable' of life as a constant 'flow and ebb of death and love and birth' (*TGB*, p 177), the Golden Age which she comes to appreciate with Keith Sinclair involving a life of completely spontaneous sensuous indulgence unhampered by any moral constraints or spiritual considerations. Death is presented as simply a formal part of the human experience and, as Sinclair tells Clair with an equanimity so typical of Mitchell, it is neither to be regretted for its physical inevitability nor made the basis for religious promises and superstitious fears. Clair's distress at the seemingly callous behaviour of the hunters with regard to Sir John's corpse is thus convincingly overcome by the logic of Sinclair's argument that, 'Death is of no account in fundamental human values' (*TGB*, p 171). Here, death is less the Lawrentian 'joy of moving on with the invisible',[28] or the spiritual fulfilment found by Chris at the climax of the *Quair*, than a fact of life apprehended with the strict kind of scientific neutrality which governs Gorky's assertion in *Mother* that 'the pleasure of living entails the necessity of dying'.[29] Sinclair's argument that 'there is nothing horrible in death' is acceptable enough, as is Clair's own understanding of the act as the forfeiture of life which produces the inanimate state of 'not being' (*TGB*, p 191); yet generally, Mitchell prefers to steer clear of such profound subjects altogether in this book.

Clair can believe in Christ and Buddha but not in God, and her original objection to the theist argument, given in agreement with diffusionist policy, is subsequently backed up by more decisive appreciation of the non-rational nature of the universe. Cast adrift in the 'frozen wastes' of atheism, she receives a discomforting vision of the futility of her own existence and of human life in general, her romantic sensibilities alone saving her from the cosmic despair that Mitchell's earlier heroes experience. Only by dint of romantic assertion can Clair avoid the anguish which Mitchell felt was the logical response for human beings gifted with the powers of reason to make when confronted with the stark reality of their existence. However, Keith Sinclair, the most scientifically-minded of the book's protagonists, puts Clair's viewpoint into something like its true perspective in the real ideological crux of the book by discriminating between the received and perceived images of God. Thus, he does not supply Clair with the confirmation she is seeking for her 'wild hope', her earnest yearning after God, telling her brusquely:

> An honest god's the noblest work of man. I don't believe there's anything to shield us from the darkness, Clair. And not even for the sake of poetry do I think we should carry the idea to our hunters in that world we're to make beyond these mountains . . . (*TGB*, p 210).

God is thus an artificial concept created by man, and one which is ultimately irrelevant to his spiritual well-being. This disbelief in the existence of a supreme deity outwith the human imagination. or at least outwith the human sphere, foreshadows the distinction drawn at the close of *A Scots Quair* between the political cause espoused by Ewan and the spiritual fulfilment found by Chris. Mitchell here seems to be edging towards the identification of the true religious impulse as being the province of the individual, and yet this tantalising snatch of things to come is short-lived, as the dissemination of the idea of God comes to a premature close, Mitchell turning his attention to the considerably lighter matters associated with diffusionist ideology for the last fifty pages of the book.

Thus, although the tone of *Three Go Back* is completely different from the bleak note struck in his earlier novels, beneath it all Mitchell's fundamental outlook does not appear to have changed. The optimism exuded at the close seems illusory, just as the principles of diffusionism, being only loosely related to the concerns of modern life, appear nebulous. As in *The Thirteenth Disciple* and *Image and Superscription*, this idealism is largely displaced by the contrastingly disquieting impression given of the Absurdity of life, admittedly much less firmly established in this novel. Written, as Mitchell admitted, as 'a holiday from more serious things', *Three Go Back* arguably makes easier reading than the early novels and is perhaps more coherent than both *The Thirteenth Disciple* and *Image and Superscription*; and yet inevitably, it has a less lasting effect because it deals with less momentous themes.

The *Lost Trumpet* appeared only six months after *Three Go Back*, and although this book witnesses a slight improvement in the handling of theme, it also falls prey to the same intellectual privations which affect its predecessor. In this second romance, the reader is transported to Egypt and the Oriental world which provides the setting for Mitchell's three story-cycles. The novel is described on the fly-leaf as 'Swansong of Colonel Saloney', the narrator in the *Polychromata*. Mitchell tries to exploit this connection by making gratuitous references within the text of the novel to incidents which feature in the stories collected in *The Calends of Cairo*. This exercise merely underlines the novel's 'pot-boiler' status.

The artistic impoverishment of *The Lost Trumpet* is further indicated by the dubious quality of the fragment in which it had its origins. Judging by its style, this fragment predates 'It is Written', the *Cornhill* story upon which the novel is loosely based. For while *The Lost Trumpet*, like Mitchell's other two romances, seems intellectually threadbare, even the book's typically prolix diffusionist argument is an improvement upon what it came from. This early draft, 'Precis of THE LOST TRUMPET', is an innocuous exercise in the indulgence of the romantic imagination, and although the original script makes passing reference to two of Mitchell's pet subjects, the innate benevolence of the 'children of Nature' and the consistent brutality of the physical atrocities perpetrated throughout history, the author's main interest at this stage rests with the magic trumpet itself. This is endowed with substantially greater powers here than it is finally accorded in the novel, causing an actual earthquake which is mysteriously linked with 'the cessation of war in Siberia' and with 'The Jew-Arab conflict that died suddenly in the streets of Jerusalem'.[30] These miraculous provisions do not augur well.

Considering the inauspicious beginnings of *The Lost Trumpet*, the novel itself is surprisingly successful among Mitchell's romances as regards both the ideas expressed and the manner of their literary expression. And perhaps it is worth considering the extenuating factor, that at the time the author was working on this novel a substantial proportion of his creative energies was being diverted to the writing of *Sunset Song* which burst upon the scene the month after *The Lost Trumpet* made its appearance.

The sharply observed characterisation of Mitchell's second romance looks back beyond *Three Go Back* to *Stained Radiance* in particular, and the character types are largely similar in these two books: Esdras Quaritch may be regarded as a later version of John Garland, the tortured and disillusioned writer who figures in the first novel; the erudite Saloney and the scholarly Dr Adrian are basically romantic characters who have a strong affinity with the loquacious poet Andreas van Koupa before he suffers his loss of faith; and the Communist Marrot has much in common with the early doctrinaire James Storman, or indeed with John Garland as he appears at the end of the novel, as practising Marxist.

Of the seven main figures in *The Lost Trumpet*, Dr Adrian is the least convincing, for he, like Keith Sinclair, is little more than spokesman for the diffusionist viewpoint. Periodically, he adumbrates the stock diffusionist theses, and he does so in a characteristically pedantic fashion, stressing how the moral goodness of mankind endures despite the challenging evidence provided to the contrary by the contemporary evils of war and poverty, the latter of which is observed at its very worst by Saloney and Pelagueya when they visit the Warrens of Cairo. Although this novel contains its full complement of didactic passages, however, Mitchell's actual application of the diffusionist argument is more convincing in this book than in *Three Go Back*.

In the earlier romance, diffusionism itself seems to offer some kind of universal panacea, inspiring Clair and Sinclair to embark upon a mission to save the world, but this mission is not given any explicit purpose or direction. In *The Lost Trumpet*, the lesson taught by diffusionism is garbed in a more modest guise, Adrian observing, 'The cure in diffusionism—well, it is very simple: *Be your essential self*' (*LT*, p 139). The discovery and sounding of the magic trumpet frees the protagonists from the repressions and inhibitions which hold them captive but, although each finds his or her 'essential self' at the end of the book, each reacts to this self-discovery in his or her own way, Saloney and Pelagueya returning to their native Russia and the Communist dream, Heubsch returning to his own colony in Jerusalem, Marrot to his native America, and Quaritch and Auslag going back to work in the streets of Cairo. This process of the discovery of purpose in life is thus taken further in *The Lost Trumpet* than in *Three Go Back*. As Adrian acknowledges, diffusionism in itself is of limited importance in modern life, providing basic inspiration, but neither the goal this inspiration should be directed towards nor the means by which it should be sought, Mitchell's historical expert informing his companions:

> I can diagnose your complaint with the aid of the Diffusionists: I can diagnose the complaint of the world. But how to effect the cure . . . (*LT*, p 141).

The positive political dimension of *The Lost Trumpet* is thus crucial to the impact the book makes as a whole, for whereas Clair and Keith Sinclair in the end make vague pledges to 'preach Atlantis' and to return to the natural mode of existence which reigned in prehistoric times, the protagonists of the later novel, having heard the 'trumpet-voice of human sanity' (*LT*, p 141), proceed to direct their fervour into channels which are more sharply defined; ultimately they devote themselves to a variety of political or pseudo-political causes. While in *Three Go Back* Mitchell does little more than articulate the need and the desire to find a cause in life, in *The Lost Trumpet*, he goes some way towards bringing this unspecified urge to some sort of practical fruition.

Mitchell seems as politically unsure in this second romance as he appeared in *Stained Radiance*, but the political alternatives he outlines here are very similar to those provided in his first novel, the principles he recommends being the same humanistic ones of the freedom of the individual, and of the fundamental equality of men. The author's social conscience is comparatively well represented in *The Lost Trumpet*, especially in the passages dealing with the destitution of the Warrens, and this moral force recommends some form of radical political commitment, most fully realised in Saloney's and Pelagueya's return to Stalinist Russia. This signifies the triumphant fulfilment of their destiny in the renunciation of the social privilege they both enjoyed as White Russians in their former life, in favour of the willing acceptance of the constraints and sacrifices demanded by the Communist programme, eulogised as the effort 'to work and talk and fight for daylight and sanity' (*LT*, p 279).

Marrot is the main political figure in the book, however. Although he is in no way a paragon, the two qualities which Mitchell deemed to be most admirable in the political activist are combined in his portrait. Firstly, he is well grounded in formal political theory and in official Communist policy, which gives some kind of scientific justification for his efforts. His personal aims are drawn straight from Marxist ideology, and he himself admits the orthodoxy of his ideal of a classless society when he tells two of his colleagues, 'If either of you knew the elements of communist philosophy you'd be aware that the communist's only interest in the proletariat is its abolition' (*LT*, p 179). Marrot thus sticks firmly to the Party line, but an equally important factor in his political make-up is his sympathy and compassion. Early in the book, Heubsch expressly describes his friend as a sentimental politician as opposed to a scientific one, observing that, 'he's a communist more from sentiment than economics' (*LT*, p 67). It is worth remembering in this context, then, that Mitchell himself has been berated over the years by the more rigidly Marxist critics, including James Barke and Hugh MacDiarmid, and praised by some of the more neutral commentators such as his biographer Ian Munro, for the very same reason—that he was a communist of an emotional kind.

Marrot therefore is made very much in his creator's image, exemplifying the marriage of the moral and intellectual qualities of the 'reformer' which Mitchell felt to be most worthy of praise in the politician. Accordingly, the one flaw which Heubsch distinguishes in his friend's political standpoint—when he remarks that, 'His failing is that he lacks a purpose' (*LT*, p 67)—is duly corrected when, upon hearing the inspirational sound of the trumpet, Marrot realises that he must put his political principles to work in his native America.

In *The Lost Trumpet*, therefore, communism emerges as the most likely solution to the social ills of the world, but the political meaning uncovered in the book is itself underwritten by a deeper theme. Saloney tends to confine his attention to what he calls the 'concrete realities' of life (*LT*, p 163), and yet early in the novel he shows an appreciation of the greater dimensions lying beyond the human sphere, with all its elaborate political and religious 'supposings', when he observes simply that 'the morning was unaware of all concepts economic or religious ever fathered by men on nature' (*LT*, p 85). As is so often the case with Mitchell's protagonists, Saloney comes to view the major themes of existence with painful detachment, apprehending death, for example, as a dark journey 'into that which, spite all my romantic dreamings, I still knew for an end and no beginning' (*LT*, p 119). All this builds up to a typically stark vision of human Absurdity, Saloney again portraying human life as 'the mean whining of carrion-starved animals under the jeering indifference of the stars' (*LT*, p 218). And yet again the novel follows the familiar pattern from this point, with Saloney eventually finding a form of escape from these harsh realities in the personal happiness afforded him by his romance with Pelagueya and by the political purpose he discovers, both of which again appear rather vapid, despite the fact that in this book, as in all three of the imaginative romances, Mitchell gives a more muted impression of the darker aspects of the human condition.

As in its two companions, one specific passage stands out in *The Lost Trumpet* as the intellectual crux of the novel. This is situated two-thirds of the way through the text, involving an animated debate over the most important matters of life. The decisive philosophical exchange between Saloney and Esdras Quaritch is completely dominated by the embittered young writer. Mitchell himself seems much more involved in the argument put forward by the younger man than in Saloney's urbane but somewhat equivocal comments, and ultimately the sceptic's argument weathers the mild criticisms raised by the narrator.

Quaritch's elaborate metaphor, which explodes man's conviction of his own importance by apprehending him in a universal context as a minute liver-fluke, is unusually suggestive among Mitchell's conceits in that the beguilingly simple parallel he draws between the worm and the body it inhabits and man and his universe finally touches on profound spiritual themes. Quaritch's sobering vision of the physical triviality of the human adventure and of the non-rationality of existence fully reflects all the qualities of 'confidence and uncertain cruelty and the bright, shining rebelliousness of youth' which his elder credits him with (*LT*, p 190). Mitchell supported Quaritch's vision of the bold 'search for reality' (*LT*, p 189) undertaken by the rebellious young flukes who are shocked into action by the sudden realisation of the limitations and deprivations of their physical and spiritual circumstances. The challenging forthrightness that Quaritch associates with the flukes' quest—'Anarchy of thought and immorality of deed' in their elders' estimation—is one of the author's main *idées fixes*, while the questioning of the established conception of God comes especially easily to Mitchell as a diffusionist. And above all, in view of the beliefs of the 'blasphemer', it is safe to assume that Quaritch's disbelief in the existence of a 'great Super-Fluke . . . in the Beyond' is his also.

Saloney's vain attempt to refute the starkness of Quaritch's sardonic allegory fudges the issue, the dragoman arguing on the following page that, 'though the poor flukes are unable to comprehend it, there *is* a meaning. . . . The liver is part of a body, the body of some biological species, the species of some social group'. Quaritch's riposte, that 'That isn't a meaning, it's merely a multiplication', is sharp and incisive, however, and provides a key to the unravelling of the two main ideological strands which run throughout Mitchell's work.

When Saloney projects his belief in mankind and in the universe to which he belongs as a near-religious affirmation, Quaritch, alive to the distinction between the secular and spiritual, points out the inadequacy of such a procedure. Here Mitchell seems to recognise the schism that runs throughout his work between secular and spiritual matters, between what Ewan defines as GOD and FREEDOM respectively. In the imaginative romances as a whole, however, the author confuses the two strands, attempting to subvert the profound sense of despair manifested in relation to the universe at large by merely accentuating the optimism he expresses in man's moral and social welfare. This is a most unsatisfactory operation for, to use Quaritch's terminology, it constitutes a 'multiplication' rather than a valid affirmation of 'meaning'.

Although Quaritch's astute comments suggest that Mitchell himself appreciated the major thematic discrepancy that had infected his latest novels, *The Lost Trumpet* itself closes on a very similar note of unbridled idealism which could legitimately be condemned as a 'multiplication'. Perhaps Mitchell needed to cling to this reassuring dream of mankind's glorious destiny because he, like Koupa or Robert Colquohoun, found the greater realities of existence too hard to bear. Or perhaps under the guidance of his publisher he believed his readership looked to fiction for some kind of message of hope. Most probably the thematic shortcomings of the book can be attributed to sheer pressure of work, and to the author's own awareness of his latest novel's comparative insignificance within his canon.

A general improvement in Mitchell's literary powers from *Three Go Back* is signified by the author's easy recourse to metaphor in *The Lost Trumpet*, as, for instance, in the early representation of Saloney's middle-age nausea as 'the grasshopper of futility' (*LT*, p 85). The most successful of the experimental passages in this novel is the remarkable extended metaphor of the 'search for reality' which Quaritch elaborates for Saloney's benefit. The other major symbolic passage, located a third of the way through the text, also happens to be inspired, in true Beckett-like fashion, by the bleaker aspects of human existence—what Jan Kott has called the quality of the 'grotesque'.[31]

Saloney's six-page 'fairy-story' of three brothers who each set out on a journey, and who each end up dying at the hands of robbers (*LT*, pp 109–14), is a curious distorted pastiche of the parables of 'The Good Samaritan' and 'The Prodigal Son' which has a flatness of style and a pessimistic tone reminiscent of the Kafka of *The Trial* and *The Castle*. It constitutes one of the most puzzling passages in all Mitchell's work. This is the one instance in all his writing when the oblique approach he adopted in stories like 'Vernal', 'Gift of the River' and 'Greenden' deteriorates into cryptic depths which defy comprehension. Pelagueya cannot fathom the meaning behind the story and, enigmatically, Saloney refuses to enlighten either his listener or the reader.

Perhaps, as in *The Trial* and *The Castle*, the whole point of the tale is its very inconclusiveness, suggesting the inscrutability of life itself: this in fact is the theme of the poem by R L Megroz which Mitchell used as the inscription for the American edition of the novel, in which the poet concludes, 'Mysterious still to me/ is my reality'.[32] Although the novel does not contradict this proposition, the ancillary themes of human resilience, and of moral fervour translated into political mission, merely highlight the incongruousness of Saloney's parable within the novel. Happily, Mitchell confined his subsequent literary experimentation to more practical limitations.

Overall, *The Lost Trumpet* is an improvement upon *Three Go Back* for it gives a truer reflection of the author's own thoughts and ideas, particularly those of the 'reformer'; it relegates the artistically and ideologically restricting theories of diffusionism to a more realistic position within the book's framework, and it heralds a slight development in Mitchell's technical skills. As with its predecessor, however, the novel is ultimately more noteworthy for what it excludes, and its thematic shortcomings may be attributed in part to Mitchell's decision to stand by a relatively lightweight fictive form which had already been seen to be largely unsuited to his particular gifts and to be less capable of carrying the profound themes which enriched the early novels.

In his last romance, Mitchell forsakes the central plot of the search for buried treasure and returns to the fantasy of time travel which featured in his first novel of this kind. In the dedication which opens *Gay Hunter* the author introduces his latest work as a companion book to *Three Go Back*. The idyllic natural world which the protagonists of *Gay Hunter* visit lies in the post-apocalyptic future, whereas in the earlier volume it lay in the primitive past, but the exploitation of the situation is similar in the two books; and again, the plot appears all too convenient for Mitchell the proselytising diffusionist, setting up the decisive contrast between society in a civilised and in a pre-civilised—or, in *Gay Hunter's* case a post-civilised—state.

The situation described in *Gay Hunter* thus has a clear didactic purpose, the central confrontation that it arranges between primitive and civilised standards ultimately condemning civilised man and commending his primitive counterpart. In the book's dedication, however, Mitchell denies that it serves any dogmatic function:

> . . . this book has no serious intent whatever. . . . It is neither prophecy nor propaganda. It is written for the glory of sun and wind and rain, dreams by smoking camp-fires, and the glimpsed immortality of men.

Shortly after the novel had been published, the author repeated this profession of flippancy in a letter to Helen Cruickshank in which he wrote, '*Gay* isn't very serious stuff: it's a fairy tale for fun'.[33] Mitchell certainly plays up the more whimsical qualities of his story in *Gay Hunter*, and consequently even the diffusionist message falters, appearing especially subdued when the heroine expresses her newly discovered *joie de vivre* as a romantic celebration of uninhibited sensuous indulgence. And just as Clair Stranley's romance with Aerte in *Three Go Back* facilitates her rejection of civilised values, so Gay's assumption of the spontaneous life-style of the hunters is directly assisted by her affair with Rem.

The general romantic theme of natural harmony culminates in the symbolic fusion created towards the close of the novel, with the hunters 'merging in and out of the brown gold of the autumnal landscape as though part of the play of sun and shadow themselves. (And out of the earth and sky)' (GH, p 277), a conceit which harks back two years to Chris's mirage-like vision of Ewan's and Rob's assimilation within the surrounding fields in 'Harvest' in Sunset Song. Gay's own heavily Lawrentian rapport with the 'living quick' of the elemental world gives her a mystical kind of spiritual assurance:

> Knowledge of that kinship entered your heart and you walked the ways of the wind and the ways of the sun of no volition of your own at all, but the volition of all life that was, that moved to being in grass and tree and the flicker of a bright bird's wing (GH, p 277).

Again there is a strong parallel here with Chris, who has a similar empathy with the natural world in A Scots Quair. The Scots heroine eventually attains a form of spiritual fulfilment by coming to terms with the essentials underlying human existence, and the physical freedom which Gay discovers with the hunters instils in her an ancillary sense of mental and spiritual liberation, as she considers:

> Winter in a cave, the roar of a fire within, the roar of storms without, no clothes or furnishings to bedevil life or hide the stark, fierce face of things. Life like a song, terrible and true, stark as themselves (GH, p 276).

The 'Paean of all life' which Rem sings to Gay at the close of the book just before she drifts back to her own epoch thus brings this romantic theme to its climax:

> For he sang of Life as a fine bright fire, tremulous, tremendous, against the dead wastes—Life and its splendour in the touch of hands, in the touch of lips and bodies and words, in its pain, in its pleasure, its tiredness, its madness (GH, pp 280–1).

Mitchell thus takes the romantic theme of the novel about as far as it can legitimately go, providing a vivid celebration of 'the glory of sun and wind and rain, dreams by smoking camp-fires, and the glimpsed immortality of men'. However, although he more than succeeds in achieving what he set out to do, ultimately endowing life itself with a spiritual importance in an otherwise dead universe, evidently he was dissatisfied with this particular aspect of the novel. Gay reacts laconically to the bizarre situation she finds herself in after she has been transported to the idyllic life of the future, condemning it as 'the kind of thing that sick little imaginative novelists had dreamt of in the smoke and squalor and the unemployment queues of the fourth decade of the twentieth century' (GH, p 93). This hints strongly that Mitchell —who by then had Spartacus and the first two parts of the trilogy under his belt—reproached himself for devoting his book to frivolous romantic topics when there were much more pressing contemporary issues demanding his attention. This brief allusion to the social reality of the thirties contrasts with the sentimental romance which encloses it, and ultimately it reflects back upon Mitchell himself. Consequently, appreciating the limitations of his romantic theme, and perhaps recognising at the same time the limited significance of diffusionist doctrine, Mitchell attempts a more realistic approach to political and philosophical matters in this novel than in his previous romances.

Discounting the mild left-wing sentiments of the diffusionist argument, *Gay Hunter* has enough political mettle to put a questionmark against Mitchell's claim that his novel was 'neither prophecy nor propaganda', for it is the most ardent of the three imaginative romances. On one level, it is a mild political allegory warning against the nascent evils of fascism—of which Mitchell, writing in 1934, was fully aware, and to which he was violently opposed. As a diffusionist, he regarded this despicable movement as the final barbarity of a decaying civilisation, and as a communist, he interpreted it as the most extreme manifestation of capitalist doctrine. Gay's two companions from her own time, Ledyard Houghton and Lady Jane Easterling, are both sardonic figures representing the evils of fascist fundamentalism, which upholds the position of social privilege they themselves have been born into and establishes the imperious call for 'discipline and breed and good taste [to] come into their own again' (*GH*, p 19). The sympathy which Gay extends to her companions is perhaps the logical response of the diffusionist determined to affirm man's inherent goodness, but the emphasis she puts upon the influence of their environment and their privileged upbringing recalls Engels's postulation in *Socialism: Utopian and Scientific* that 'man's character is the product, on the one hand, of heredity, on the other, of the environment of the individual during his lifetime'.[34] In fact, Gay's antipathy towards her adversaries relaxes noticeably towards the end of the book, as she accepts the Marxist explanation for the arrogant delusions of grandeur shown by her former companions, and realises in a revelatory moment:

> Yet—were even they to blame? The were no more than victims of their one-time environment and education and social-caste; and the aberrant culture that companioned that caste in the days of its economic straits (*GH*, p 250).

The characterisation of *Gay Hunter* thus has an implicit political significance, and the plot has a similar relevance, the disastrous ending which Mitchell forecasts for civilisation, as related grimly to Gay by the Voice of the Tower, being attributed to social and political factors. Mitchell's symbolic demarcation of the perversity and corruption of the pre-apocalyptic dystopia, by substituting the traditional religious icon of the cross with the symbol of the phallus (*GH*, p 228), is reminiscent of the modern cinematic technique of Ken Russell in its heavy-handedness, yet Mitchell's analysis of the situation has a contrasting power and validity. With society in his own time already being caught in the grip of fascism, Mitchell simply follows this trend to its logical conclusion in the novel. In the age which he sardonically calls the age of the Hierarchies, increasing social polarisation culminates in the creation of a whole new subordinate species of Sub-Men. Inevitably, this subservient body rebels against its oppressors, chaos ensues, and from this chaos War States emerge which eventually destroy each other. The mature political beliefs of the 'reformer' thus play a considerable part in this very Wellsian scheme.

Thus, Mitchell's final imaginative romance reflects the radical sympathies of the 'reformer', indicating that the author had a sure grasp of the main issues at stake in Europe in the early thirties. As in *The Lost Trumpet*, however, this political theme is integrated within the materialistic approach adopted throughout the novel in regard to life in general; and again this pragmatic quality appears sadly out of place in imaginative romance.

At the beginning of the novel, Gay comments flatteringly, 'salt of the earth, the materialists' (*GH*, p 18), and she obviously inherits this opinion from her father, whose outlook, concentrating chiefly upon the 'hopelessness' of life (*GH*, p 22), is quite intimidating in its austerity. Gay's own view of the world at this stage is also deeply pessimistic, as her grim conception of the unhappy relationship between man and his civilisation shows. Mitchell's heroine observes that, 'the world was one great pounding machine, pounding the life out of humanity, making it an ant-like slave-crawl on an earth turned to a dung-hill of its own futilities' (*GH*, p 22).

This sense of human futility and insignificance is tied to a deeper conviction of spiritual barrenness, indeed to a universal vision of a truly 'grotesque' character. Gay includes herself in the Absurdity of her vision later on by contrasting the rational intellectual powers which she believes to be her birthright as a human being with the aridity of the universe at large: with a tinge of self-pity, she declares herself 'Damn young to be launched out in the wastes of time and space, with a vexing intelligence' (*GH*, p 45). As in *Image and Superscription*, the simple human quality of romance provides the one redemption in this context of universal inertness, as Gay observes in her celebration of 'lust and love':

> They were the ultimate and lovely mystery, she had thought, gay little materialist, seeing all mystic philosophies and hopes as the play of diseased reflexes only, the wind and gusty regurgitation of human life. And all the world, whatever the names and sickened stomachic dreamings of gods and heavens and hells and codes they had shielded behind, had believed with her in the tremendousness of lust and love (*GH*, p 86).

Gay thus mirrors the philosophical disposition of the 'blasphemer' by expressing a belief in natural and material reality itself, as opposed to the diaphanous 'philosophies and hopes' which men drape upon it. And at its most profound, *Gay Hunter* dramatises Mitchell's effort to come to terms with the hard facts of existence, for Gay's physical experience of life in its most rudimentary form among the Golden Age primitives introduces her to the greater realities. Thus, midway through the novel, Gay contemplates the night sky and asks herself, 'what were stars to her, what had men ever seen in them but their own fancies?', affirming conclusively, 'And she had ceased to play with the cloacal fancyings of men' (*GH*, p 144). Eventually, Gay consciously perceives the final truth in an extended passage which, like those given to Keith Sinclair in the first romance and to Esdras Quaritch in the second, stands out sharply from the rest of the book. And the obvious link which Gay's vision has with the central theme of *A Scots Quair* reflects how Mitchell's philosophical thinking had developed from his earlier novels.

The English heroine is actually prepared for her role as 'Seeker' (as Chris is termed) in exactly the same way as the Scots character, being symbolically divested of all the superfluous effects, of the mental and physical diversions of ordinary life which could come between her and what Mitchell defines in the *Quair* as 'the truth, and the only truth that there was' (*SQ*, p 207). More than fifty pages before she finally apprehends this vital 'truth' Gay achieves a state of grace similar to that which Chris attains in the trilogy, the Englishwoman's return to the bucolic life of the hunter granting her experience of the sensation of 'Night and darkness and the wind upon one', which leaves her ultimately, very much like Chris at the end of *A Scots Quair*, 'naked and unshielded and unafraid' (*GH*, p 164).

Chris's dying vision of the ruling power of Change is at once more lyrical and explicit than Gay's reverie, but the latter's elucidation of Heraclitus's classical postulation that 'nothing endures' has an immediate and fascinating affinity with the quasi-religious theme enshrined in the *Quair*. Initially in the English novel, this principle is applied by Gay with commendable frankness to both the personal and universal situation, promoting the stark conclusion that, 'death waited on all life that ever was' (*GH*, p 220). Finally, however, probably out of deference to the romantic form which the novel takes, Mitchell reduces this stirring nihilistic affirmation to the banal level of romantic fancy, Gay deciding in the end that 'in this evening quiet, you could sit and doubt even the endurance of change'. The passage as a whole proves that the 'blasphemer's' thinking when he wrote *Gay Hunter* was at a similar stage to his thinking when he wrote *Grey Granite* almost six months later, but ultimately the romantic form proves obstructive and he relegates the key passage from its rightful place at the book's climax, as is the case in *A Scots Quair*, to a comparatively innocuous position—and, more harmfully, dilutes its message.

Thus, more so even than *Three Go Back* or *The Lost Trumpet*, *Gay Hunter* demonstrates just how badly matched the form of the imaginative romance was to Mitchell's particular literary gifts, for even when he seemed disposed to consider those penetrating themes which had featured so strongly in his early fiction, his good intentions were thwarted by the conditions imposed by romantic conventions. It is too easy to criticise the romances for merely employing a literary form which now appears stereotyped and outmoded, but these three books invite the more severe criticism that, despite the greater imaginative freedom they gave the author, ultimately they boast nothing like the philosophical breadth and depth of vision of his more heavily realistic work.

SPARTACUS

Mitchell introduced *Spartacus* in direct contrast to *Gay Hunter* when he wrote to Helen Cruickshank in 1934:

I've had a long letter from Fritz Wölcken about all that he's thought and believed regarding the works of L.G.G. and J.L.M. Nice letter. But I wish he'd read 'Spartacus'. . . . He seems to think and hope that *Grey Granite's* (Ewan's) solution of the world's ills will be—return to Nature à la Gay Hunter! This is shocking.[35]

The author's own implication is that *Spartacus* is attributable to the pragmatic side of his character while *Gay Hunter* stems from his more romantic persona. This would suggest that *Spartacus* belongs more with the early novels than with the imaginative romances, and yet Mitchell's is a historical novel of an unorthodox kind, for it is far more than the 'splendid reconstruction in fictional form of the slave revolt in Ancient Rome' which Hugh MacDiarmid hailed it as.[36] Just as the mature political role of the 'reformer' incorporates both a disciplined pragmatism and a lofty idealism, so the realistic qualities of *Spartacus* are balanced by highly romantic properties. Indeed, in the final analysis, *Spartacus* combines the best features of the early novels with the more worthy attributes of the imaginative romances, producing a work that is at once a vivid account of a particular episode in Roman history, and a political abstract embodying the principles and ideals which the author held most dear.

Mitchell habitually provided explicit justification for his various literary manoeuvres either within the work in question (as in John Garland's critical theorising in *Stained Radiance*), or in the form of an independent preface (as in *Sunset Song*), or in an entirely separate work, and his opinions upon the imaginative fabrication of history are most directly expressed in *The Conquest of the Maya*, the author observing in this, his most intensively researched historical study:

> The imaginative interpretation of puzzling, dazzling, or inexplicable personalities or epochs in history by poets and story-tellers is both legitimate and useful, as much for the light it throws on the psychology of the artist as for the fresh light his mendacity throws upon history (*CM*, p 133).

Again, although this statement is not applied directly to his own work, the author consciously invokes the familiar licence to introduce a profoundly personal dimension to his art, and this isolated sentence thus gives belated explanation for *Spartacus's* powerful blend of recorded fact, imagined fact and poetic transmutation.

Mrs Mitchell told me she helped her husband piece the Spartacus legend together in preparation for his novel by sifting through the main classical sources of the writings of Appian, Plutarch and Sallust in the British Museum in the early nineteen-thirties, but Mitchell's knowledge of the Spartacus myth, and especially of what it represents in the socialist pantheon, goes at least as far back as his first novel, which makes passing reference to Spartacus as a political figure of symbolic stature (*SR*, p 66). In fact, as early as October 1929, Mitchell was praising the earnest and compassionate character of Friedrich Freligrath in 'A Volcano in the Moon' by calling him a 'Spartacist'.[37] It is also noteworthy that Mitchell's poems include panegyrics on both Karl Liebknecht and Rosa Luxemburg, who called themselves Spartacists, and upon the legendary figure from whom they drew their name, which suggests that Mitchell came upon the historical legend of the slave revolt indirectly, through the dramatic modern episode of the heroic martyrdom of the German Spartacists. Whatever the actual procedure was by which he originally encountered the historical legend, however, the fact remains that he was aware of the myth itself and of its political connotations several years before he came to write a novel around the story.

Despite the artistic inadequacies of the poem upon 'Spartacus' (published in *A Scots Hairst*), it establishes beyond doubt that the author's primary interest in the legend was political. The subject is hailed as the living embodiment of the spirit of 'Freedom', and Mitchell employs fairly orthodox light imagery to represent his enduring influence; but more important is the final encomium that Spartacus paved the way for 'the lordship of the slave' (*SH*, p 186), for this reveals the author's true colours as champion of the proletariat. These sympathies are also uppermost in the novel, which shows ultimately how much more assured Mitchell was in his political attitudes in the last years of his life than he had been in the late twenties.

Of the three novels written out of the classical legend of the Spartacist revolt, Mitchell's was the first, and in my own view it remains the best, as he exploits his material less pedantically than Howard Fast, whose *Spartacus* (1952) is more melodramatic than Mitchell's original, and hence offered suitable material for translation into the celluloid Hollywood 'epic' that it became. And while Arthur Koestler's *The Gladiators* (1939) is more exacting in its psychological and economic analysis of the historical situation than both Mitchell's and Fast's versions, ultimately it falls down by failing to exploit the epic qualities of the legend.

Mitchell's treatment of the Spartacus myth constitutes his second greatest achievement behind the trilogy itself. In purely literal terms, it stands head and shoulders above his other English novels. The dramatic action of Spartacus's violent rebellion against his Roman oppressors is vivid and swift-moving, and Mitchell's descriptive work is graphic without being overstated, bringing the whole spirit and atmosphere of the time vitally alive in much the same way as Fionn MacColla recreates the strife-torn days of sixteenth century Scotland in *Scottish Noël* and *Ane Tryall of Heretiks*. In fact, Mitchell frequently displays the same ability as MacColla shows in *Scottish Noël* in particular, to 'paint a battle in a paragraph' as Ivor Brown put it.[38] In one way, the most frequent criticism levelled at this novel, that it lays undue stress upon physical atrocities and acts of violence, may be interpreted as an inverted compliment to the brisk impression of realism that it creates. Both Mitchell and MacColla revel in the imaginative task of fleshing out the historical facts, and the blood and gore are necessary parts of the exercise. Indeed, *Spartacus* and *Scottish Noël* are in good company, for there are few gorier works than the classical epics, and *The Iliad* in particular.

Even the very language that Mitchell uses to describe the historical action is admirably functional, the author forsaking the overelaborate approach he adopts elsewhere in the English fiction in favour of a style which has a biblical simplicity and which, possessing a slightly archaic tone, seems uncannily apposite. This is especially true of the final chapter of the novel describing the intense suffering that Kleon experiences before he receives his dying vision fusing the inspirational figures of Spartacus and Christ. Mitchell relates in a rarefied prose style:

> On the third night the insects left him and the beasts came. But they found him still living, and all that night he lived; and they came not near him, tearing at other flesh in the dark. And the last time he awoke he found the morning in the sky, and before his swimming gaze saw the world lighten, greater and strange (*Spart*, p 286).

The novelist also exploits the climatic nature of his plot in the way he paces the book, which steadily gathers momentum from the initial rebellion and escape of the gladiators at Capua through to the time when the Free Legion stands poised to conquer Rome itself. The tragic fate to which the slave insurrection comes sets Mitchell with a minor problem, but his symbolic conclusion, pointing optimistically to the future, circumvents the harsh historical truth by providing a compelling climax to the political theme. Whereas Howard Fast reduced the sense of tragic finality by concentrating upon the promise boded by an apocryphal 'Son of Spartacus', Mitchell does so without actually tampering with the facts, by the poetic expedient of simply casting Spartacus as a forerunner of Christ himself. Kleon's confusion of images is highly symbolic, but it is nonetheless immensely suggestive and inspiring.

The characterisation in *Spartacus* is arguably the single most important factor in the exposition of the political theme, and just as much of the success of the book as political propaganda is due to the marriage of realistic and romantic elements throughout the volume as a whole, so these properties are particularly finely balanced in this specific aspect of the work.

Although his proletarian sympathies encouraged him to take the side of the slaves throughout his account of their fight against the masters—and the conflict is described predominantly from their point of view—astutely, Mitchell resists the temptation to draw a simplistic contrast between their moral worthiness and their adversaries' corruption, as Howard Fast tends to do. The early novels and the mature Grassic Gibbon works demonstrate that Mitchell always tried to guard against idealising the working classes, despite appealing eloquently on their behalf in his writing, and thus he gives a tolerably realistic impression of the diverse character types gathered within the slave host and of the disputes and arguments which ensue. Over and above this, the physical atrocities perpetrated by the victorious slave army upon the defeated forces of the Roman legate Furius are described in their full horror in the first book (*Spart*, pp 64–5); and conversely, the Romans are not uniformly villainous, the sympathetic description of the painful death of the kindly general Cossinus at Salenae in the second book evoking special pathos (*Spart*, p 92).

As in *A Scots Quair*, Mitchell has the political assurance in *Spartacus* to dramatise the obstacles standing in the way of his hero's—and his own—main objectives, the direct opposition presented to the revolution of the lower classes by those whose power is threatened being supplemented by the disorder in the revolutionaries' own camp and by the gladiators' inability to win the unanimous support of the general public. The senseless intractability which is the older slaves' response to Spartacus's heroic efforts to improve their lot rings as infuriatingly true as the Kinraddie crofters' political recalcitrance in *Sunset Song*, Mitchell writing in the historical novel that, 'In Calabria the old slaves of the farms heard the news and shook their heads, knowing that always, till the world ended, there must be masters and slaves' (*Spart*, p 221). Similarly, certain illustrious members of the slave army remain fatalistically convinced of the permanence of their servile status and identity, Gershom the Jew arguing with resignation, for example, that 'no man may ever be a slave but he bears the stigma until he is dead', explaining blackly that, 'that stigma is on his soul' (*Spart*, p 106).

Spartacus himself absorbs some of the pessimism circulating in the ranks of his army, but eventually he overcomes the personal doubts about the validity of his efforts, although he does so at the expense of the confidence he held previously in his fellow generals, affirming that 'his tribunes questioned his plans: the great host never did—unless deserters like Gannicus or Castus misled it with lies and rhetoric' (*Spart*, p 264). Within the context of the irresistible progress of the slave army as it sweeps through Italy, however, these troubles emerge as little more than temporary setbacks, and therefore they do not seriously undermine the faith which Mitchell places in their motives and intentions, and indeed in their ultimate ability to bring about the desired changes in society.

Much of Mitchell's confidence in this revolutionary activity is founded upon Marxist theory, and in fact the aims of the slave revolt are frequently presented in formal Marxist terms. Beneath the petty squabbles within the ranks there is a mutual recognition among the slaves of their common bond. Early on in the proceedings, this feeling of political solidarity actually triumphs over the fiercest religious differences, promoting a conciliation between Gershom ben Sanballat and Kleon, Jew and Gentile respectively. This turns out to be the rule rather than the exception, for whenever it comes to the crunch internal disputes tend to be forgotten in the face of the one overriding purpose.

However, Mitchell makes it clear that the slaves are not fighting for political supremacy but for their own freedom and, ultimately, for a free world. The long-term objective of a classless society, as articulated earlier by the Communist Marrot in *The Lost Trumpet*, is recognised within both communist and anarchist theory. The proclamation that Spartacus issues before he marches on Rome in book four thus emphasises the fundamental aim of liberty, here opposed to that of vengeance, the Strategos announcing, 'that we come to free all slaves whatsoever, that in the new state we'll make even the Masters will not be enslaved' (*Spart*, p 190). This ideal is briefly realised in the poignant episode in the following book, in which Kleon liberates the captive Roman girl Puculla, an act which involves the assertion of this greater humanity, signifying for Mitchell that 'they had laid aside master and slave' (*Spart*, p 226). And on the very next page Spartacus himself formulates the aim of a society in which all class differences are abolished:

I know nothing of the histories or plans of men, but there'll never be peace or the State unshaken, with women suckling their children at peace and men at work in the fields with quiet hearts, but that slave and master alike is unknown in the land. . . . If ever we build our slave state, there'll be no slaves in it at all.

No matter how noble the ideal of a free society may be in itself, however, Mitchell can foresee it being attained only through violent revolutionary action, and in this he is in direct agreement with the communist stipulation that bloody class warfare is a necessary preliminary to the achievement of the millennium. Thus, where Hiketas believes that 'only by perfect freedom may life be perfect again' (*Spart*, p 188), such idealistic sentiments are qualified by the pragmatic Kleon, who warns the hero tersely earlier in the book that 'we must destroy before we build' (*Spart*, p 125).

Although the noble ends which Mitchell promotes are perhaps most strictly anarchist, therefore, the unglamorous revolutionary means that he advocates in order to secure their fulfilment are conventionally Marxist. His vision of the proletariat abolishing social privilege by means of a concerted revolutionary effort directed against the ruling classes is, more precisely, Marxist-Leninist: he sees the emergence of an altruistic leader to discipline and orchestrate the mass movements in a primitive 'dictatorship of the proletariat' as being essential to the success of the venture.

Spartacus's development from simple para-military opportunist to messianic freedom fighter is quite superbly done, making him for me Mitchell's most memorable character—and I include Chris Guthrie in this judgement. For Spartacus is a Marlovian figure who has appreciably human characteristics but is essentially larger than life, whereas Chris's most striking quality is her intense humanity, her truth of life. Spartacus has a romantic grandeur which Chris does not have, and the hyperbolic elements in his portraiture are therefore completely justified.

The political role which Spartacus fulfils in his book is based principally upon the Leninist ideal, in that he is less an authoritarian figure than a paternalistic representative who is subordinate to the people's will. His lover, Elpinice, who generally expresses Mitchell's own opinions, stresses more than once the subservient part the leaders must play in the communal movement, and Spartacus acknowledges his own subordination when he tells Kleon in the second last book:

> It is only the slaves themselves that can do that [build the slave state]. Not you or I alone. We are here to lead. We pass. But they endure (*Spart*, p 227).

Spartacus thus stands with the people rather than above them, but he is also the quintessential revolutionary, the living incarnation of the spirit of freedom, and consequently he stands out from the crowd, very like Ewan in *Grey Granite*, as the noble proletarian hero in a Marxist novel. Mitchell himself linked Ewan with his earlier historical figure in the letter to Helen Cruickshank cited earlier. Indeed both characters define their political intentions in similar, basically religious, terms, identifying the goals to which they are dedicated as their God. Referring to his gathering sense of political mission, Spartacus remarks midway through the novel that, 'a God drove him on' (*Spart*, p 187), and his God stands for the same sympathetic motives and exalted ideals which Ewan describes to his mother at the end of *Grey Granite* as a rock propelling him up a hill.

As the portraits of Rejeb ibn Saud in 'One Man with a Dream' and of Marrot in *The Lost Trumpet* indicate, Mitchell considered the quality of compassion to be every bit as important in the political champion as intellectual prowess. In *Grey Granite*, Ewan gravitates towards his role of communist agitator through his emotional and sympathetic identification with the downtrodden Duncairn workers, and Spartacus's political development is of a similar exemplary character.

Very like Ewan at the beginning of *Grey Granite*, Spartacus originally appears distant and preoccupied, and initially he stands apart from the other gladiators in his wistful withdrawal from reality. His early aims are romantic and self-indulgent: as such, they are unhappily reminiscent of the intentions expressed by the protagonists of the imaginative romances, the hero virtually dissociating himself from the fighting in its initial stages. In fact, the slave uprising only wins his support in the first place as a potential means of removing the threat which the Romans pose to his personal dreams of happiness. By the end of the first book however, Kleon notices the temperamental transformation, manifested in his physical appearance, which has begun in Spartacus, indicating the dawning of new purpose. Yet he still lacks the compassionate affiliation with the people he is leading, and indeed when he finally emerges as sole leader of the slaves in the second book, the reasons lying behind his assumption of power are not wholly laudable, the new commander savouring 'the taste of power already strong in his mouth' (*Spart*, p 93).

The final four books in the novel chart Spartacus's progress to selfless champion and eventually, to symbolic martyr. The relationship with Elpinice stabilises the behaviour of the slave leader in much the same way as John Garland is humanised by his romance with Thea Mayven in *Stained Radiance*; and again like Garland, Elpinice's pregnancy brings out the mellower side to his character, which sorely disappoints the pragmatic Kleon who has earmarked the gladiator as the chief protagonist in his attempt to realise his fine Republic. Thus the Greek complains of his Strategos that 'he had halted the march like a midwife—he who had shaped so sure in the seeming, cold and passionless, of Plato's Prince!' (*Spart*, p 113).

The rape and murder of Elpinice midway through the novel finally removes this distraction and goads the gladiator on in his efforts on the slaves' behalf, just as Thea's near-death releases John Garland to dramatic new heights of political commitment, and just as Zenocrate's passing galvanises Tamburlaine into performing even greater feats of conquest in Marlowe's play. Crucially, however, Spartacus retains his compassion: his clemency in refusing his victorious prerogatives of both torture and looting sustains the rumour circulating in Roman society that their adversary is mentally unbalanced, which of course he is within the terms of their own perverse definition.

Eventually, Spartacus achieves a heightened state of awareness by which ultimately he becomes the living personification of those whom he represents, as Ewan becomes identified with the Duncairn proletariat in

Grey Granite, and as Wallace comes to represent his 'Army of Commons' in the unfinished extract of the Gibbon biography. The gladiator first experiences this mystical transportation in book four. Mitchell attributes to him 'a warmth of care and pity new in his heart' which graduates into a sublime conviction:

> As though he were all of the hungered dispossessed of all time: as though at moments he ceased to live, merging his spirit in that of the horde, his body in that of a thousand bodies, bone of their bone, flesh of their flesh (*Spart.* pp 173-4).

This compelling humanitarianism holds Spartacus 'bound in a mystic kinship of blood' with the body of the slaves from this time, and his passionate identification with the masses is constantly reiterated throughout the remainder of the book. Appropriately, the finest passage on this theme appears towards the close of the novel when, newly resigned to the fact that his army is no longer capable of conquering Italy, Spartacus reaffirms his devotion to the slaves' cause, apprehending himself finally in a marvellously expressive metaphor as' 'but a voice for many, the Voice of the voiceless' (*Spart*, p 264).

Spartacus's social and moral sympathies thus mark him out as the natural representative for the slaves who turn against their Roman masters. However, he also has a genuinely inspiring symbolic stature which Ewan understandably lacks, and this sets the historical figure on a plane above the Scots hero, with whom otherwise he has much in common.

The symbolic status which Mitchell gives Spartacus is truly, and surely consciously, Marlovian, the superhuman appearance he presents to his future opponent Gnaeus Manlius before the Battle of La Fata Pass being especially reminiscent of Marlowe's apparently invincible hero in the first Tamburlaine play. Manlius perceives his charismatic adversary high up on the opposite ridge, mounted and armed for battle, his towering stature and burnished armour making him seem a 'terrible figure' who is 'like a God'. Indeed, his awesome presence takes on an even greater significance, Manlius finally considering that, 'he saw more than the Strategos Spartacus, he saw THE SLAVE himself' (*Spart*, p 179).

Mitchell again seems to have been thinking of Tamburlaine, the demi-god who 'held the fates bound fast in iron chains', when he endowed his hero's march upon Rome with a kind of supernatural sanction in the episode in which Spartacus interprets the shooting star as an omen, claiming it for his own and observing to Kleon that 'our star leads us south to Rome' (*Spart*, p 192). And this suggestion is repeated on the following page in the description of the hysteria engendered among the Roman slaves who see in the celestial portent intimation of Spartacus's approach, and with it the possibility of escape from the death sentence.

Like Tamburlaine again, Spartacus also possesses an ageless quality, although this serves a more practical purpose in Mitchell's book, demonstrating the enduring nature of the values he represents. Thus the hero contrasts the physical strain which has taken its toll upon his body with his surviving spiritual ardour, considering how 'he himself felt strangely little of this [physical] ageing, as though, a mirror for them, and no more, he reflected their lives, but in his inner self remained un-old' (*Spart*, p 216).

The novel's climax has been criticised on the grounds that Mitchell's appropriation of Christian symbolism is unethical, but I feel this is a justifiable feature in that it makes for a much more inspiring ending than the bombastic vision which brings *The Thirteenth Disciple* to a close. The apotheosis which ends the historical novel is actually heightened by the veiled Christian reference contained in the apparently innocuous sentence which introduces the action of the book as taking place 'a hundred years before the crucifixion of Christ' (*Spart*, p 15). This direction is repeated at the climax, by which time it has gained much greater weight in view of the concluding parallel drawn between Spartacus and Christ. Mitchell also prepares for this highly symbolic ending within the actual narrative by connecting the action of Spartacus sharing his meal with his comrades with the Last Supper, the author describing how his hero 'stared down into the future, as the three broke bread and drank wine, and saw for a moment an alien table, with alien faces about the board' (*Spart*, pp 200–1). Judiciously, Mitchell does not dwell on the allusion or try to make too much of the association at this stage, but this fleeting analogy does much to enhance and sustain the quite glorious vision apprehended by the dying Kleon:

> And he saw before him, gigantic, filling the sky, a great Cross with a figure that was crowned with thorns; and behind it, sky-towering as well, gladius in hand, his hand on the edge of the morning behind that Cross, the figure of a Gladiator. And he saw that these Two were One, and the world yet theirs: and he went into unending night and left them that shining earth (*Spart*, p 287).

Thus, although Spartacus is portrayed in convincingly human terms, his figure also has a tremendous symbolic power, and both these factors are of vital importance to the political theme of the novel. While much of the moral fervour and the rousing idealism of Mitchell's political theme depends upon the hero's characterisation, however, the more rational quality of intellectual understanding is transmitted primarily through the figure of his acolyte, Kleon.

In *The Lost Trumpet*, Marrot possesses both the emotional and intellectual qualifications which Mitchell deemed to be necessary in the political activist. In *Spartacus*, he divides these two qualities between the protagonist and Kleon, Spartacus's henchman and mentor. In his own way the Greek is as fine a figure as Spartacus. In one sense, Kleon is a satirical character whose physical emasculation reflects the barrenness of his political ideas, which initially are founded upon the vision enshrined in Plato's *Republic* rather than upon the moral indignation and emotional commitment of Spartacus. To begin with, Kleon's political abstraction is an intellectual compensation for his physical and sensual deprivations, presented with due sympathy by Mitchell. Kleon's meeting with Spartacus is truly opportune, however and, as their subsequent relationship shows, each becomes equally important to the other, for the man of action requires the backing of the political scientist, and he for his part needs the man of action to realise his aims. Kleon is thus largely responsible for Spartacus's transfiguration into the great proletarian leader, Mitchell directly referring to his hero on one occasion in particular as 'the strange barbarian moulded from a wayward slave to an archon-tyrant under the hands of a dreaming eunuch' (*Spart*, p 119). And yet while Kleon's dispassionate detachment allows him to shape Spartacus into the formidable political champion, for much of the book his own political hopes rest on insubstantial bureaucratic and constitutional theories: his early standpoint is encapsulated in the ascetic belief he expresses that, 'only by Law may the perfect State and citizen be created' (*Spart*, p 188). Through his active involvement in the slaves' fight for freedom, however, Kleon's ideal attains a more red-blooded aspect, with his methodical plans being invigorated by Spartacus's infectious idealism. Eventually, therefore, he looks forward to a society which is anarchistic in the true sense of the word (being free from all laws and rules of government), the Greek hankering after the return of 'that Golden Age of which Hiketas had dreamed' (*Spart*, p 227). Finally, Kleon's political maturity is epitomised by the fact that he receives the stirring symbolic vision which is the climax of the book.

It is not only for his political role that Kleon is crucial in the novel for, as the sceptic who is almost as familiar a figure in Mitchell's work as the revolutionary, he provides the philosophical 'blasphemy' which habitually goes in tandem with the political urge for 'reform'. In *Spartacus*, political action is authorised and fortified by a deeper philosophical vision: in the relationship between Spartacus and Kleon, Mitchell shows this ideological liaison off to its best advantage.

Where Spartacus is the main political figure in the book, expressing Mitchell's 'Angry' impulses, Kleon is the spokesman for the Absurd. At the beginning of the novel, Mitchell introduces three slaves who among them cover the spectrum of religious belief: Titul is a devout believer in the god Kokolkh who, very Calvinistically, is for him 'Pain and Life', the other two being, 'Brennus the agnostic and Kleon the atheist' (*Spart*, p 21). Over the course of the novel, Kleon's attitude prevails, due mostly to the disciplined logic which he applies to the major themes of existence.

The Greek's physical mutilation severs his sentimental and superstitious ties with the human world, elevating him to a privileged vantage point from which he, like Chris at the end of the *Quair*, can come face to face with the true realities of life. Thus, he confronts the physical universe with the candour of the scientific rationalist as opposed to the charmed romantic spirit of Spartacus, so that when Titul indulges in sun-worship Kleon, along with Gershom and the other Ionians, looks on contemptuously, 'knowing the sun to be but a ball of fire three leagues away' (*Spart*, p 34). Similarly, towards the end of the book, when all around are reading prophetic meanings into the shooting star which travels across the sky above Rome, Kleon alone preserves his equanimity, resting secure in the knowledge that 'the stars were bodies of fire circling about the earth at a little distance, and had no bearing on the fates of men' (*Spart*, p 192).

Kleon is thus the philosophical pragmatist who regards the universe as a physical phenomenon utterly devoid of spiritual meaning. Indeed, lowering his sights to his own world, he can see no greater harmony existing between man and his earthly environment; his immediate surroundings have the same Hardyesque remoteness from human affairs as the 'greater singing', Mitchell writing in book four:

> And it came on the eunuch, as so often, how strange it was that men should toil and moil on this little earth that knew them not—that knew only its winds and rains and the suns that ripened the crops, and the light and glow of the imaged sun, never the seedsmen or reapers. It was the Fear of the Fates and the Gods that drove men, shadows they made in their own dark hearts (*Spart*, p 171).

This conception is obviously bound up with the diffusionist view of the alienness of agriculture and of civilisation in general within the organic motion of the universe, and yet Kleon acquires a deeper sense of the Absurdity lying at the heart of the contradiction. Human life itself is presented as an Absurd affair, for death mostly appears physical and final, with the preceding life seeming equally pointless as a paradigm of universal meaninglessness. Kleon declares phlegmatically early in the novel that, 'all we do or dream are but blowings of dust' (*Spart*, p 79).

As in his other English novels, therefore, the existential vision extended in *Spartacus* is basically Absurd, and yet Mitchell faces up to this idea directly in the latter without shirking its harsh and painful implications. Indeed, having acknowledged the Absurd truth in the book, he then becomes free to build positively from the honesty of the proposal, and he does so in a manner which reminded me of André Malraux's first novel, *The Conquerors*, published in English four years before *Spartacus*. Malraux's hero realises that although life is spiritually pointless, his subsequent response to this situation need not be one of nihilistic despair, and this finally galvanises him into action as a political revolutionary. A very similar procedure is involved in *Spartacus*.

There are four main passages strategically spaced throughout the historical novel in which Mitchell forges a dynamic connection between his bleak philosophical outlook and his political idealism: in these the 'reformer' builds upon the achievement of the 'blasphemer'. The first occurs on only the second page, in which Kleon makes a tentative link between the secular and spiritual, between his personal physical situation and the image he creates of God when, ruminating upon the human importance of 'a divine plan', he like John Garland achieves a suitably jaundiced impression of a Setebos-style deity, Serapis, who is insane.

Having established a loose connection between social and philosophical concerns, Kleon receives a more penetrating vision of man's cosmic insignificance and of spiritual 'negation'. He then flies off at a political tangent from these profound propositions, turning to a Platonic dream of a social utopia 'for ease', in much the same way as Mitchell's romantic heroes and heroines turn to diffusionism in order to avoid the 'grotesque' realities of existence. Deprived of his manhood, Kleon is denied the possibility of romantic involvement, an outlet which enables other of Mitchell's pro-tagonists to overcome the more depressing aspects of life. This leaves him with the choice of committing suicide or embarking upon a search for an alternative god to fill the spiritual void.

The central passage on this whole theme of the relationship between political and philosophical initiatives appears midway through the book, where Kleon defines his revolutionary ardour as not so much an escape from the conviction of universal Absurdity, as a logical sequitur to it, as a positive rather than a negative response. Thus, when Gershom ben Sanballat tells Kleon that he is 'impatient with this plotting and planning . . . this building of sky-republics, these secret raids and hopes' and complains further that 'you and your Thracian build a house in sand', Kleon rises magnificently to the challenge, replying astutely that 'sand or rock, their end is the same, a dream of order on a planless earth, of endurance where all things meet and melt' (*Spart*, p 117). This is a remarkably concise and 'modern' expression of the benefits to be gained from the frank acceptance of the Absurdity of existence, and Kleon's explanation has much in common with the philosophy of Albert Camus, of whom Arnold Hinchliffe has said:

> The Absurd, for Camus, is an absence of correspondence between the mind's need for unity and the chaos of the world the mind experiences, and the obvious response is either suicide or, in the opposite direction, a leap of faith.[39]

The most constructive response is radical political involvement, and thus Camus's distinction between Absurd and Angry impulses is roughly analogous with Sartre's dual interests of existentialism and communism, Mitchell's distinction between Freedom and God fitting in neatly with this general scheme, as the twin goals of what Quaritch calls 'a search for reality'. Kleon's own assertion of the political stability he finds in an otherwise uncertain life reappears towards the close of the book, although the two main articles are shared between Kleon himself and Spartacus. The Greek thus opens with the typically austere asseveration, 'There are neither Gods nor devils. Only the Fates, who are mindless', and Spartacus subverts this pessimistic vision—which again has familiar Hardyesque undertones—by affirming, 'There's a God in Men. But an Unknown God' (*Spart*, p 266). Admittedly this conclusion is bordering upon the bombastic style of writing which characterises the imaginative romances, but the clarity and sharpness of Mitchell's distinction between the secular and spiritual in *Spartacus* helps set the historical novel far above everything else published under his own name.

In *Spartacus*, therefore, Mitchell squares up to the idea of a meaningless universe more courageously than in any of his other English novels except the first, and consequently he wins the reward from his efforts of a surer grounding for the political theme expounded in the book. Whereas the 'reformer' and the 'blasphemer' frequently seem to work against each other in the imaginative romances, with Mitchell attempting to represent the search for God as a direct substitute for the quest for Freedom, *Spartacus* shows the effective dovetailing of the two initiatives, the political argument being enhanced by the acceptance of existential Absurdity to which it is anchored.

SIX

A Scots Quair

THE BACKGROUND

I observed earlier how it was virtually inevitable that Mitchell would eventually turn his full attention as an artist upon his native land. It was equally predictable that the final product would reflect the generosity of his philosophical outlook. In keeping with his general perspective, Mitchell's specific aims with regard to his trilogy were universal in their scope.

The language of *A Scots Quair* is undoubtedly much more resonant and appealing than that of Mitchell's English fiction and fully bears out the author's belief, expressed most firmly in the essay on 'Literary Lights' and in the unpublished satire of Wallace Mongour, that Scots is capable of producing literature of the very highest order. However, it is particularly revealing that in *Grey Granite* Mitchell should have a sly dig at Hugh MacDiarmid, the dedicatee of the novel, on account of the contrastingly obscurantist approach that MacDiarmid adopted towards Scots in his early poetry, Ewan responding to Archie Clairmont's reference to 'Hugo MacDownall [*sic*], the chap who wrote in Synthetic Scots' by asking him with disarming ingenuousness, 'Why synthetic? Can't he write the real stuff?' (*SQ*, p 378). Notwithstanding the deep respect each had for the other's work, this jibe indicates the difference of opinion which lay between Mitchell and MacDiarmid concerning the use of Scots in literature, the novelist's lightly Scoticised English prose contrasting sharply with the poet's arcane Jamieson-inspired Scots lexicon.

Over and above the purely aesthetic considerations involved in Mitchell's recourse to his native vernacular, the experiment had a critical bearing upon the actual creative process, and in my opinion the single most important aspect of Grassic Gibbon's whole linguistic enterprise is that it gave Mitchell a completely serviceable and responsive medium in which to pursue the themes and ideas which interested him most. Thus, what MacDiarmid once said with particular regard to William Soutar is equally applicable to the novelist Gibbon:

> Many critics have pointed out in relation to modern Scottish poets writing in both languages that Scots invariably proves their happier medium and that, through it, they were able to liberate faculties of their personalities for which their English work afforded no outlet.[1]

Certainly the clarity of thought and the coherence of theme which mark the trilogy out as Mitchell's most profound and enduring work are attributable in large part to the creation of a prose style most sympathetic to his personal requirements.

Mitchell's literary approach in the trilogy is as functional and ambitious as his use of language, and here his general procedure is to exploit established modes already at his disposal and finally extend beyond them by force of personal innovation. Although Scots life itself commands the poetry of *A Scots Quair*, the artistic fulfilment of this aim owes more to classical and international influences and to Mitchell's own powers of invention than to Scottish literary traditions. And just as the linguistic theory behind the trilogy is covertly represented in the text itself in such features as the joke directed at MacDiarmid, so Mitchell gives some indication in the *Quair* of the literary context within which he wants his book to be appreciated.

The author first sets his literary parameters in the final paragraph of the 'Prelude' in *Sunset Song* through the Reverend Gibbon's literary riddle. His definition of Kinraddie as 'the Scots countryside itself, fathered between a kailyard and a bonny brier bush in the lee of a house with green shutters' (*SQ*, p 31) seems to suggest that Mitchell is placing his novel within the Kailyard and anti-Kailyard tradition, as some kind of compromise between the two modes: and the fact that the speaker is given the author's own pseudonymous surname strengthens this suggestion. However, the highly satirical nature of his portraiture prevents the reader from accepting his remark at face value, and indeed the climactic sentence of the section is decisive, the anonymous narrator rejecting the minister's analogy outright, commenting—

> And what he meant by that you could guess at yourself if you'd a mind for puzzles and dirt, there wasn't a house with green shutters in the whole of Kinraddie.

The Reverend Gibbon and the disingenuous rustic are both held up to ridicule, therefore, and yet the folk-narrator's postscript, placed in such a prominent position in the text, rings more compellingly true than the minister's rather esoteric analogy. As a whole, this final paragraph is thus subtly self-recriminatory, Mitchell poking fun at all attempts to capture the reality of the Scottish countryside in fiction, including his own: the gulf separating art and reality appears final and conclusive, no matter how elaborate are the representational techniques which the writer employs. More explicitly, the rustic's impatient dismissal of the Reverend Gibbon's allusion dissociates Mitchell's novel from attempts by Barrie, Maclaren and Douglas Brown to capture Scottish country life in their literature. Mitchell himself evidently felt he was doing something more than them, and this is confirmed by the uniformly critical (and frequently calumnious) references he makes in letters, articles and books to these authors, which condense finally into the vilification of 'the scum of Kailyard romance' made in 'Literary Lights' (*SH*, p 69).

Considering how dismissive Mitchell was of the whole Kailyard tradition, therefore, and considering also the universal scope of his general artistic precepts and his philosophical outlook, I feel that Ian Campbell is wrong to regard the trilogy, or *Sunset Song* on its own, as simply a modern response to the whole Kailyard ethos.[2] Mitchell's frame of reference in the trilogy is much wider than that of Maclaren, Crockett or Barrie, or indeed than that of their most notorious traducer, George Douglas Brown.

There is a cavalier quality about the statement of intent which Mitchell made to George MacDonald in response to Cuthbert Graham's expression of faith in Mitchell's ability to write a major novel about his homeland. The novelist affirmed to MacDonald that 'one of these days I'll write that north-east novel he talks about—so Scotch I'll make it that people will tear out leaves to suck in church'.[3] In fact, the trilogy was much more carefully planned and was conceived on a much grander scale than this remark would suggest.

The Scottish episodes which feature in Mitchell's first two novels indicate that he was fully aware of the possibilities of turning to his native land for literary inspiration. Mrs Mitchell told me that the motivation for his writing a major work of Scottish fiction went even further back than this: she wrote in a letter to me that, 'regarding Leslie considering writing a Scots novel, his brother John had been urging him to write such a novel in the twenties and many of us hoped he would'.[4] The final product surely bears full testimony to such a lengthy period of gestation, the actual speed of Sunset Song's composition having been made possible in large part by the time the author spent mulling the project over beforehand.

The aim of quintessential Scottishness which Mitchell expressed for his Scottish novel in his letter to George MacDonald was realised in a typically generous manner in the trilogy. A Scots Quair operates upon two basic literary levels. The mimetic deals primarily with social concerns, with the concerns of the 'reformer'. The transcendental deals with more profound matters, with the interests of the 'blasphemer'. It is on the former level that the quality of Scottishness is most important.

In 'Literary Lights', Mitchell argues that the novelists working in modern Scotland are effectively English novelists (SH, p 147). He makes this claim despite his enduring belief that an accessible literary compromise can be created between the compatible languages of Scots and English, and despite the faith he held in the prose medium, and in 'the major art of the novel' in particular. Above all, Mitchell's wholesale dissatisfaction with the efforts of his fellow Scottish novelists reflects the ambitious aims that he had for the form of the Scottish novel. When he refuses to acknowledge the existence of any author worthy of the description of modern Scottish novelist, he is not just lamenting the contemporary failure to strike the crucial balance between authentic Scottishness and universal relevance but is also deploring the inability of modern Scottish fiction writers to come to terms with the social realities of Scottish life. Modern society makes extremely heavy demands upon the skills of the writer seeking to represent it in fiction, and the trilogy is Mitchell's most sustained attempt to meet this challenge.

On a mimetic plane, A Scots Quair reflects in condensed form the main transformation going on in Scottish society, as all over Europe, from a rural, feudal type of existence to an urban and industrial one; and the only literary form with the scope to deal with the panoramic scale of this theme is a modified type of epic. The Quair is a modern epic, produced, for convenience, in a tripartite form, in which the author mirrors the changing face of modern Scottish society and works through this to the universally relevant political and quasi-religious responses which the situation recommends.

I will deal later with the themes uniting Mitchell's trilogy which provide conclusive proof that the trilogy requires to be regarded as a single unit, but it is worth noting here that the *Quair* was by all accounts originally conceived as a uniform whole.[5] The earliest surviving written reference that the author himself made to *A Scots Quair* by name actually dates from a time after the appearance of the first volume, Mitchell referring in a letter written to Helen Cruickshank in December 1932 to his efforts in 'copy-hunting for the second part of *A Scots Quair*',[6] but evidently he took the work's corporate identity for granted, observing in 1934, for instance, again to Helen Cruickshank, in relation to the three Gibbon novels in general that, 'surely they would never be allowed publication in Nazi Germany or Heimwehr Austria?'.[7] The author's own tendency to accept the uniformity of purpose behind the components of his *Quair* adds significantly to the claim for the trilogy to be appreciated as a single volume, and this is backed up by his widow's informed conjecture as to the work's original conception. She wrote to me in 1978:

> I have but a vague recollection regarding a trilogy but it would seem reasonable to suppose that Gibbon had that in mind—surging around in that amazing brain. Also it was customary for a publisher to request—nay demand—two works to follow an initial one when an author is a beginner. And who, then, knew Lewis Grassic Gibbon. . . .[8]

The Scottish element in the trilogy is superficially important, the author using his own native land as a medium through which he can reach general truths. In fact, Mitchell himself showed his awareness of the typicality of the experience depicted in national epic when Anton Saloney gave the following description of Connon's 'Epic of the Khalig's soul' in the *Cornhill* story published in 1929:

> For it was the song of the Khalig he had written, the song of all Cairo, the song of Egypt and the world and the days unnumbered since first the brown Stone Men drifted their dusk hordes across the Nile. In the Khalig's colours and voices he had found the tale of all humanity and told it as I had never read it told before. . . . Of the daedal wars and love and death and the birth was his tale; sunset and morning and the travail of heat and the lash; the battle-song ringing across the waiting lines at dawn; the bridal song and the birth-night agony, and all the quests and fulfilments of men. All the voices that Cairo has ever known cried from his pages—the emir's voice and the voice of kings and the love-song of the slave outside his wattle hut. . . .[9]

Despite the romantic vagueness afflicting Saloney's definition, the comprehensiveness of Connon's achievement in working through the regional and national to find 'the tale of all humanity' foreshadows Mitchell's own practice in the trilogy of penetrating beyond life in the Mearns to themes of national and ultimately universal significance.

Mitchell's awareness of the universal nature of the basic peasant experience represented in *Sunset Song* is reflected in the literary works that influenced him, which in the main are not Scottish at all, but international.

Douglas Young has fully defused the charge that Mitchell plundered the translation of the nineteenth-century German novel, *Jorn Uhl* by Gustav Frenssen,[10] and yet there is little doubt that the Scots author did read this book, and learned a certain amount from its treatment of peasant life in Germany. The same country also provided the model for the episode in *Sunset Song* of Ewan's sudden and tragic recovery of his sanity in the midst of the madness of the First World War: Mitchell owned a copy of Eric Maria Remarque's eloquent anti-war novel, *All Quiet on the Western Front*, in which the German farmer Detering, like Ewan, suddenly remembers the contrasting sanity and tranquillity of farm life back home, and dies making the vainglorious attempt to win back to it from the battle-front.[11] It is significant that Mitchell should also have had a copy of Ignazio Silone's trenchant anti-fascist novel set in the eponymous Italian peasant community of Fontamara, which actually appeared after *Sunset Song*, but which itself demonstrates the common lot of the peasant way of life. Silone's intimate knowledge of 'the monotony of the sky, the earth, the rain, the snow', which promotes the view that 'the life of men, of the beasts of the field, of the earth itself seemed destined to revolve in an everlasting cycle, a natural cycle, insusceptible to the changes of time',[12] has much in common with the vibrant picture painted by Mitchell in 'The Land', and it is also heavily redolent of the endless trauchle of the Kinraddie crofters as this is dramatised in *Sunset Song*. The kindred attitudes of Silone and Mitchell also anticipated the conclusions John Berger reached more recently in his fictive analysis of peasant society in France in *Pig Earth*. Thus, Ian J Simpson underrates *Sunset Song* when he says that it 'can be fully appreciated only by north-east folk',[13] and a more sensitive critic, Marion Nelson, corrects this blinkered provincial view when she asks rhetorically, 'Who better than the Scottish crofter . . . would understand *Fontamara?*'.[14] Ultimately, *Sunset Song* stands firmly in the European tradition of the rural novel embracing such masterpieces as Zola's *The Earth* and Hamsun's *Growth of the Soil* as well as the more obscure offerings by Frenssen, Silone and Berger.

The problems caused by increasing urbanisation in modern Scotland are problems which Mitchell felt duty-bound to address as a novelist, and yet he was fully aware that this process was continuing on a world-wide scale. The modern reality of urban Scotland is just as universally significant as the rural reality it is destroying: in fact indigenous Scottish customs and traditions are much less in evidence in the city, as Edwin Muir observed when he considered Edinburgh on his *Scottish Journey* in 1935, and concluded that, 'the past is a national past; the present . . . is as cosmopolitan as the cinema'.[15] A year before this, Mitchell had found the pulse of modern Scotland in a Glasgow slum, which, he discovered, 'is incredibly un-Scottish', adding that, 'it is lovably and abominably and delightfully and hideously un-Scottish', and concluding, 'It is not even a Scottish slum' (*SH*, p 90).

The dramatic change in the face of modern Scottish society leads Mitchell to alter the design of the epic art form in which he intends to deal with the subject, and a critical review that he made of recent Scottish novels in *The Free Man* several months before the publication of *Grey Granite* contains the most illuminating outline of his artistic aims for the urban novel. Firstly, in considering James Barke's latest fiction work, *The Wild MacRaes*, Mitchell acknowledges the need for literary reorientation, for the discovery of a mode which fulfils the lofty universal ideals of classical epic but which is better equipped to deal with the problems inherent in modern society; he remarks, 'In another age Mr Barke might have been a great epic poet; in this one, with poetry the most minor and affected of the arts, he employs the major art of the novel with a fine skill and freedom.' The subsequent definition of 'the major art of the novel' is typically audacious, involving the dynamic fusion of classical and international influences, the integration of the epic form with the politically enlightened mode of socialist realism; Mitchell writes further of Barke's book:

> His crofters and fishers and village folk are faithfully living and life-size; the Wild MacRaes themselves—four sons of a gamekeeper—are heroic figures of myth, and not the less real for that. They centre and epitomise the struggle of the classes that is waged just as bitterly in the remote glen as in the nearby factory. . . . Their countryside . . . seems on the verge of rising to their leadership in a miniature peasant rebellion. . . . There is this glimpse of a possibility, then it fades, as in real life it would fade. The weakness of even heroic peasants without a definitive creed or code of revolt destroys them; one by one they are lopped down, farcical or tragic in their fall.[16]

Here Mitchell is commending *The Wild MacRaes* as a compromise between epic and socialist realism, between traditional and modern responses to life. In his own art, and in *Grey Granite* in particular, his approach to modern society in its cosmopolitan industrialised form involves substantial use of literary techniques commonly associated with the school of socialist realism.

The socialist motivation behind Mitchell's writing is reflected in his literary tastes, and in particular in his interest in the Russian experiment in socialist realism at the beginning of the century. Mitchell read the two definitive prototypes of this genre which dated from the first quarter of the century, and later he gave them both the credit they deserved. The author of *Cement* receives praise in an early story in which Anton Saloney refers to a militant Russian, Alexandr Sergeyvich, who wrote 'with the starkness and simplicity of a Gladkov';[17] and when Gorky used his early novel *Mother* as the model for the school of socialist realism which he formally established by name in 1932, it is no coincidence that Mitchell's original attempts with Grieve 'to form a section of the Revolutionary Writers of the World' were made that very same year.[18] *Grey Granite* especially betrays considerable signs of influence by *Cement* and *Mother*, first in characterisation, with the redefined concept of heroism which Ewan epitomises when he pledges himself to the proletarian struggle, second in the narrative structure involving heavily polemical passages, and third in the use of Marxist imagery on a descriptive level.

Mitchell acknowledged his political intimacy with Gladkov and Gorky when in his letter to *The Left Review* in 1935[19] he stated unequivocally, 'I am a revolutionary writer.' Nevertheless in the same letter he played down their contemporary relevance as writers of fiction. Mitchell pointedly criticised utopian socialists 'still in the grip of wishfulfilment dreams' who 'never read their contemporaries (they wallow instead, and exclusively, in clumsy translations from the Russian and German)'. Again, therefore, Mitchell is calling for the correct balance between the universally relevant, eclectic elements, and the distinctively national and original qualities in art. The excellent modern analysis of the genre of socialist realism by the Hungarian critic George Lukács makes out a strong case for the inclusion of a sense of national identity within the general demonstration of the irresistibility of the radical socialist imperative,[20] but socialist realism, in common with the other literary influences in the *Quair*, is drawn upon initially, and finally superseded.

Ultimately, the only group with which the Gibbon trilogy could legitimately be identified is one as elastic as David Lodge's genre of 'the modern experimental novel',[21] which manages to gather the original talents of Lawrence, Woolf and Joyce under the same banner, by virtue of the sheer inimitability of the work they produced. Although no great claims have as yet been made for *A Scots Quair* as a 'modern experimental novel', significantly it has elicited comparison at various times with Lodge's experimental novelists; and, more pertinently, Mitchell himself indicated that his literary horizons extended beyond his native land for in 'Literary Lights' especially, the criteria which he applies to the Scottish novel are appreciably broad in scope. Early in the essay, he speaks of the Scots literary ideal as being 'a Scots Joyce, a Scots Proust' (*SH*, p 143), and the European frame of reference is revived two pages later when the author represents the modern Scottish novelist lagging behind his European counterparts, advancing his countrymen's belated use of the technique of photographic realism as example. However, literary awareness in itself is adjudged to be relatively unimportant in comparison with original creative enterprise, and consequently Mitchell's great desire for the modern Scots novel is that it will have a character and an originality all of its own. Of all the Scottish novels which have appeared this century, Mitchell's own trilogy still comes closest to realising his greatest hope that 'a Scots Virginia Woolf will astound the Scottish scene, a Scots James Joyce electrify it' (*SH*, pp 145–6). *A Scots Quair* has many influences and points of reference, but its success is finally a tribute to Mitchell's unique creative powers.

THE ACHIEVEMENT

In his obituary of Mitchell, Edwin Muir observed that of all his books the trilogy 'reflects more adequately than any of his others the qualities one felt in him as a man'.[22] Indeed, the two main thematic shafts which run through the *Quair* represent the twin meanings which Mitchell found in life itself. In this instance, however, the undoubted honesty and integrity of his intellectual and emotional response to life is given the sophisticated artistic expression it deserves.

In a newspaper interview given a few months after the publication of *Sunset Song*, Mitchell described his novel as 'a realism-romance of Scotland'.[23] This definition corresponds with the recipe for national epic which he provided a year later in reference to Barke's *The Wild MacRaes*, integrating the realistic elements of the novel with the poetic, visionary qualities of the epic, and in fact Mitchell's definition of *Sunset Song* may be applied to the trilogy as a whole, the duality of the volume as a 'realism-romance' being reflective of the two levels of reality, the one social and the other transcendental, which the work presents.

The political and philosophical themes are less closely related in the trilogy than in *Spartacus,* in which Mitchell's Angry sentiments are indirectly endorsed by the affirmation of universal Absurdity. Yet in the *Quair* the efforts of the 'reformer' and the 'blasphemer' are brought together as alternative approaches in what Quaritch called the 'search for reality' (*LT*, p 189). In fact, these two initiatives turn upon the same pivot, for the principle of change is the touchstone in both the political and philosophical themes, the quest undertaken by both the 'reformer' and the 'blasphemer' in the volume hinging upon what Mitchell described in his first published book as 'the upbuilding of a workable Philosophy of Change' (*Hanno*, p 77).

The thematic continuity of the trilogy upon both the mimetic and transcendental planes has often been played down by critics, but in the final analysis *Sunset Song* is just as vital to the political theme as *Grey Granite*. Conversely, *Grey Granite* provides a fitting climax to the trilogy's search for a deeper meaning to life and explores this profound subject just as thoroughly as either of its predecessors.

One of Mitchell's main motivating forces was his humanitarianism, and this is a prominent feature of the Grassic Gibbon work. The two extant manuscripts which show Mitchell feeling his way towards the original prose technique of *A Scots Quair* are almost completely lacking in the technical sophistication and philosophical depth of the trilogy, and yet both reveal the author's consistent preoccupation with the plight of the Scottish people. In a short introductory fragment simply titled 'Curtain Raiser', a rather crude early version of the 'Prelude' which sets the appropriate social and historical context for *Sunset Song*, the author draws a contrast between the bright heroic legends of Scottish history and the sombre social conditions of the times in which they were set. Thus, Mitchell writes sarcastically in the early fragment:

> Those were fairly the times, there's little doubt, when Scotland had its glory bright and untarnished, folk went half-starved, when they weren't that they were being broken on the wheel or hanged at the tail of a cart of manure for stealing a penny's worth of meal, or led out and butchered on the dreich Mearns hills, in rain and the dirty on-ding of sleet, white pelting, for the sake of Scotland and god and the wealth to fill up the gentry's pouches.[24]

In the substantially longer manuscript of the half-finished novel published in 1982 as *The Speak of the Mearns*, Mitchell once more subordinates all national concerns to the welfare of the peasantry and the proletariat of Scotland, writing, again with some bitterness:

> And the tenant if he had any wisdom left from the grind and chave of his sweating days would 'gree to . . . pay more rent; if he didn't he was chased from the land he held and hounded south and out of the county, maybe strayed to Fife and was

seized on there and held a slave in the Fifeshire mines, toiling naked him and his wife and bairns, unpaid, unholidayed in the long half-dark. For that was the Age of God and King when Scotland had still her Nationhood.[25]

In both these works, Mitchell's uppermost concern is with the 'common folk', and his approach to history is fundamentally socialist, for he sides with the people throughout. The *Quair* itself is unified in a similar way by the author's moral preoccupation with the welfare of the Scots folk, whether they be the peasants of Kinraddie, the rustics and spinners of Segget, or the Duncairn proletariat. Consequently, a certain part of Mitchell's general endeavour to create 'the free and undefiled illusion' in his trilogy is devoted to the changing of the traditional socio-historical perspective to a basically socialist viewpoint. And the manner in which he achieves this reorientation in *A Scots Quair* is as sophisticated as the two trial runs cited above are crude.

The main force governing human society in *A Scots Quair* is that of change, and Mitchell attempts to come to terms with this in the volume within a Scottish context by monitoring it, setting it in a positive political light, and finally identifying a means by which this process may be exploited for the general benefit of the people. Much of the political impact of the *Quair* is thus directly attributable to the author's representation of this universal dialectic of change.

The omnipotent force of Change which Chris apprehends at the close of the *Quair* is reflected in the disciplined symbolic superstructure governing the individual volumes, in the organic cycle with which the Kinraddie crofters and Chris herself are bound up in *Sunset Song*, in the strict meteorological progression of *Cloud Howe* which moves from innocuous Cirrus clouds to ominous Cumulus and Stratus ones and ends with gloomy Nimbus ones, and in the steadily hardening mineralogical sequence which reflects the thematic development of *Grey Granite*. This principle is also prominent in the book's thematic infrastructure.

The quintessence of modern Scottish society whose story unfolds throughout the volume is itself introduced against a historical background of change. The social history of the Kinraddie crofters represented in *Sunset Song* is shown taking over where the baronial history of the Kinraddies, related in the first section of the 'Prelude', leaves off, with the conclusive image of Cospatric's castle which 'crumbled to bits like a cheese' (*SQ*, pp 17–18). The 'Proem' to *Cloud Howe* fulfils a similar role to the 'Prelude' in the first volume, counterpointing the legendary history and baronial usury of Hew Monte Alto, as Segget's equivalent to Kinraddie's Cospatric, with the less dramatic activities of the Segget populace. The rise of the Segget worthies who animate *Cloud Howe* thus coincides with the demise of the baronial Mowats, whose mutability and transience provides a timely reminder of the inevitable universal process of decay and change; just as Cospatric's castle degenerates into a derelict ruin in the 'Prelude' signalling the end of the Kinraddie dynasty, so at the end of the 'Proem' the baronial Mowats come to an equally inglorious end, Mitchell's sardonic chronicler merely recording that 'they lived and they died and they went to their place' (*SQ*, p 203).

As a more modern phenomenon, the city of Duncairn lacks the legendary background of Kinraddie and Segget, and therefore *Grey Granite* naturally begins without an introductory chapter, but the prefatorial sections of the first two volumes do more than enough to establish the background of historical change. And just as the alteration in social conditions represented within these opening sections stimulates a demand for a modification in the subsequent political and literary responses to the situation, so the three distinct phases which Mitchell apprehends in the evolution of modern Scottish society, from country to town, to city, each recommend a particular literary mode of approach and serve a distinctive political purpose. It is thus unfair to criticise *Grey Granite* by comparing it with the preceding volumes, as each novel employs different techniques to make its point.

While *Sunset Song* has a less pronounced political character than the later volumes in the trilogy, it contributes significantly to the final impact of the work's political theme by establishing the moral obligation for the radical programme elucidated at greater length in *Cloud Howe* and *Grey Granite*.

As an elegy lamenting the passing of the crofting class, *Sunset Song* concerns changes of the past, and inevitably this historical distancing detracts from the work's sense of political immediacy. Nevertheless, this first volume is invested with a fierce moral power of implicit political significance which draws much of its strength from the realism and the poignancy with which the community of Kinraddie is portrayed. The language, narrative technique, characterisation and plot of *Sunset Song* are all consciously calculated to heighten the impression of reality, and these all combine to great effect to suspend the reader's disbelief and submerge him in the community whose passing Mitchell is lamenting.

Mitchell's literary approximation of peasant speech in both narrative and dialogue not only gives a passable sense of authenticity, but it also affords Gibbon a descriptive particularity not available to his rather stilted English counterpart. This licence 'to call a graip by its given name' (*SQ*, p 331)—to use Grassic Gibbon's own rustic analogy—where his English 'cousin' showed, by his own admission, 'a disposition to call a spade a sanguinary shovel'[26] gives his descriptions a vigour and intensity seldom evident in the English writing; and his increased confidence is displayed in his greater willingness to innovate, manifested most frequently in vivid onomatopoeic and animistic effects.

In addition to these intensifying descriptive techniques, throughout the trilogy the representation of both action and scene has an immediacy which comes from what can only be called a consciously cinematic method of description, in which movement and sound and even particular camera techniques such as panning and zooming are used to embellish the fixed visual image. Together with Mitchell's personal predilection for description of smell, this gives the final picture a comprehensiveness essential to his aims of creating 'the free and undefiled illusion'. Chris herself, as heroine, is frequently employed as the camera eye, the scenes she witnesses constantly achieving a rigorously methodical completeness which has a cinematic immediacy and clarity. The account of Rob's violent reaction to the attentions of the local jingoists in 'Harvest' shows this technique off to fine advantage, the distancing effect of Chris's detached observation of the skirmish imbuing the incident with a mock-heroic flavour by reducing the protagonists, who appear 'like beetles in the distance' (SQ, p 151), to sardonic miniature.

In the first volume of his trilogy in particular, Mitchell shows this ability to set a scene in a single sentence and capture a whole episode within a single paragraph. And this striking descriptive realism is abetted in the narrative itself by his success in combining the omniscient scope of third person narrative with the personal intimacy and authenticity of the first person in Sunset Song's uniquely flexible narrative mode.

Being channelled mainly through the protagonist's consciousness, the narrative of Sunset Song carries all the spontaneity of first hand experience, and the descriptions of Chris's domestic situation at Blawearie and her romance with Ewan gain added poignancy by being related by Chris herself. As heroine, her sensibility is normally the dominant one, and as her thoughts are used to frame the individual narrative blocks in the flashback technique employed throughout the trilogy, her consciousness could also be described as the controlling one. However, in Sunset Song especially, the narrative voice changes with quite bewildering frequency, usually without warning, to both defined and undefined narrators. This is particularly the case in the opening sections of the book, in the 'Prelude', and in 'Ploughing'.

After the pseudo-legendary chronicle which provides a false opening for the 'Prelude', Kinraddie as it stands in 1911 is described from the viewpoint of a variety of narrators. This makes the descriptions of the local worthies throb with a vitality which was conspicuously absent in the earlier section. The individual portraits of the Kinraddie inhabitants possess a remarkable roundness and depth. The assumptions, criticisms and prejudices contained within the narrative itself frequently hold the narrators themselves up to ridicule. This adds significantly to the picture of the communal psychology of the people being described. In this way, Mitchell's narrators are directly connected with the plot, and they seldom detract from the sense of authenticity. Indeed, the very opposite is most usually the case, for the blatant hypocrisy and mischievousness of Mitchell's 'malignant'—to use George Douglas Brown's pungent term[27]—who shows an obsessive interest in gossip and scandal and tends to call a 'daftie' a 'daftie' and any innocent romantic an adulterer, are themselves the focus of much ribaldry.

Mitchell's characterisation also achieves a greater degree of realism than is customary in the English fiction, Sunset Song possessing, in addition to the main protagonists, secondary characters who are equally heavily individualised, physically, psychologically and morally. The physical descriptions have an originality and atypicality right from the original roll-call of dramatis personae provided in the 'Prelude'. And there is an equally healthy sense of variety in the inventory detailing the distinctive foibles and quirks and idiosyncracies of the various worthies, from Rob's disproportionate fondness of horses, Chae's stubborn political idealism and Mistress Munro's mutually exclusive social senses of humility and pride, to the Sinclairs' untarnished romantic innocence, Pooty's stutter and Mistress Mutch's fatalistic self-assurance. This sustains Chris's later meditation upon the challenging diversity of personality she has seen on parade even within the confines of a small place like Kinraddie: she exclaims incredulously:

> How funny were folk! . . . You knew them, saw through them, tied them up in little packets stowed away in your mind, labelled COARSE or TINKS or FINE; and they came tumbling from the packets at the very first shake, mixed and up-jumbled, she'd never known a soul bide neat and sure in his packet yet (SQ, p 110).

This sense of the integrity of the individual and of the inadequacy of classification is reasserted in the following volume, in which Chris no longer judges her compeers as morally black and white and settles instead upon a more realistic scale of judgement, observing of the inhabitants of Segget that, 'They gossip and claik and are good and bad, and both together, mixed up and down' (SQ, p 230).

In Sunset Song, and, to a lesser extent, Cloud Howe, Mitchell thus adopts a candid approach to the characterisation, indicating the limitless permutations possible overall and striving to create a realistic balance in his own figures between their less worthy qualities, such as are called into play by Chris's stoic reaction to her father's death, and their more generous instincts, which are seen to best effect in the description of Chris's wedding. This realistic ambivalence is perhaps most obvious in a single individual in the portrait of John Guthrie, whose brutality to his own family is mitigated by his redeeming sense of justice and social equality. However, Mitchell also seeks this balance among his secondary figures, and the introductory sketch of Mistress Munro in the 'Prelude' provides a particularly fine example of his method of tempering the satirical edge of the portrait with a redeeming sympathetic appeal, for the narrator's picture gradually mellows as it develops, his subject's sharp manner eventually paling into insignificance in comparison with the diligence with which she discharges her duties as the local 'howdie'.

Mitchell's characters in Sunset Song are thus suitably and sometimes infuriatingly human and emerge from the pages satisfactorily 'mixed and up-jumbled'. This moral sense of truth to life is accompanied by a psychological sensitivity in the handling of the major protagonists, and this is epitomised in Chris herself.

Although Chris is just one part of the rich human tableau of Sunset Song, Mitchell takes special care in his treatment of his heroine's development. In fact this aspect of the book has much of the simple immediacy of the bildungsroman, as a sensitive study of the experience of a young girl as she grows up. The metaphoric cycle governing Sunset Song, justified literally by the straightforward descriptions given in the text of the chief activities of the farming year, also mirrors Chris's own development from the naivete and innocence of pre-adolescence through the painful learning of adolescence to the Lawrentian 'harvest madness' of early womanhood, blossoming finally in the maturity of wife and mother. Secondary influences in this central pattern of evolution, such as the emotional experience that she gains by proxy from Will's affair with Mollie Douglas and the adult poise she acquires from her early assumption of the matriarchal mantle following her mother's suicide in 'Drilling' also add considerably to the sense of authenticity. Such is Mitchell's insight into the psychological, emotional and sexual maturity of his heroine, in fact, that Helen Cruickshank was led to believe that the author of *Sunset Song* was female, and Chris's development is indeed described with a frank intimacy and understanding fully befitting the modern novel.

Thus, Mitchell's portrait of Chris, which traces her domestic development from daughter through to matriarch and her romantic development from adolescent to lover, bride, wife and mother, epitomises his endeavour to create a high sense of psychological realism in *Sunset Song*. The plot of the book, based upon the ordinary life of the Kinraddie peasants seen both at work and play, also adds to the irresistible illusion of reality.

The action of *Sunset Song* is designed to arouse the optimum emotional response in the reader, and to this end Mitchell occasionally introduces highly melodramatic incidents to the narrative, such as Jean Guthrie's poisoning of herself and the twins, John Guthrie's tormented lusting after his daughter, the various supernatural visions, and the tragic deaths of the individual Kinraddie crofters in the war. However, the actual proportion of melodrama contained in the novel as a whole is relatively small, the genuinely moving effect of the plot overall being as much due to Mitchell's dynamic treatment of the more mundane aspects of Kinraddie life as to the individual dramatic episodes dotted throughout the narrative.

The emotional bitter-sweetness of *Sunset Song* is especially seductive, due in large part to the author's successful exploitation of the tragi-comic form, both within individual episodes and in the general plot sequence in which the emotional peaks and troughs are exaggerated by their close juxtaposition. This deliberate swing from one emotional extreme to the other is particularly effective in the description of the fire at Peesie's Knapp in 'Drilling', in which the tension and pathos created by the destruction of building and beasts are actually intensified by the comic relief found fleetingly in the middle of the narrative, when one of Chae's cows betrays humorously incongruous signs of life within this context of death and destruction, the narrator describing how, when the byre wall caved in, 'Chae's oldest cow stuck out its head and said *Moo!* right in Chae's face' (*SQ*, p 77).

Mitchell makes conscious efforts to preserve the emotional balance of his narrative by periodically changing the pace of delivery and the emotional pitch. *Sunset Song* contains a superabundance of extraneous anecdotal episodes which give humorous counterbalance to the tragic and lyrical element. The narrative thus contains a generous smattering of farce in such episodes as Andy the Dafty's dramatic escape from Cuddieston related in 'Ploughing' and the Reverend Stuart Gibbon's eventful expedition to Aberdeen described in 'Drilling'. And although the war and its disastrous aftermath results in a progressive seriousness throughout the final sections of the novel, the insertion of a semi-comic rustic review of the state of post-war Kinraddie—between the description of the events of the war given in 'Harvest' and the subsequent politically orientated conclusion drawn from this by Robert at the close of the book—heightens the impact of the climax by force of contrast.

The plot of *Sunset Song* also has an important social function, of reflecting everyday life in the community of Kinraddie. The couthy contentment of the traditional hogmanay festivities shown in 'Drilling' and of the wedding celebrations represented in 'Seed-Time' are introduced against a heavily realised backdrop depicting the Kinraddie crofters' endless struggle to win sustenance from the soil. Thus, Mitchell's narrative has a lyrical naturalism and offers graphic descriptions of the cardinal agricultural tasks as they were performed by the crofting farmer at the turn of the century, from ploughing (*SQ,* p 133), drilling (*SQ,* p 163) and sowing (*SQ,* p 48), to harvesting (*SQ,* pp 61-3; p 144) and stooking (*SQ,* p 174).

The language, narrative mode, characterisation and plot of *Sunset Song* combine in this way to create an exuberant sense of realism, and this is of critical importance to Mitchell's theme; for the brisk vitality of the social picture increases the sense of loss the reader feels at the end of the novel. And this of course makes Robert's rousing conclusion all the more impressive, for its apparent grounding on reality: it is admittedly too late to do anything to help the Kinraddie crofters themselves, but the poignancy of their condition adds urgency to the moral obligation to learn from their tragic experience.

'The Unfurrowed Field' sandwiching the 'Song' itself as 'Prelude' and 'Epilude' fully captures the social changes which have taken place throughout the intervening 'Song' by systematically comparing the state of the holdings of Kinraddie before and after the war. And because the author's sympathies rest throughout with the engagingly simple and straightforward peasant farmers like Chae and Rob who are the main victims of this historical process, this finally generates in the reader an overwhelming sense of moral dissatisfaction with the course that history has taken and produces an accompanying desire to change things in the future. This leads on naturally to the search for political solutions enacted in *Cloud Howe* and *Grey Granite.* In *Sunset Song*, the main stimulus for change comes from the outside, and the peasantry's inability to move with the times or conquer the hostile social forces condemns them to their fate.

The events depicted in *Sunset Song* thus endorse Robert's call for radical political action, and yet the candid characterisation of the book realistically reflects the inconsistency and diversity of political opinion prevailing in Kinraddie, which runs the whole gamut from Chae's radicalism, through Rob's emotional humanism, to the Conservatism of Ellison. However, the peasants upon whom Mitchell concentrates in particular throughout the novel, John Guthrie, Chae, Long Rob and Ewan, all exhibit a 'smeddum', a sense of pride, and consequently all stand opposed to the forces of social injustice.

Thus, for all her father's faults, at his funeral Chris is moved to remember, 'his justice, and the fight unwearying he'd fought with the land and its masters to have them all clad and fed and respectable' (*SQ,* p 95). Six pages later, she herself is shown to have inherited 'that hatred of rulers and gentry a flame in her heart, John Guthrie's hate', and later her husband reveals a comparable 'flame' when the wealthy Fordoun farmers incur his wrath and move him to exclaim angrily, 'To hell with them and their fine land too, they're not farmers, them, only lazy muckers that sit and make silver out of their cotters' (*SQ*, p 135). Chae Strachan similarly 'wasn't well liked by them that set themselves up for gentry' (*SQ*, p 21), and his flagrant disregard and disrespect for social status, like John Guthrie's, proves costly to his own welfare. Chae's socialist idealism, however, is more a mark of characterisation than an integral part of Mitchell's political theme, and the eccentric nature of his stance within the context of Kinraddie is frequently pointed out by Long Rob, whose socialist sympathies are of a more commonsensical kind.

Despite their admirable principles and sentiments, however, the crofting farmers are not equipped to cope with the changes taking place in society. John Guthrie himself realises the threat posed to his own way of life by the advancing forces of agrarian capitalism which herald 'the day of the fine big farm' in the 'Prelude' (*SQ*, p 17). When he goes to view a tenancy in Banchory, he discovers that 'the rent was awful high and he saw that nearly all the district was land of the large-like farm, he'd be squeezed to death and he'd stand no chance' (*SQ*, p 40). And following his move to Blawearie, this gloomy realisation gathers even greater force:

> Now also it grew plain to him here as never in Echt that the day of the crofter was fell near finished, put by, the day of folk like himself and Chae and Cuddieston, Pooty and Long Rob of the Mill, the last of the farming folk that wrung their living from the land with their own bare hands (*SQ*, p 67).

This prognosis naturally leads on to an indictment of the increasingly unequal social polarisation developing in the rural areas, 'with the country-folk climbing on silver, the few, back in the pit, the many'. And the Great War witnesses a substantial upsurge in this greedy materialism and sounds the final death-knell for the Kinraddie crofters towards the end of the novel.

The change taking place upon a social level is also mirrored throughout the book on a cultural level: as the social structure changes, so the established cultural traditions die out. This is what Will means when he tells Chris that Scotland is 'dead or it's dying' (*SQ*, p 165), and this is what Robert is referring to when at the book's climax he looks back on the fate of the Kinraddie peasants and states that 'it was the old Scotland that perished then' (*SQ*, p 193). Just as the old farming ways are being threatened by the attempts at mechanisation and collectivisation, therefore, so the linguistic register is changing accordingly. Pooty, the oldest indigenous inhabitant of Kinraddie, is already something of an anachronism by the time of his original introduction in the 'Prelude', Mitchell's narrator observing, 'He was a shoe-maker, the creature, and called himself the Sutor, an old-fashioned name that folk laughed at' (*SQ*, p 30). And despite Rob's noble defence of his native vernacular at Chris's wedding, Gordon's argument sadly smacks of the truth:

> You can't help it, Rob. If folk are to get on in the world nowadays, away from the ploughshafts and out of the pleiter, they must use the English, orra though it be (*SQ*, p 123).

Similarly, Gordon's own social advancement after the war is demonstrated linguistically, Mitchell's anonymous narrator relating in the 'Epilude' how, 'you couldn't get within a mile of the Upperhill without you'd hear a blast of the English, so fine and genteel' (SQ, p 186).

Social developments in the countryside also mean that the traditional songs delivered at Chris's wedding which ring true to the old farming life are now giving way to, among other things, 'the sugary surge of Auld Lang Syne' (SQ, p 130), with the result that Rob's happy homecoming from prison in 'Harvest' is noteworthy for bringing about the welcome return of the sound of his personal anthem of 'Ladies of Spain'. Indeed, the whole repertoire which Rob draws upon in order to sing young Ewan to sleep in his father's absence is now outmoded and part of the life of the past, Mitchell describing how Chris and old Brigson listen nostalgically, and liken the experience to 'listening to an echo from far in the years at the mouth of a long lost glen' (SQ, p 175).

By the time of the methodical survey in the 'Epilude' which records the alterations in Kinraddie since the war, the traditional folk ballads have been almost completely supplanted by alien importations presaging the twenties, Mitchell's trendy young narrator observing that, 'You heard feint the meikle of those old songs now, they were daft and old-fashioned, there were fine new ones in their places, right from America, folk said' (SQ, p 186). The lament of 'The Flowers of the Forest' played by McIvor at the close of the novel after Robert has delivered the epitaph for the dead crofters is thus appropriately old-fashioned and, belonging to the crofters' own bygone age, the dirge itself symbolises the passing of an era:

> It rose and rose and wept and cried, that crying for the men that fell in battle, and there was Kirsty Strachan weeping quietly and others with her, and the young ploughmen they stood with glum, white faces, they'd no understanding or caring, it was something that vexed and tore at them, it belonged to times they had no knowing of (SQ, p 194).

The vivid realism of Sunset Song conveys with a convincing impartiality the sense of the worthiness of the Kinraddie community whose passing is being lamented. The narrative establishes a firm moral base of implicit political import, and Robert's credentials for the task of elaborating the political significance of the story at the book's close are presented in old Brigson's recommendation, 'that many a decent thing had gone out of Kinraddie with the War but that only one had come in, and that was the new minister' (SQ, p 190). Robert brings a socialist perspective to bear on the story, exploiting the pathos generated by the extinction of the Kinraddie peasants. For Sunset Song is an elegy in that it provides an eloquent swansong for the Scottish crofting farmer, but it is not merely a passive exercise in nostalgia—which would be understandable from someone of Mitchell's pedigree. Robert's epitaph is, indeed, 'just sheer politics' (SQ, p 193), and as such it points the way forward from the pain of the past to the promise of the future.

It is a tribute to Mitchell's personal integrity and to the strength of his political beliefs that he, like Edwin Muir in Scottish Journey, could face up so candidly to the fact that the whole way of life from which he himself came and for which consequently he preserved a great love, was finally dying out. Even the essay on 'The Land' which is his explicit homage to his roots is courageously realistic and forward thinking: Mitchell resists his personal sentiments and confesses that 'when I read or hear our new leaders and their plans for making of Scotland a great peasant nation, a land of little farms and little farming communities, I am moved to a bored disgust with those pseudo-literary romantics playing with politics' (*SH*, p 69). A central part of Mitchell's honest social 'illusion' is thus a determination to face facts and to look forward to the future rather than back to the past.

Likewise, it is Robert's duty at the close of *Sunset Song* to suggest a way in which the gravest social consequences, epitomised in the recent historical past by the demise of the crofting farmers of Kinraddie, may be obviated. Thus, the moral thrust of the first volume of the trilogy sustains Robert's call for political action which looks forward to the political involvement of the later volumes: Robert affirms that, 'They died for a world that is past, these men, but they did not die for this that we seem to inherit' (*SQ*, p 193). He finds political inspiration even in the tragic past of *Sunset Song*, and although the sunset of the book's title relates to the final eclipse of the Kinraddie peasantry, the significance of the event lives on in the search for the 'morning star' of Robert's text. It is worth remembering here also that Mitchell's original title for the second novel in the trilogy was itself 'The Morning Star'.

Mitchell's demonstration of the Kinraddie peasants' vulnerabilty to the forces of change provides the pressing incentive to seek a practical method by which these forces may be controlled. This search is the political theme of *Cloud Howe* and *Grey Granite*.

Cloud Howe is the transitional book in the trilogy, and its locale is at an intermediary stage of social development between country and town. This social shift is represented within a move away from the historical past of *Sunset Song* to a more immediate present (the small industrial town being basically a nineteenth century phenomenon), and thus, Chris formally renounces the rural reality of Kinraddie at the very beginning of *Cloud Howe*:

> . . . now as she looked on the land so strange, with its tractors and sheep, she half-longed to be gone. It had finished with her, that life that had been, and this was her's now . . . (*SQ*, p 208).

Opposed in this way to the modern rural reality, Chris finds a willing ally in her husband Robert, who harbours a guilty conviction that by staying on in Kinraddie he is avoiding the modern social issues and thereby betraying his own political—and pastoral—calling. His feeling that, 'here he could never do good or do ill, in a countryside that was dying or dead' naturally promotes the following resolution to 'try to find something betwixt and between' (*SQ*, p 213). This is realised in the village of Seggett.

Much of the rustic vitality of Kinraddie spills over into Segget, calling the same vigorously realistic literary techniques into play. The narrative authenticity, the earthy humour, the gratuitously anecdotal flavour of the plot and the lifelike characterisation of *Cloud Howe* all refer back directly to the first volume. In fact, several of the Segget worthies take over exactly the same roles within their community as existed in Kinraddie, with Ake fulfilling Long Rob's function as the irreverently witty voice of common sense in Segget and Ag Moultrie playing Mistress Munro's part of the malicious slanderer of character. *Cloud Howe* also demonstrates Mitchell's enduring interest in the quality of psychological realism, in his treatment both of the individual and the community; Chris's development is just as sensitively dealt with in *Cloud Howe* (although obviously she now has less dramatic leaps towards maturity than she had in *Sunset Song*), and young Ewan's childish world described in 'Cirrus' has all the vivid spontaneity of Gunn's little hero's world in *Young Art and Old Hector* and *The Green Isle of the Great Deep*.

As in the earlier volume also, the descriptive realism which Mitchell achieves is supplemented by the impression of honesty given in the characterisation, which highlights the less worthy attributes of the Segget folk as well as their more admirable features. On the whole, the indigenous population of the village of Segget are as unenlightened politically as were the Kinraddie folk, even though their own welfare and livelihood also come under threat from the steadily advancing forces of 'progress'. Their political position in the modern world is at best neutral: at worst it is one of complacent conservatism, Peter Peat declaring stubbornly early on in the book, for instance, that 'folk wanted no changes here' (*SQ*, p 240), and the taciturn folk-narrator reiterates this towards the end of the novel when he asks gruffly, 'who the hell wanted alterations in Segget?' (*SQ*, p 348).

This conservatism appears self-defeating in view of the lesson taught by the Kinraddie crofters' elimination in the previous volume, and indeed in a very similar manner, the traditional Segget ways come under progressively graver threat of extinction as the novel develops. Dite Peat and old Leslie are eventually faced with financial ruin and, like Pooty the Sutor in the 'Prelude' to the first volume, old Rob Moultrie the saddler appears early on in *Cloud Howe* as a sad reminder of a more prosperous time in the past: Mitchell relates how 'his trade had gone, and his sweirty had come' (*SQ*, p 224). Accordingly, Rob's death is invested with a poignant symbolic significance, John Muir the gravedigger reflecting as he contemplates Rob's freshly dug grave at the end of the book, 'that something was finished and ended in Segget, more than old Moultrie, older than him' (*SQ*, p 336).

The encroachment of capitalist methods carries grave consequences for the people of Segget as well as the crofting farmers of Kinraddie. However, the original pictish stock of Segget has been contaminated first of all by the weavers introduced by Hew Monte Alto in mediaeval times and then by the Bervie spinners drafted in by Mowat, in the wake of the Industrial Revolution, and this industrial element—which eventually comes to account for half of the burgh's population—gives *Cloud Howe* a decisive political dimension lying beyond the relatively innocent rural world of *Sunset Song*.

The characteristically opinionated Kinraddie artisan who anonymously delivers much of the narrative has a successor in *Cloud Howe* who makes no attempt to hide the enmity which he and his fellow rustics feel towards the spinners, and young Ewan, as neutral observer, visualises this principle of mutual antagonism in terms of small-town class warfare, in which the people of Segget 'hated capitalists, if they were spinners, and hated spinners if they were New Toun' (*SQ,* p 279). The eccentric political position of the indigenous Segget population thus confuses the neat Marxist opposition between the industrial proletariat and their capitalist oppressors. However, just as the voice of the Kinraddie crofters is a voice of the past, so the rustic accent of Segget has lost much of its immediacy in a world of increasing industrialisation.

The process of social decay affects the indigenous population of Segget badly enough, but the spinners suffer dreadfully at the hands of a capitalist system which not only is harmful to them but develops in inverse proportion to their personal welfare. Where the traditional rustic sector of the population maintains its habitually diffident political status throughout the book, therefore, the spinners naturally develop a self-protective sense of political identity and solidarity in response to the worsening social situation. Mitchell's political theme in the novel is thus focused through Robert upon the spinners' attempts at political mobilisation. Where *Sunset Song* was an elegy, *Cloud Howe* is a social tragedy tracing the frustration of Robert's vain but noble efforts to harness the change for the benefit of the working men.

Robert is both 'the comrade of God' (*SQ,* p 222) and 'a go-ahead billy' (*SQ,* p 265): his sincere humanitarianism transmutes on a political level into a fairly radical form of Christian Socialism, as his Armistice Day sermon in 'Cumulus' prophesying mankind's heroic recovery from the carnage of the war demonstrates. *Cloud Howe* follows Robert's quest to put his political ideals into practical operation, and as the spinners emerge as the most socially repressed body within Segget, and also the most politically active and aware, at the end of 'Cumulus' his political hopes, to the dismay of the local bourgeoisie, inevitably come to rest on them.

Robert's idealism described in 'Cirrus' gains much of its moral strength from Chris's reference at the end of the section to the catastrophic events of the preceding volume, and this carry-over of the earlier elegiac tone adds substantially to the sense of political urgency. Mitchell writes of his heroine:

> . . . and she thought of Robert—his dream just a dream? Was there a new time coming to the earth, when nowhere a bairn would cry in the night, or a woman go bowed as her mother had done, or a man turn into a tormented beast, as her father, or into a bullet-torn corpse, as had Ewan? (*SQ,* p 223).

And suddenly, from the poignancy of the past, Mitchell switches to the political prospect of the future, when Chris turns to consider, 'a time when those folk down there in Segget might be what Robert said all men might be, companions with God on a terrible adventure?', and relates this vision incredulously to their present locality, 'Segget: John Muir, Will Melvin, Else Quean; the folk of the grisly rees of West Wynd-'.

Thus, the crofters' extermination presented in the previous volume combines with the social threat facing Segget, articulated mainly through Chris's and Ewan's sympathetic affiliation with the spinners, to lend weight to Robert's subsequent conclusion, 'that men must change, or perish here in Segget, as all over the earth', and to his following affirmation that, 'Necessity's the drive, the policeman that's coming to end the squabbling stupidities of old' (*SQ,* pp 230-1).

Robert's consuming interest in the general welfare of his fellow men naturally graduates into an essentially Marxist exhortation of the imperative for change, and the high moral ideal of humanity forging its own destiny in a glorious communal effort throughout the world remains his abiding obsession to the end. The campaign that he launches upon Segget against the background of the increasing social unrest of 'Cumulus' is sustained by a near-Marxist view of the changes past, and of the social change to come: Robert observes that, 'change, imperative, awaited the world, as never before men could make it anew, men of good will and a steadfast faith' (SQ, p 240).

This aim to determine the way in which society develops is irreproachable, but the success of the social tragedy of *Cloud Howe* largely depends upon the realistic impression that Mitchell gives of the modern social situation and of the spinners who live in this environment. They must appear credibly fallible and yet deserving of Robert's sympathy and confidence, for the stress in the tragic hero should not be upon how wrong he was but upon how nearly right he was; and, as with Hardy's later protagonists Tess and Jude, Robert's relative lack of responsibility for his own fate lays the blame even more firmly at society's door.

The means by which Mitchell establishes the urban milieu which his spinners inhabit in *Cloud Howe* are more sophisticated than the vividly realistic descriptive techniques employed in *Sunset Song*. The emotional practice of presenting the spinners' houses as 'pig-rees' is overused but the increasing urbanisation of modern society is also represented in more subtle metaphor.

Throughout *Cloud Howe*, Mitchell seems more inclined to use industrial analogies in his descriptive work, and this disposition is not merely a self-conscious Lawrentian attempt to move with the times in his art, but a functional ploy which adds significantly to the impression of the contemporary social movement away from the country to the industrial towns. Descriptions of human behaviour and of nature now draw heavily upon less traditional and more urban material, without sacrificing any of the author's customary representational sharpness. Appropriately, too, this technique becomes steadily more apparent as the book progresses and the spinners' cause gradually dominates the proceedings, with metals such as iron and steel appearing increasingly within the imagery. While it would be facile to make too much of this modification between *Sunset Song* and *Cloud Howe*, it would also be unfair to ignore one of the subtler ways in which Mitchell signifies the social shift that takes place between the first two novels of his trilogy.

As a group with a uniform identity and a conscious role to play in the future war of the classes, the spinners themselves also demand a different literary form of approach. Thus, in *Cloud Howe*, Mitchell employs a generally more stylised mode than in *Sunset Song*. Mitchell exploits the dual character of this work-force to the full by representing them as a single corporate body made up of individuals of common social background, occupational experience and political mettle, and yet, as the fairly sharply individualised members of the Cronin family testify, each member of this group has a distinctive personality and separate hopes and aims and fears. Young Ewan's friendship was Charlie Cronin and the affectionate romance between Dod Cronin and Cis Brown are the two main sub-plots by which Mitchell reflects the individuality of the various characters lumped together under the single pejorative heading of 'spinners'. Indeed Charlie himself is assigned the most important role in the expression of this theme when he tells Ewan that 'the folk in New Toun were daft to speak of the folk in the Mills as only spinners, there were foremen and weavers, and a lot more besides; but they all *looked* like spinners' (*SQ*, p 282). Significantly, Charlie's description presents the textile workers from both angles, in their individual and collective identities. However, although Mitchell sticks up for the spinners as individuals, wisely he resists the temptation to idealise them.

At the end of 'Cumulus' Mitchell is unduly hasty in his dismissal of the possibility of political reform being implemented from above, resorting to crude caricature in his treatment of the various candidates whom Robert tries to coerce into joining his Socialist League. The stuffy representatives of the Segget bourgeoisie gathered together in the manse after the Armistice Day service—Mrs Geddes, Miss M'Askill, Miss Ferguson, Mr Geddes, and even Jeannie Grant, who is meant to condemn the others by her contrasting liberatedness—are all flat figures, and Stephen Mowat, who represents Robert's last hope with regard to the prospect of social reform being introduced from above, is too stereotyped a villain to give much credibility to Robert's subsequent affiliation with the spinners themselves. However, Mitchell largely compensates for this shortcoming in his convincingly impartial portrayal of the spinners.

Even allowing for their poverty, the early scenes which introduce the spinners cast them in an unfavourable light. They are generally hostile and resentful towards the rest of the town, which, true to form, returns the sentiment with interest. Less forgiveably, they also mock Robert for his political idealism, and the antipathy between the minister and the truculent jute workers comes to a head in the Homeric hammer competition at Segget Show presented in 'Cumulus', where their taunts rouse Robert to heroic efforts to beat their champion, Jock Cronin. Even after Robert pledges himself to the spinners' struggle in 'Stratus', Mitchell questions their ability to succeed where the traditional political channels have failed to bring about the requisite improvements in the standard of living among the lower classes. 'Nimbus' contains a sharp satirical scenario which describes the political defection of Jock Cronin from the front line of the battle, the narrator describing his meteoric promotion in Glasgow with wholly misplaced admiration.

Although the reader is led to sympathise with Robert's conclusion that only the lower classes themselves can improve their own lot, as in *Spartacus*, Mitchell's awareness of human fallibility means that he refuses to give any political guarantees. Personal idiosyncracies are rightly accepted as part of the human character, and of course as such they cannot be legislated for. Against this honest approach to the human character, however, Mitchell retains a redeeming optimism in the collective power of the lower classes to overcome these inevitable setbacks in their mass effort to reform society.

Accordingly, he lays considerable emphasis upon the spinners' identity as a single unit.

The political force which the spinners represent is graphically captured within the narrative. The rustic narrative voice, which in *Sunset Song* incorporated various—mainly unspecified—personae, now acquires a representative capacity which generalises the experience described. And latterly, this common response is elicited by the hostile presence of the spinners, whose own status as a political unit gains force indirectly from association with the uniform reaction they thus provoke even in' the politically diffident folk of Segget. This sense of class solidarity and of the growing social stratification of the village is best seen in the incident of the Armistice Day service related in 'Cumulus', where the spinners' personal experience of the war stands in direct contrast with that of the narrator. The Segget population is thus neatly divided into two camps, signified here by those who are entitled to wear medals, and those who are not, Mitchell's narrator remarking when faced by the impressive array of honours displayed among the spinners that, 'you hadn't been able to get to the War, you'd been over-busy with the shop those years, or keeping the trade going brisk in the Arms, or serving at Segget as the new stationmaster' (*SQ*, p 267).

The war thus reappears as a political motif in *Cloud Howe*, and it is particularly appropriate that Robert's death which follows his political disillusionment is physically attributable to his gassing. The First World War finally kills off the Scottish peasantry already under severe threat of extinction at the hands of the forces of agrarian capitalism in *Sunset Song*, and this same external agency is responsible for Robert's death in *Cloud Howe*, thereby intensifying the book's impact as social tragedy.

Perhaps the single most prominent technical modification in *Cloud Howe* is the greater interaction between the personal and the political. In *Sunset Song*, the political impact of Robert's concluding threnody depends heavily upon the pathos evoked by the peasants' gradual demise. In *Cloud Howe*, however, there is a direct interaction between the personal and political spheres. The social tragedy of the failure of the General Strike is accentuated by Robert's personal tragedy. The social decay in Segget which escalates as the book progresses introduces increasingly urgent demands for political reform, and the symbolic meteorological progression of the individual sections in the novel reflects both this general development in political awareness and Robert's own political experience, both of which, as the darkening cloud formations indicate, are ultimately tragic.

Ewan's death at the end of the previous volume is built on a tragic pattern, arousing tragic pathos by demanding that the ultimate penalty be paid for an understandable mistake. Ewan's error is that he defies his own better judgement and goes against everything his simple lifestyle has taught him when he joins in the war. When he recovers his sanity, it is too late to repair the damage, and the agency whose inflexible code of justice demands that he must pay the ultimate price is not, as in classical tragedy, a divine force, but, as in the later Hardy novels, an uncaring and hostile society. Ewan should not have been in the war in the first place, and when he is shot as a deserter he is being punished for an act which the reader is disposed to approve, and, more importantly, he is being punished by an agency which is unfit to judge him, and which the reader is disposed to condemn. Robert's experience follows a similar course, only his tragedy has a more explicit political significance.

Robert's tragedy stems from his inability to cope with the frustration of his political hopes rather than from any actual mistake, with the result that his death seems even more unnecessary than Ewan's and so the powers which demand the forfeiture of his life stand condemned. Until the end of 'Stratus', his fortunes, centred principally upon his efforts to drum up political action in Segget, rise steadily, so that ten pages from the end of the section he finally looks forward to the General Strike as the event which promises to bring about the realisation of his greatest ambitions, to usher in the era of 'Man made free at last' (*SQ*, p 301).

Chris endorses Robert's political ideal as 'a dream that at least had the wind in its hair' (*SQ*, p 321), but the failure of the General Strike gives his vision a contrasting ethereality and an impracticality, so that Christ is no longer apprehended as a social reformer, but as a remote spirit. In 'Nimbus', Robert's Christianity is seen to have deteriorated from an inspiring creed into an amorphous hallucination. When Robert tells his wife desperately, 'I've thought Him only a Leader, a man, but Chris—I've looked on the face of God' (*SQ*, p 321), Chris's response, mixing pity and revulsion, throws his madness into sharp relief.

Robert's political disillusion thus manifests itself as a religious mania which is disconnected from contemporary social and moral concerns, but his death is tragic because, like Ewan's it is preceded by the recovery of his sanity. Robert's realisation of the factors behind his failure provides the tragic climax to the volume, whereas the significance of Ewan's death with his fellow crofters in 'someone else's war' had to be elucidated afterwards by Robert, as the new minister. The social conditions prevailing in Segget continue to deteriorate steadily: Ewan is physically sickened by Charlie Cronin's description of conditions in Old Toun, and Mitchell follows this up immediately with the poignant, if stylised, episode relating the Kindnesses' traumatic social experience, an episode which owes something to the example of earlier socialist writers such as Dickens and Robert Tressell, and which is particularly closely related to the much maligned 'Father Time' episode in *Jude the Obscure*. In his final sermon, Robert rises above his political disappointment and manages to come to terms with this marked deterioration in living standards. His final call for a more radical political approach than that which fuelled the General Strike has an apocalyptic urgency, as he writes the world off as a lost cause whose future well-being rests solely upon the miraculous discovery of 'a stark, sure creed that will cut like a knife, a surgeon's knife through the doubt and disease' (*SQ*, p 350).

Cloud Howe thus charts the tragic inability of Robert's Christian Socialism to bring about the social changes which the increasingly desperate plight of the lower classes demands. And just as *Sunset Song* ends climactically but inconclusively, so *Cloud Howe* points the way forward from the insubstantial political efforts of Robert and the Segget spinners to the more pragmatic measures of *Grey Granite*.

The social change established in *Grey Granite* brings the reader face to face with the modern urban reality which, as in 'Forsaken', intensifies the demand for a fool-proof political solution. This transformation to the fully developed industrial town again requires an altered literary approach, and Mitchell himself expressed misgivings as to his ability to deal with this new social environment when he wrote apprehensively in 'Literary Lights' in 1934:

> His [Gibbon's] scene so far has been a comparatively uncrowded and simple one—the countryside and village of modern Scotland. Whether his technique is adequate to compass and express the life of an industrialized Scots town in all its complexity is yet to be demonstrated . . . (*SH*, p 154).

Certainly the urban novel does not seem to have 'written itself' in the same way as *Sunset Song* and, to a lesser extent, *Cloud Howe* did. In fact, during the writing of the last volume of the trilogy, Mitchell appeared dissatisfied with his efforts, writing in a letter sent to Helen Cruickshank to apologise for his enforced absence from an impending PEN meeting that he was 'too busy with this abominable *Grey Granite*'.[28] Mitchell may have found the composition 'abominably' difficult, but the final result is more successful than most critics care to acknowledge.

In *Grey Granite*, Mitchell comes fully up to date: this final novel deals with the social changes taking place in the present, and even contemplates the future. The basic transformation to an industrialised society is represented with a conviction surprising for someone of Mitchell's rural background. To establish this new social reality, the author employs a combination of trusted techniques carried over from the preceding volumes, and techniques custom-made for the new task in hand.

By the end of *Cloud Howe*, modern society, even within Segget, is acquiring an increasingly urban character, as Chris realises when she is lying in bed at night, near the end of the volume, for, 'the curlews had ceased to cry on the Kaimes and of nights the sounds [of] the trains came blurred, those nights that the great lighted buses would lighten, suddenly, firing the walls of the room where she lay' (*SQ*, p 340). Thus, just as Chris formally rejects the alien capitalist form which Kinraddie society takes after the war as a necessary preliminary to her involvement in the more pressing social concerns of Segget, so before Mitchell establishes the city of Duncairn as the modern social reality in *Grey Granite*, he also formally dismisses Segget as an outmoded social form. Just after his arrival in Duncairn, Ake Ogilvie, the native wit from the previous volume, describes Segget's gradual decline to a stagnant social backwater when he thinks back to his original arrival in the burgh, 'not near so dead in those times as now, the joiner's business with still enough fettle to bring a man a bit meal and drink', and he recalls further how 'he'd settled down there . . . till the place was fairly all to hell, with unemployment and all the lave' (*SQ*, p 403).

This passing of old ways is vividly enacted in *Grey Granite*, as in the earlier volumes, upon a cultural level. The fashionable young city dwellers now openly deride traditional Scottish music as old fashioned, the narrative representative at Ewan's Young League dance criticising the Scottische as, 'a daft old dance, not up to date' (*SQ*, p 430), and appearing much more at home with the modern waltzes. The urban population now finds its entertainment in the Music Hall, where Snellie Guff and Gappy Gowkheid—cruel parodies, perhaps, of the popular Aberdeen comic Harry Gordon—in Ewan's term, 'assassinate' music, and in the cosmopolitan entertainment of the cinema, which creeps insidiously into the communal psyche, promoting the bizarre misconception that all orientals are, 'coarse little brutes . . . like that Dr Fu Manchu on the films' (*SQ*, p 478).

As in the previous volumes, the change of social circumstance is also designated linguistically. The flashback to Segget with its rustic narrative representative in 'Epidote' acquires an antediluvian air in view of the contemporary urban episodes framing it, which introduce Chris's new urban environment and her new domestic routine in the guest house respectively. This sense of the archaic nature of small town life is emphasised within this particular section by the indigenous narrator's reference to the Segget Provost as 'Hairy Hogg the sutor' (*SQ*, p 360); for Mitchell's deliberate use of the term 'sutor' refers back to the 'Prelude' to *Sunset Song*, in which the unspecified Kinraddie spokesman mocks old Pooty for his stubborn adherence to this old-style term which even then is 'an old-fashioned name that folk laughed at'. By *Grey Granite*, then, the term has become positively obsolete.

In 'Apatite', social developments are again mirrored on a linguistic level when Ewan's temporary lapse into his native vernacular is regarded as a rare enough event for the narrator to remark that he was 'speaking Scotch who so seldom spoke it, that blunted and foolish and out-dated tool' (*SQ*, p 464). Subsequent references to this linguistic development impart a greater sense of regret, however. In 'Zircon', John Cushnie's 'feeungsay' comes under the cosmopolitan influence of the cinema and cultivates a false gentility which encourages her to pour scorn on the country folk, 'with their awful Scotch words' (*SQ*, p 474). Eleven pages later, Mitchell again satirises this form of snobbery when his apocryphal representative of the popular press is criticised for being 'full of dog Latin and constipated English, but of course not Scotch, it was over-genteel'. Thus, Mitchell's reaction to the contemporary decline in the use of Scots is ambivalent. For although on the one hand he accepts its deterioration into a 'blunted and foolish and outdated tool' as an inevitable sign of the times, on the other he defends it stoutly against the 'genteel' English which is replacing it. Where he laments the passing of Scots on aesthetic grounds, socially he can accept its demise as part of the inevitable process of decay and change: and to Mitchell, social matters always outweigh purely aesthetic concerns.

Other of Mitchell's methods used to establish the change of social circumstances earlier in the trilogy carry over to *Grey Granite* with comparable success. The direct descriptive work in this novel is not as consistently lyrical as in the earlier books and in *Sunset Song* in particular, and yet Mitchell's sharp poetic eye also brings the city of Duncairn convincingly to life. Again, as in the earlier volumes, the scene is set with a striking cinematic vigour, as on the second page of the book, which vividly captures the noise and the motion and the sheer scale of Chris's new urban environment as a dizzily spinning maze populated by trams and trains. In this passage, Mitchell still uses Chris as his camera eye, but this capacity is exploited less often in his heroine within this final volume; indeed, towards the end of the book, other characters such as Ewan and Ellen Johns are used in the very same way. In addition, balancing this first-hand view, Mitchell provides an omniscient perspective which has a descriptive intensity and an imaginative sweep that first hand experience cannot offer, and at its best, as in 'Sphene', this leads the reader into the very bowels—or sewers—of Duncairn, Mitchell following in intricate detail the progress of the rainwater deposited by a downpour from its collection in the gutter through its journey out to the open sea (*SQ*, p 423).

As ever, then, in *Grey Granite* Mitchell seeks a descriptive faculty which is capable of giving a comprehensive picture of the physical locale. And as in the earlier volumes, this descriptive method, frequently pursued at the expense of grammatical orthodoxy, augments the formal cartographical-style descriptions of the topography of the respective locations provided in *Sunset Song* (*SQ*, p 63), *Cloud Howe* (*SQ*, pp 215–16, p 220), and *Grey Granite* (*SQ*, p 368).

Mitchell's vivid descriptive technique adapts especially well to the new urban environment, primarily because the city, as a more lively place than either the country or the village, lends itself more dramatically to the author's talent for describing motion, the trams and buses which constitute the main method of transport within Duncairn being particularly receptive to this descriptive technique, assuming an independent life of their own as toiling mechanical beasts of burden.

The initial transformation to the urban environment is also exacted upon a metaphoric level. The Homeric dawn epithet which in the previous volumes presents the arrival of morning in lyrical terms takes a radically different form in *Grey Granite*, with the lightening mornings which announced 'summer coming, marching up each morning with unbraided hair' in Kinraddie (*SQ*, p 141) metamorphosing at the beginning of *Grey Granite* into the substantially less attractive figure, 'lacing its boots and grabbing its muffler and pelting across the roofs of Duncairn' (*SQ*, p 362). And this transmutation is recreated in 'Apatite', when Chris observes that, 'Spring was coming clad in pale saffron—the sun hardly seen all the winter months except through the blanket of Duncairn reek' (*SQ*, p 443).

As in *Cloud Howe*, these descriptive techniques are backed up in an indirect way by the author's increasing recourse to industrial, or at least modern, elements in his imagery. In 'Apatite', Ake dreads a showdown with his old friend who is now the Provost, which he feels would give himself 'as much chance of getting home safe as a celluloid cat that had strayed into hell' (*SQ*, p 442). In this section, this modern kind of slang starts to creep into the narrative, with Alick Watson referring to his mother as 'the old woman' (*SQ*, p 447), and Ewan himself remarking fifteen pages later how the road is 'chockablock with traffic'. In 'Zircon', Mitchell establishes the sense of modernity in a more formal way: his analogy to describe the voice of John Cushnie's fiancee is 'as though her throat were chokeful up of old razor blades' (*SQ,* p 475). And, more instructively, Mitchell describes Ewan, who represents the apotheosis of Marxist heroism, in suitably modern industrial terms. Eight pages from the end of the novel, the author demonstrates his hero's political determination by observing that 'there was steel in his voice, the steel of a cold, unimpassioned hate', and on the second last page, the completion of his heroic transfiguration is signified by the closing reference to him as 'the hard young keelie with the iron jaw'.

However, although Mitchell establishes the city itself with roughly the same realistic techniques as he used in the earlier volumes, the element of characterisation in *Grey Granite* lies predominantly beyond the grasp of naturalism. And it is in this realm that Mitchell has to alter his literary mode of approach most radically.

Many writers from rural backgrounds have viewed the modern pheno-menon of the city with distrust, as a subject inherently unsuited to art. In her second novel, *Glitter of Mica,* Jessie Kesson, who, hailing from the rural North-east, proudly defends the land of her upbringing against the expanding modern urban reality of Scotland, considers thoughtfully:

> Edinburgh. Glasgow. Aberdeen. Dundee. How small Scotland sounded, summed up by its four main cities, but what a width of world its little villages stravaiged.[29]

Almost thirty years before this, Edwin Muir's tour of his homeland had provoked a similar conclusion, and although he badly overstates his case, and although his main interest in the subject is sociological rather than literary, Muir's application of this observation to character is of direct relevance to the modern novelist, the writer contending:

> For variety and originality of character are produced by an immediate and specific environment; and that, in modern life, counts for less and less; it is being disintegrated on every side, and seems to be, indeed, a life-form of the past.[30]

Muir's socialist ideals helped him to come to terms with this situation, and similarly, as a practising communist, Mitchell makes this modern erosion of the 'specific environment'—represented deliberately throughout the trilogy —work towards his own advantage. Thus, where someone like Jessie Kesson finds the steady industrialisation of modern society a handicap in that the specifically rural experience from which she draws her strength is becoming progressively rarer in real life, Mitchell manages to cope with the situation by political means, and this subsequently is reflected in his art.

Strangely enough, the rural novelist Hardy, not the urban Dickens, provided the most apposite comment upon the particular problems of characterisation introduced by modern industrialisation for the novelist when, in a rather laboured passage in one of his early pastorals, his description of John Smith the mason leads to a general comparison between rustic figures and urban ones:

> In common with most rural mechanics, he had too much individuality to be a typical "working-man"—a resultant of that beach-pebble attrition with his kind only to be experienced in large towns, which metamorphoses the unit Self into a fraction of the unit Class.[31]

Hardy's personal preferences lead him to overgeneralise, and many modern urban novelists, from Alan Sillitoe and David Storey in England, to George Blake and William McIlvanney in Scotland, have successfully represented the often heroic survival of the human spirit within even the most socially deprived urban environment. However, the sheer magnitude of the city and the sheer size of its population do indeed introduce problems for the urban novelist, and this largely explains the greater stylisation of *Grey Granite*.

The main problem facing Mitchell here is that, as a city, Duncairn has a population which in force of numbers defies the kind of individualisation which the inhabitants of both Kinraddie and Segget demanded, and received. Mitchell therefore requires a means by which he can convey the typical experience of the city dweller without completely sacrificing his personality as an individual. The main method by which he achieves this is by extending the narrative device used in *Cloud Howe* to represent the increasing social and political polarisation of Segget, where the multiple-voiced narrator gave a sense of class solidarity completely lacking in the portrait of Kinraddie. In *Grey Granite*, the customary anonymity of the narrator who relates the experience of the typical 'keelie' deliberately degenerates into a vague facelessness which Mitchell uses to reflect the widespread social hardships endured in the city and the urgent need for practical political solutions. And, appropriately, this device is used more and more towards the end of the book, as the political theme gathers momentum.

In 'Epidote', Mitchell allows father, mother and daughter in an unspecified Paldy Parish household to relate their personal responses to urban life in an episode containing a starkness strongly reminiscent of the introductory chapter of Walter Greenwood's celebrated portrait of the life of the proletariat, *Love on the Dole*. Towards the end of the section, Mitchell articulates the compelling demands made by Jim Trease's Communist rally upon the working man of Duncairn by giving the witness who describes the scene a multiple personality in spite of his lively status as a character in his own right, being hailed by his wife as '*Will!* or *Peter!* or *Tam!* (*SQ,* p 393). In 'Sphene', Mitchell employs exactly the same method in the description of the Young League dance from the inside, only this time the narrator is appreciably younger and his girlfriend calls him, '*Bob!* or *Will* or *Leslie*' (*SQ,* p 429). In 'Apatite', the most successful use of this unspecified urban narrator occurs in the description given of Ewan's release from prison (*SQ,* pp 456–7), although here Mitchell demonstrates the anonymity of the narrator by the more obvious means of denying him a name altogether. In the rather whimsical passage in 'Zircon' which focuses upon the typical concerns of a young city couple, however, the man is no more heavily particularised by being accorded the name of John Cushnie (*SQ,* pp 474–6), and the same goes for the sympathetic 'keelie' simply called Bob through whom Mitchell represents Ewan's increasing political credibility (*SQ,* pp 478–80). Four pages later, however, the author evokes sympathy by concentrating upon the natural concern of a Footforthie wife for her husband's welfare after the explosion at Gowans and Gloag's, and the sympathy gains a political edge when he generalises her experience by providing a multiple choice of names for her spouse. The wife considers fretfully, 'And John—Peter—Thomas—Neil—Oh God, he was there, in Furnaces, Machines—it was and it couldn't be Gowans and Gloag's.' Finally, four pages from the end of the novel, Mitchell emphasises the almost irresistible claims of Jim Trease and his Communism, when the multiple narrator, 'Jim . . . or Sam . . . or Rob' defies the injunctions of his multiple wife, and promises to support the hunger march.

As Cloud Howe suggested, therefore, with the move to the city Mitchell's characterisation had to move from dealing with the unit of the individual to embrace whole groups. The narrative technique examined above gives both a suitably animated and appreciably broad picture of the Duncairn pro-letariat. However, Mitchell's equally formalised attempt to represent the sectors opposed to the proletariat is less successful.

In Grey Granite, the forces opposing the proletarian motion for political reform are divided into two groups, the popular and the official, and both of these reactionary elements are condemned through caricature. The respectable bourgeoisie who resent this threat to their security are conveniently gathered together in Ma Cleghorn's guesthouse in true stage convention, in the same way as the Segget bourgeoisie are grouped together in the passage describing Robert's afternoon tea party in Cloud Howe. However, as in the earlier episode, the satiric execution is too easily effected, and therefore the reactionary political force which Miss Murgatroyd, Ena Lyons, Mr Quaritch and Mr Piddle are meant to signify appears negligible.

Mitchell himself was under no illusions about the magnitude of the task facing those who, like himself, were intent on destroying the capitalist structure of modern society, and he fully appreciated the size of the 'knock-out blow' (to use John MacLean's combative phrase[32]) that it would take for the working classes to emerge victorious from the class struggle. In this light, then, it is strange that he should have been accused of a kind of dogmatic complacency in his representation of the official reactionary forces opposing the proletariat in Grey Granite, and I feel that much of this criticism arises from a misunderstanding of his purposes.

Throughout Grey Granite, concise impressionistic vignettes are run together to pillory the forces pitted directly and indirectly against the proletariat, from the hostile press and corrupt city councillors to the traditional parliamentary representatives, the clergy and the police. Undeniably, the means of pillorying these sacrificial victims—the Reverend Edward MacShillock, Bailie Brown, Lord Provost Speight and the Chief Constable—are fairly crude, and yet it is unjust to criticise the author on the grounds that he fails to make these figures any rounder than the boarding-house residents. The whole point that Mitchell is making about these official reactions is that the roles themselves, and not just the people fulfilling them, are effectively redundant. As the book progresses, the systematic satirical episodes increase from the token examples contained in 'Epidote' and 'Sphene' to two in 'Apatite' and three in 'Zircon', and this methodical pattern underlines the monotonous formality of reactionary official policy, which becomes increasingly set in its opposition to the call for reform the more apparent the need for that reform becomes. Of course, Mitchell must plead guilty to the charge that he did not take sufficient care over the individual satirical portraits, but in this case the basic reason for resorting to caricature in the first place is itself wholly justifiable.

As the element of characterisation indicates in particular, therefore, *Grey Granite* is generally a more sophisticated work than *Sunset Song* and *Cloud Howe* although, as the transitional book in the trilogy, the latter does prepare the way for the more formal approach of the urban novel. The greater stylisation is in fact hinted at in the 'Cautionary Note' pinned to the start of *Grey Granite* in which Mitchell explains that he altered his city's name from Dundon to Duncairn when over-zealous critics latched on to the derivative nature of his original compound and identified his fictive locale with actual Scottish cities: instead, he insists, 'it is merely the city which the inhabitants of the Mearns . . . have hitherto failed to build' (*SQ*, p 356). Duncairn, then, is a representative setting which is not as heavily particularised as either Kinraddie or Segget.

The granite image of the title of the urban novel obviously refers literally to the basic building material used in Duncairn, and metaphorically it also describes Ewan's unflinching and forthright temperament, which dates back to the days of his youth and contrasts so sharply with Robert's dreamy political aspirations in *Cloud Howe*. Mitchell describes the substance of grey granite in his essay on 'Aberdeen' as 'one of the most enduring and indestructible and appalling building-materials in use on our planet', and his subsequent reference to its 'starkly grim and uncompromising' property (*SH*, p 97) provides a neat summary of Ewan's austere political disposition. However, nowhere in the actual text of *Grey Granite* itself does the author make reference to the terms which provide the headings for the individual sections of the novel, and it seems that these terms are more than mere synonyms for granite, for they are loosely arranged in ascending order of hardness. As in *Cloud Howe*, this symbolic progression reflects thematic developments (although I would dispute the elaborate meanings Douglas Gifford reads into the gradation), the hardening granite representing both the general theme of the book and Ewan's personal political maturity. Nevertheless, the obscurity of this symbolic pattern indicates the greater degree of stylisation in the novel as a whole; and significantly, much of the more formulaic element of *Grey Granite* comes from the genre of socialist realism, whose influence had first become apparent in Mitchell's writing in his 1931 story, 'Thermopylae'.

The opening paragraph of *Grey Granite* plunges the reader unceremoniously into a modern urban environment without the cushioning effect of a formal introductory prelude. Both the abruptness of this opening and the intense sense of squalor conveyed within the passage itself strongly resemble the opening of *Mother*, the novel Gorky had presented only two years earlier as the model of socialist realism. Although the narrative voice is different—Chris's sensibility directly describes her new urban surroundings in *Grey Granite*, whereas the opening to *Mother* is omniscient in tone—both introductory paragraphs are literally packed with toxic and fetid allusions. In Duncairn, 'the street walls were dripping in fog', 'yellow fog' hangs on Chris's eyelashes, and she has 'the acrid taste of an ancient smoke' in her mouth, while the 'hand-rail like a famished snake' is 'warm, slimy' to her touch (*SQ,* p 357). The urban setting of *Mother* is no less sordid than Duncairn, Gorky describing how:

Every day the factory whistle shrieked tremulously in the grimy, greasy air above the workers' settlement. And in obedience to its summons sullen people, roused before sleep had refreshed their muscles, came scuttling out of their little grey houses like frightened cockroaches. They walked through the cold darkness, down the unpaved street to the high stone cells of the factory, which awaited them with cold complacency, its dozens of square oily eyes lighting up the road. The mud smacked beneath their feet. . . . Tall black smokestacks, stern and gloomy, loomed like thick clubs above the settlement.[33]

It is surely no coincidence that the writers who share this conception of the unhealthiness of the city are both of peasant extraction. And while there are other points of contact between *Mother* and *Grey Granite,* on the whole, these are more general, showing that Mitchell's intentions were roughly equivalent to Gorky's, although his book was not modelled specifically upon the Russian novel.

I indicated earlier how there is a greater interaction in *Cloud Howe* between the personal and political planes than in *Sunset Song,* and this development continues in *Grey Granite,* with the main protagonists shouldering greater responsibility for the elaboration of theme. In this final book, Chris and Ewan directly represent the two thematic strands emerging from the earlier volumes, and, as the political protagonist, young Ewan contrasts with the tragic figures of his father and his step-father by being presented as the typical Marxist hero who traditionally dominates the novel of socialist realism.

EWAN

Even in *Cloud Howe,* Ewan is being groomed for the heroic role he assumes in the urban novel, with Mitchell taking particular pains to stress—mostly through Chris's consciousness—Ewan's fearless and forthright qualities, his self-assurance and his enlightened moral attitude. His heart is also clearly in the right place, as his revulsion at Charlie Cronin's description of the squalor persisting in the Wyndes of Segget proves, and it is of moment to his later status as proletarian hero that his mother should view this act as something of a blooding, observing that her son 'was turning to look in the face of Life' (*SQ,* p 342). Despite Ewan's preoccupied detachment from contemporary standards at this juncture, therefore, his social sympathies are in no way stunted or misplaced.

Much of Ewan's subsequent development is treated on the level of metaphor. The granitic imagery employed to represent his 'starkly grim and uncompromising' temperament is really done to death. Indeed he is more of a symbolic figure than his mother. And although Chris's experience has its own sense of logic, the procedure by which Ewan transmutes to the diamond hardness of Zircon has, like the evolving heroism of Gladkov's Gleb and Gorky's Pavel, a compelling inevitability.

Ewan's major characteristic as a youth in *Cloud Howe* is his cool self-possession, and although self-assurance is a crucial property in the mature Marxist hero, before this quality can be put to its full use, he must first be won away from himself. Throughout 'Epidote', Ewan remains detached from his fellow workers at Gowans and Gloag's steelworks; Chris remarks generally that, 'human beings were never of much interest to him' (*SQ*, p 380). Despite standing aloof from social reality, however, he remains intensely serious, as both Robert, who 'had once told him he was born a prig; he'd no humour' (*SQ*, p 380), and Chris, who feels that 'fun was beyond Ewan' (*SQ*, p 382), acknowledge. This seriousness is manifested in his rather esoteric and self-indulgent interest in scientific progress, expressed most graphically in a paragraph placed midway through the section which could have been lifted from one of Mitchell's imaginative romances. His hero hails science as the key to mankind's glorious future, and looks forward to the human race storming the heavens. This *per ardua ad astra* form of idealism is not wholly reproachable in itself, but it does have an obvious romantic remoteness as an imaginative pipedream when not constrained by any practical consideration. The socialist realists were attempting to inject a practical sense of purpose into the traditional idealistic mandate embodied in the utopian literature of their predecessors. This practice is exemplified in one particular passage in *Mother* where Pavel's romantic idealism is qualified by an almost fanatical purposefulness. Gorky's hero proclaims that 'for the sake of that [future] life I am ready to do anything at all'.[34] Ewan is thus not wrong in a socialist sense to dream of mankind conquering the stars, but without the support of a practical scientific creed his ideas seem untenable. He, like Pavel, should be committed to working towards his goal, rather than just dreaming of it.

Ewan's sense of self-possession reaches its zenith in 'Epidote' when he earnestly declares to his mother, 'I'm neither you nor my father: I'm myself' (*SQ*, p 375); and, very much like *Spartacus*, the subsequent pages of the novel trace the steady erosion of this insular quality in the protagonist as he progressively adheres to communism.

Ewan, like Robert in the previous book, has to find out for himself the best political mode of approach, but he has two major advantages over his step-father in that his naturally sympathetic temperament is accompanied by an almost ruthless purposefulness and, unlike Robert, he is a child of the town, 'by love or by nature', his mother observing in 'Epidote' that 'Ewan born in a croft in Kinraddie knew little of the land, cared less, not his job— that was stoking a furnace in Gowans and Gloag's!' (*SQ*, p 385). His gravitation towards the Communist Party is thus both emotionally motivated, through his sympathetic affiliation with the working classes, and intellectually sustained by the formal education he receives in political theory from Ellen Johns—who as the typically liberated Marxist heroine of the novel of socialist realism is particularly closely related to Dasha in Gladkov's *Cement*—and, later on, from Jim Trease. By the close of 'Epidote', Ewan has advanced in both these ways, Ellen's pedagogic arguments, while not convincing him fully, at least forcing him to doubt himself, with the result that he becomes much more sympathetic to the general concerns of the workers in Duncairn and patches up his differences with Alick Watson and Norman Cruickshank at the smelter. An even more decisive step in his development is taken when the sight of police brutality towards the Communist marchers moves him to physical action to help defend the demonstrators.

In 'Sphene', Ewan is still haunted by the major act of violence he witnessed at the rally, although he remains unsympathetic in the main to Ellen's 'blah about history and Socialism' (SQ, p 404). He is still overly attached to his scientific manuals and is cynical about Ellen's faith in the proletariat as political instruments, asking himself, 'what was there in them that wasn't in the people of any class?', and contending haughtily, 'Some louts, some decent, the most of them brainless, what certain tool to be found in crude dirt?' (SQ, pp 404–5). However, he himself is being accepted, almost unwittingly, into the working classes who 'took you for one of themselves nowadays' (SQ, p 405); and now he has to make a conscious effort to resist the compelling claims they make upon his sympathies by telling himself peremptorily, but with a singular lack of conviction, 'They DON'T concern you. BREAK with it all' (SQ, p 405).

Ewan's loyalties are by now inescapable, and his visit to the Museum Gallery merely confirms him in his 'flaring savage sickness' at the atrocities perpetrated upon the lower classes throughout history. Not even his persisting incredulity, wondering, 'oh hell, what had it to do with you?', can prevent his socialist 'flame' from acquiring the all-consuming radiance of a Spartacus, Ewan now feeling, 'as though 'twas yourself that history had tortured, trodden on, spat on, clubbed down in you, as though you were every scream and each wound, flesh of your flesh, blood of your blood' (SQ, p 407). This marks another important step in Ewan's integration with the working classes, and his subsequent quest for practical political solutions— 'not oratory, please' (SQ, p 413)—through the Workers' League, and his efforts to provoke the Union into action at the steelworks are undertaken in complete disregard of his own welfare and seem especially creditable following his promotion to the Stores at Gowans and Gloag's. However, as Ellen points out midway through the section, 'your heart's not in it at all. Only your head and imagination' (SQ, p 414), and Ewan's non-Marxist rejoinder, 'You don't quarrel with History and its pace of change any more than you quarrel with the law of gravitation' shows his political immaturity.

The official political commitment continues, however, as Ewan tries vainly to oppose the factory's conversion to armaments manufacture towards the end of the section by arranging strike action and organising the more successful Young League dance at Hogmanay. In fact, this latter episode signifies his final assimilation within the proletariat, the anonymous narrator remarking that 'he didn't look a toff a bit, just one of the lads' (SQ, p 430). And after he delivers the closing speech, Ewan receives another Spartacus-like vision of his political destiny, of the communal demands of the proletariat for whom he must sacrifice his own independent identity, with the result that finally, 'that Ewan Tavendale that once had been, the cool boy with the haughty soul and cool hands, apart and alone, self-reliant, self-centred, slipped away out of the room as he stared, slipped away and was lost from his life forever' (SQ, p 430).

Having finally 'entered into the souls of the workers', as Gladkov says of Lukhava in *Cement*,[35] at the close of 'Sphene', the following section is devoted to Ewan's formal political indoctrination and his final initiation into the Communist Party. Through his experience of the strike, which recreates the open war of the classes upon a smaller scale, the hero exchanges the early belief in non-violent revolution for the more severe 'stark, sure creed that will cut like a knife' which is invoked again a third of the way through 'Apatite' (*SQ,* p 447). His traumatic prison experience finally kills off all his hopes of the proletariat ever achieving power without violence and, as Jim Trease predicts, Ewan emerges from prison converted to the communist viewpoint that, 'Only by force could we beat brute force, plans for peaceful reform were about as sane as hunting a Bengal tiger with a Bible' (*SQ,* p 457).

In 'Zircon', Ewan finally merges with the working class and his political maturity comes to a climax, leaving him fully engaged as a Communist agitator. Although his political activities prove detrimental to his personal welfare, precipitating his departure from Gowans and Gloag's and limiting his stay at Bailie Gawpus's shop to a term of a few days, Ewan stands by his principles, with the result that the last job he is seen to secure, at Stoddart's the granite-mason's, is of the most menial kind, Chris naturally enough experiencing considerable difficulty in coming to terms with the idea of, 'EWAN A LABOURER!' (*SQ,* p 474). Homogenised by his dusty overalls, Ewan merely appears 'a chap from the granite-works' (*SQ,* p 479), and finally even Ellen is forced to realise his representative status as the definitive working man when she concludes that 'he was the keelies, all of them, himself' (*SQ,* p 489). Four pages after this, Mitchell extends this symbolic image of his hero when he depicts Ewan and Trease, the two main Communist Party activists, as, 'soldiers who met a moment at night under the walls of a town yet unstormed', and the last time the reader meets Ewan his political metamorphosis is complete, as he himself is now just one member of the industrial proletariat, albeit a politically committed one, ending up as 'the hard young keelie with the iron jaw' (*SQ,* p 495).

Throughout the latter stages of *Cloud Howe* until the end of *Grey Granite* Ewan's character develops in specific stages, so that the insular and independent youth of *Cloud Howe* gradually merges with the proletariat and ends utterly devoted to the Communist offensive. In the process, Mitchell adheres to the Marxist concept of heroism established in the novel of socialist realism such as *Cement* and *Mother*.

The major characteristic of this Marxist hero is his capacity for self-sacrifice, for self-abnegation, as opposed to self-advancement and self-aggrandisement. This is introduced as the main requirement in *Cloud Howe*, where the spinners' rendition of 'The Red Flag' reminds Chris of Chae Strachan, 'who had said the mission of the common folk was to die and give life with their deaths forever' (*SQ,* p 269). This is also the implication of Robert's politicised view of Christ, whom he feels 'was no godlet, but a leader and hero' (*SQ,* p 301). It is significant that in his dissatisfied survey of the exhibits in the Museum Gallery in 'Sphene' Ewan should specifically question why there is no bust of Spartacus on show, for in the historical novel Mitchell presents the gladiator as the definitive altruistic proletarian hero—indeed, according to his correspondence with Helen Cruickshank, as the very model for Ewan himself. The pivotal moment in Ewan's political development could in fact be straight out of the English novel, the Scots hero finally affirming of the working folk that 'the blood and bones and flesh of them all, their thoughts and their doubts and their loves were his, all that they thought and lived in were his' (SQ, p 430).

In both *Mother* and *Cement*, one of the ways in which the protagonist demonstrates his heroic fortitude is by resisting the threat made to his greater political destiny by romantic involvement. Gladkov's hero Gleb finally comes to accept this condition of self-denial in both himself and his wife Dasha in *Cement*, and in *Mother*, Gorky's stern hero Pavel has to reject the advances of Sasha before going on to consolidate his heroic status. In *Grey Granite*, Ewan's political future is directly threatened by his relationship with Ellen, and he must show his dedication to the main cause by quashing his romantic instincts.

The relationship between Ewan and Ellen follows the general pattern set in the socialist realist prototypes, of conciliation followed by separation. The political similarities between the two idealistic socialists are formally represented in 'Sphene' in their joint involvement in the Young League and in the dance at the end of the section which links them romantically as well as ideologically. From this point on, however, Ewan's political involvement becomes more and more pronounced, while Ellen becomes increasingly prepared to sacrifice her socialist principles to her affair with Ewan: as he becomes progressively less insular in his outlook, so Ellen becomes contrastingly self-indulgent in hers. Ellen's designs upon Ewan become increasingly selfish throughout the later stages of the book, as she becomes more obsessed with the dream of acquiring middle-class comforts. Ewan's interests lie elsewhere, however, Mitchell's hero realising during his salutary visit to Jim Trease's home in 'Zircon' that everything must be sacrificed to the one overpowering mission, which means, 'Neither friends nor scruples nor honour nor hope for the folk who took the workers' road' (SQ, p 482). From this point on, the Communist struggle monopolises Ewan's attention, and this of course brings the inevitable break with Ellen ever closer.

Mitchell has been criticised on the grounds that Ewan is inhumane in his final rebuff of his girlfriend, but I feel that within the author's prescribed aims for his hero the weakness lies in a different direction. The protagonist's stern political commitment itself demands the split with Ellen, and this has already been prepared for well in advance. However, in shifting the burden of the blame on to Ellen, Mitchell weakens Ewan's status as proletarian hero. It is understandable that she should leave the Communist Party because of her dissatisfaction with their severe revolutionary methods, but the additional reasons she submits for taking this step are contrastingly unsatisfactory. She tells Ewan, 'And I've left because I'm sick of being without decent clothes, without the money I earn myself, pretty things that are mine, that I've worked for' (SQ, p 490). Although Ewan's refusal to be compromised by Ellen's personal aims of respectability becomes more admirable in the light of Jock Cronin's and Jeannie Grant's sell-out in *Cloud Howe*, therefore, Mitchell fails to exploit the break between Ewan and Ellen for its full emotional and political impact. Indeed, lacking the fine tension created even in the early story 'One Man with a Dream' between the hero's personal and communal loyalties, rather than paying tribute to Ewan's heroic fortitude, the act finally pays greater homage to Ellen's egregious failings.

The slipshod treatment of Ewan's romantic experience does minimal damage to his credibility as Marxist hero, however. The main way in which he expresses this quality is in his submission to the communist cause which, again very like Spartacus's political inspiration, assumes the all-important status of a god.

One of the less obvious ways in which Mitchell distinguishes between Ewan and Ellen is in the respective images they have of God. As a modern socialist, Ellen has a rational scientific approach to life. Her efforts to teach 'Rank Materialism' in school earns her an official reprimand in the opening section of *Grey Granite*. The only deity she finds a place for in this non-religious universe is a reprehensibly self-indulgent Lawrentian god of sensuality which she discovers after 'making Ewan whole again', Ewan's lover referring to 'the terror and wonder of those first moments that made you suddenly so frightened of God because there must be a God after all' (*SQ*, p 466). The divinity that Ewan uncovers in his transformation from heretic to communist evangelist, on the other hand, is impressive and deserving.

In *Cloud Howe*, Chris regards her son's ideological impartiality as an advantage, observing fondly that 'he'd do strange things yet in the world, Ewan, who hadn't a God and hadn't a faith and took not a thing on the earth for granted' (*SQ*, p 339). Early in *Grey Granite*, she personally endorses this freethinking attitude, and from her detached viewpoint she interprets Robert's socialism in hindsight as a substitute for the more traditional religious responses which were both socially and spiritually harmful, 'hurting life, hurting death' (*SQ*, p 375). In 'Epidote', Ewan himself, still politically uninvolved, rejects the traditional gnostic stance when he counters Alick's incredulous query that 'you surely believe there's something, man?' with 'Maybe, but I don't think it's God' (*SQ*, p 391). It is significant in view of this preliminary demand for a redefinition of religion, that the first direct reference made to Marx just over twenty pages later introduces him as an icon, an image in a picture hung above the table at Ewan's first Young League meeting. Five pages after this, Ma Cleghorn explicitly describes communism as a religion when she tells Chris:

> Och, this Communism stuff's not canny . . . it's just a religion though the Reds say it's not and make out that they don't believe in God. They're dafter about Him than the Salvationists are . . . (*SQ*, p 417).

Typically free and easy, Chris replies that 'if Ewan wanted God she wouldn't try and stop him', although she has been especially suspicious of all creeds since Robert's death.

In 'Apatite', Mitchell concentrates upon the extreme demands of self-denial and self-effacement which the communist faith makes of its disciples. The offer of help Jim Trease gives to Ewan after his victimisation by the police rests on the understanding that 'the Communists would exploit the case to the full—for their own ends first, not for Ewan's'. Trease explains further that 'Ewan was nothing to them, just as he, Jim Trease, was nothing' (*SQ*, p 454). Ewan later considers the disciplines of his creed from the point of view of a wholehearted believer:

> And he thought of Trease saying that he and the rest of the Reds were nothing, they just worked the will of history and passed. . . . And suddenly Ewan's mind trembled on the verge of something, something that he couldn't name, maybe God, that made this strange play with lives and beliefs. . . (*SQ*, p 463).

The hero's political dedication attains a religious fervour in 'Zircon'. Mitchell intensifies his efforts to identify Ewan's communism as a modern form of religion. The exercise of coming to terms with what Mitchell calls, in 'The Wrecker', 'the flinty actualities of existence' (*SH*, p 110) demands a fanatical zealousness, as Ewan confesses to his mother when he remarks, 'as for what you call my beliefs, they're just plain hell—but then—they ARE real' (*SQ*, p 470). To Chris, however, the fact that Ewan's faith is a 'real' form of religion is immaterial, and she remains doubtful to the end regarding all organised doctrine, telling Ewan bluntly on the second last page of the book:

> The world's sought faith for thousands of years and found only death or unease in them. Yours is just another dark cloud to me—or a great rock you're trying to push up a hill.

Ewan's objection, that 'it was the rock was pushing him', is indeed the apostolic proclamation of the proselyte, and his closing speech is suitably self-revealing, as he declares:

> There will always be you and I, I think, Mother. It's the old fight that maybe will never have a finish, whatever the names we give to it—the fight in the end between FREEDOM and GOD.

Like all religions, then, Ewan's communism is pursued at the expense of his personal freedom, and like Gorky's hero Pavel and Gladkov's Gleb, he ends in utter servility to its principles.

As a Marxist hero, Ewan is entrusted with the task of imposing his politically enlightened sensibilities upon the social circumstances depicted in the novel, and the more didactic portions of *Grey Granite* are split between him and his political mentors Jim Trease, and to a lesser extent, Ellen Johns. Happily, however, the Marxist solution emerges gently from the convincing portrayal of the increasingly desperate social situation prevailing in the representative city of Duncairn in the early nineteen-thirties.

As the trilogy progresses, there is a steady increase in the driving force of economic necessity as a motive for political change. Towards the end of *Cloud Howe*, social conditions become increasingly grave, with the deprivation in the Old Toun part of Segget being exacerbated by the implementation of draconian measures like the Means Test. The dreadful state in which the average Cowgate family lives, as encountered by Ewan in 'Sphene' in the urban novel, signifies a drastic degeneration. In addition, both

Ewan and Chris suffer personally from these appalling conditions, which force the former to seek work of the most menial kind in order merely to earn a livelihood, and force his mother to accept work in Ma's guesthouse and finally to enter, against her own better judgement, into a marriage of convenience with Ake, to 'sell herself like a cow, a cow's purpose, in order to keep a roof over her head' (SQ, p 447).

Throughout the trilogy, Mitchell contrasts these increasingly grave signs of social deprivation with consistent evidence of the incompetence and hostility of the traditional political bodies charged with the responsibility for improving matters. In Sunset Song, Chae looks forward cynically to the forthcoming by-election, observing that, 'it would make no difference who got in, one tink robber was bad as another, Tory as Liberal' (SQ, p 80). In Cloud Howe, Ake Ogilvie includes Labour in his political denunciation, remarking caustically that, 'there was good in none of the parties, Labour or Tory or Liberal or any' (SQ, p 326), and Chris endorses Ake's opinion when she observes fourteen pages later, 'were the liars and cheats called Labour or Tory they'd feather their own nests and lie to the end'. In Grey Granite, the anonymous narrator at Gowans and Gloag's gives Labour exemption from the main force of his political criticism but, as the book proceeds, Labour are subjected to increasingly destructive ridicule through the portrait of the complacent Bailie Brown, 'that respectable Labour man' (SQ, p 397), who is characterised by his avoidance of 'the flinty actualities of existence'.

Given the social decay as it intensifies throughout the course of the trilogy, the official political channels are thus damned by their apathy or by their sheer incompetence. However, in the minor theme of contraception which runs right through the volume as a side-issue to the main socio-political theme, Mitchell, taking advantage of the advances which Lawrence and Joyce had made in the free representation of sexual matters in fiction, indicates a way in which science may help alleviate the social destitution. And this of course is what he hopes the political science of Marxist-Communism will do on a greater scale.

In Hanno, Mitchell fleetingly considers contraception as a potential means of 'solving the world's problems of over-population' with a view to reducing the general scale of poverty (Hanno, p 36), and this theme is pursued at greater length in the Quair. In the rural areas at the turn of the century the lack of birth control results in increased social hardship due to overpopulation, as is the case with Jean Guthrie, who is one of thirteen children, and John Guthrie, who comes from a family of nine. In fact, John Guthrie's unenlightened attitude plunges his whole family into financial hardship, for when the twins are born Chris remarks that 'there'd been barely room for them all before that time, now they'd have to live like tinks' (SQ, p 39).

In Cloud Howe, despite Dite Peat's prurient interest in the methods of contraception which he discovered being advertised freely in London, the Segget burghers preserve the traditionally fatalistic attitude of the country dweller towards children, that 'folk had bairns, they came with the seasons, there was no escape were you wedded and bedded' (SQ, p 293). Chris herself is contrastingly enlightened in this matter, however, for not only do she and

Robert take contraceptive precautions themselves (*SQ,* p 334), but she tries vainly to persuade the puritanical and sanctimonious women's institute to convince others to do so. Meanwhile, over-population in the industrial sector of Segget adds significantly to the already grim social situation:

> For bairns came thick as ever they'd come, folk cut their costs in all things but cradles, down in Old Toun they squawked into life, the bairns, in rooms that were packed out already. The less the work the more of the creatures, they bred fair disgusting old Leslie would say, and it showed you the kind of dirt that they were, living crowded like that, four-five in a room, in houses that were not fit for pig-rees. 'Twas Infernal, just: the men should be libbed . . . (*SQ,* pp 337–8).

The social need for birth control intensifies in *Grey Granite.* The daughter of the representative Cowgate family introduced at the beginning of the book laments the poverty she has been born into and blames her parents, complaining that 'If they couldn't afford to bring up their weans decent why did father and mother have them?' (*SQ,* p 370). In this volume, however, Chris finds an ally in her promotion of contraceptive measures in Ellen, who in her early days as the political firebrand earns a reprimand for trying to introduce sex education into her teaching curriculum, 'So I've to leave off physiology and it's Nature Study now—bees, flowers, and how catkins copulate' (*SQ,* p 393). In 'Sphene', Ellen appears fiercely objective in the practical standpoint she takes upon the subject of birth-control, as she answers Chris's loaded inquiry that 'you'll want a baby sometime?' with the acutely impersonal observation, 'There were thousands of unwanted babies already and most of *them* should never have been born' (*SQ,* pp 410–1).

Mitchell therefore endorses contraception on the grounds that it promotes complete romantic freedom, as with Ewan and Ellen and Chris and Robert, while curbing the social problems of over-population. Through Chris and Ellen, he sets out the enlightened modern arguments for birth control.

The theme of contraception which runs through the trilogy demonstrates a minor way in which the general state of modern society can be changed for the better. This backs up the formal Marxist theme of the volume, that the universal dialectic of change can be controlled and put to work for the benefit of all.

In his essay on 'Religion' in *Scottish Scene,* Mitchell promotes this idea of man's controllable destiny when he affirms that 'men are not merely the victims, the hapless leaves storm-blown, of historic forces, but may guide if they cannot generate that storm' (*SH,* p 171). Throughout *Sunset Song* and *Cloud Howe,* he demonstrates the incentive for change in modern society, and the inability of the Kinraddie crofters and Robert and the Segget spinners respectively, as 'hapless leaves storm-blown', to dominate the historical principle has tragic consequences. However, Ewan's more disciplined Marxist approach is much more promising.

Ellen Johns, Jim Trease, and finally Ewan himself are Mitchell's three political spokesmen in *Grey Granite,* and through them the author articulates the formal Marxist arguments. All three at their most politically involved adumbrate the major doctrine of Marxist-Communism, which is a belief in the capacity of the proletariat as a concerted political force to achieve power by violent revolution and gain control over their historical destiny.

Robert's original valediction to the Kinraddie crofters at the end of the 'Epilude' to *Sunset Song* is indeed 'just sheer politics', and politics of a conventional Marxist nature at that. *Cloud Howe* carries on from this vision, plotting Robert's own despairing attempt with the Segget spinners to bring about the Marxist ideal of 'a war of the classes to bring fruit to the War' (*SQ,* p 269), the War which proved so costly to the crofting farmers of Kinraddie. In *Grey Granite*, Ellen Johns and Jim Trease regard history in an orthodox light as the conquering of the social forces of change. As the book develops, Ewan also approaches this subject from a Marxist viewpoint, coming to relish his role as being 'LIVING HISTORY ONESELF' (*SQ,* p 459), and viewing its capacity for bringing social improvement in an optimistic light in view of the formidable political force which the workers come to represent. This political optimism produces two particularly rousing idealistic Marxist visions (which appear in the later stages of the book) of the unremitting tidal wave of the proletarian revolution. The first comes upon Ewan as he is lying injured and humiliated in the police cell in 'Apatite' (*SQ,* p 452). The second appears to him in 'Zircon' in the more congenial environment of Jim Trease's house in Paldy (*SQ,* p 481). And just as MacDiarmid's Marxism produced some of his finest poetic effects, particularly in the three 'Hymns to Lenin', which Mitchell felt were 'among the world's most magnificent hymns to the high verities of life',[36] so also in *Grey Granite* Ewan's Marxist vision crystallises into superb individual images, appropriately appearing in the final two sections of the book. Mitchell's theme thus gains added strength from his impressive symbolism.

In 'Apatite', following the quasi-religious affirmation he receives upon considering Jim Trease's political philosophy, Ewan gains a heightened awareness of his own and the workers' political destiny, which endows the bus taking him home to Duncairn after the outing to Kinraddie with a symbolic status, so that, 'it seemed a moment that the shambling bus was the chariot of Time let loose on the world roaring down long fir-darkened haughs of history into the shining ways of to-morrow' (*SQ,* p 463). In 'Zircon', following his political confirmation, and again under the influence of Jim Trease, Ewan achieves an even more inspiring vision:

> Neither friends nor scruples nor honour nor hope for the folk who took the workers' road; just *life* that sent tiredness leaping from the brain; that sent death and wealth and ease and comfort shivering away with a dirty smell, a residuum of slag that time scraped out through the bars of the whooming furnace of History (*SQ,* p 482).

This climatic image is the finest in the whole book, encapsulating as it does the idea of the inevitability of the proletarian triumph over the hostile historical forces, given the benefit of time. This is the same political equation that MacDiarmid dramatises in his superb four-line poem 'On the Ocean Floor' in *Second Hymn to Lenin*, in which the formation of coral reef from the skeletons of the dying foraminifera captures brilliantly the sense of the inevitability of the workers' victory in the historical struggle. Mitchell's image is not quite as clinically precise as MacDiarmid's, but it also is a model of compression, and in fact it has a superficial advantage in that the industrial nature of the analogy forges a stronger connection with modern society.

Seven pages after this, and only seven pages from the end of the volume, Ewan again finds symbolic meaning, this time in the storm raging outside in the Glen of Drumtochtie:

> He went to the window and looked out at the storm, solid in front of the inn it went by, speckled in the lights, a great ghost army hastening east, marching in endless line on line, silent and sure; and he thought a minute *Our army's like that, the great lost legion, nothing to stop it in heaven or hell . . . (SQ,* p 489).

Again this is an impressive variation upon formal Marxist symbolism. Mitchell uses the simple image of the storm to represent the irresistible force of the proletariat as a political power. The dominant symbol in Gladkov's *Cement* conveys a very similar idea, though more soberly, and this time the Russian novelist's image is more suitably industrial and again perhaps more disciplined, the protagonist of the book averring, 'With cement we're going to have a great building-up of the Republic. We are Cement, comrades: the working-class.'[37] Mitchell, however, was typically self-conscious about using abstract symbolism, and although this has a much more functional character in the trilogy than the obtrusive symbolic passages which appear periodically in his English novels, just after Ewan makes the last allusion quoted above he is made to 'close it away in impatient contempt' on the count that, 'Bunk symbolism was a blunted tool'.

Grey Granite thus operates upon a more stylised level than its predecessors, but the formal Marxist concepts, which come to dominate the urban novel on the level of metaphor and symbol as well as theme, draw considerable strength from the earlier volumes, particularly through the affinity Mitchell establishes throughout between the peasantry and the proletariat, as the 'common folk.'

Chris is of peripheral importance to the Marxist theme of the trilogy, and she repeatedly questions both Robert's and Ewan's political activities in *Cloud Howe* and *Grey Granite*. On occasion, as the quintessential peasant, she seems directly opposed to the proletariat, replying to the political jibes of Meg Watson's father, for instance, that her peasant class, 'was digging its living in sweat while yours lay down with a whine in the dirt' (*SQ,* p 377). However, although she has inherited much of the proud peasant 'smeddum' of her class, Chris herself provides a sturdy link between the peasantry and the city proletariat as the daughter of a crofter and the mother of a 'keelie', who represents herself carrying 'the little torch' between the two (*SQ,* p 386).

Similarly, when Ewan sees the effect of the capitalist form of farming in Fordoun, he voices his objections by expressing a preference for a more humble form of existence even in the alien environment of the town, on the pretext that 'he'd rather bide in a town and wear a damned apron than work in this countryside' (*SQ,* p 135). And in Robert's 'sheer politics' which bring the book to a close by looking forward to a socialist future to follow the war of the classes, the political differences between peasantry and proletariat are again elided when he asks rhetorically of the dead crofters, 'need we doubt which side the battle they would range themselves did they live to-day . . .?' (*SQ*, p 193).

Mitchell's heroine herself drops her cloak of political neutrality in *Cloud Howe* when she tells Stephen Mowat that, 'if it came to the push between you and the spinners I think I would give the spinners my vote' (*SQ*, p 275), and this occurs only three pages after Jeannie Grant has told her with some justification, 'You're a socialist the same as I am, you know.' In the mounting political aggression of 'Stratus', Chris again adopts a less than neutral stance when she refuses to be party to Mowat's attempt to hinder the miners' strike by organising an army of volunteers to offset the worst consequences of their industrial action in society at large. In the following volume, she reacts defiantly against the prudish gentility of Ena Lyons be telling her, 'You see I'm awfully common myself' (*SQ*, p 392), without drawing any further distinction between her fellow peasants and the urban proletariat of Duncairn.

In *Grey Granite*, both Ake and Ewan ratify Chris's political synthesis of country and city dwellers. In Segget, still at the start of the book, Ake is 'aye sticking up for the working men' in general (*SQ*, p 360), irrespective of their location, and Ewan also glosses over the differences between peasantry and proletariat when, visualising radical artistic alternatives to the exhibits on show, his heart is claimed by the 'common folk' in the Museum Gallery in 'Sphene'.

Whether in the past or the present or even the future, then, and whether in the country, the town or the city, Mitchell views human history in terms of the straightforward Marxist opposition between the two social groups defined in *Sunset Song* as 'gentry and simple' (*SQ*, p 52). Whether the 'simple' be the Kinraddie crofters, the Segget spinners or the Duncairn proletariat, they are fellow combatants in the same campaign against the 'gentry'.

Although the trilogy becomes gradually more schematised as it progresses, the abstract Marxist symbolism which appears in the final volume is sustained by the thematic implications of all three of the work's components. However, Mitchell took full advantage in the *Quair* of the time which had elapsed since the publication of the two definitive Russian novels of socialist realism, which were so influential in the writing of *Grey Granite* especially. For just as the author questions the value of his Marxist symbolism in the final volume, so Ewan's political views themselves are subjected to some doubt as a means of exacting the requisite changes in society. Ultimately, Mitchell's approval of Ewan's revolutionary form of communism is discretionary, the author frankly dramatising the conditions and obstacles opposed to the fulfilment of his aims.

Throughout the trilogy, Mitchell casts aspersions upon the integrity of all those who achieve political power, whether they belong to right-wing parties or to Labour itself. In *Cloud Howe*, Robert attributes the failure of the General Strike to the selfishness of the men in charge, exclaiming that 'the leaders had betrayed the Strike, they'd been feared that they would be jailed, the leaders, they had sold the Strike to save their skins' (*SQ*, p 309). Fourteen pages further on, Jock Cronin and Jeannie Grant sell out to the politically inert Labour Party which is criticised relentlessly throughout the trilogy, and the last the reader learns of them is that Jock has become an official representative of Ramsay MacDonald's National Labour government—which Mitchell condemns savagely in 'The Wrecker'—and he finally ends poised to enter parliament, which represents the greatest defection of all. In *Grey Granite*, Selden is the villain who deserts his post, although there is something directly criminal about his act, as he absconds with the Communist Party funds. In the interests of balance, however, the author takes care to stress the understandable motives behind his action, Ewan explaining to Ellen that he had 'been sick of unemployment and his wife wasn't well' (*SQ*, p 488).

The influence of personal circumstances is particularly harmful at a grass roots level also. The anonymous Duncairn 'keelie' in *Grey Granite* is deflected from political involvement by his personal ambitions, confessing that 'if you got half a chance what you wanted was marriage and a house and a wife and a lum of your own' (*SQ*, p 390). This conflict is elaborated at greater length in the final section of the volume, in which the narrator directly presents communist agitation as being detrimental to the individual's social prospects; and of course Ewan and Ellen epitomise this conflict between personal desire and public duty, with Ewan finally accepting under Jim Trease's guidance, that romance and the Party are incompatible concerns, that 'there wasn't much time for the usual family business when you were a revolutionist' (*SQ*, p 481).

Even given the basic sympathy with the principles of communism, then, there is no assurance that the individuals in question, whether they be in the forefront or merely on the fringes of the Party effort, will stick to their task. And although Mitchell indicates that the Communist Party is in the workers' best interest, he also shows that there is no guaranteeing that the Party, deserving cause though it is, will win their support in the first place, the support which ultimately determines the success of the whole venture.

In each of the three component parts of the *Quair*, the authorial spokesmen also acknowledge the workers' general tendency to fail to either recognise or to do what is in their own best interest. In *Sunset Song*, Long Rob counters Chae's idealistic hope of a working-class revolution by observing cynically that 'the common folk when they aren't sheep are swine, Chae man' (*SQ*, p 158), and as such, clearly they are unfit political instruments. In *Cloud Howe*, Rob's astute counterpart in Segget, Ake Ogilvie, similarly frowns upon Chris's theory that the desperate plight of the people will result in violence. He exclaims sarcastically, 'Revolution? They'll starve and say nothing. Or "Come walk on my face and I'll give you a vote!"' (*SQ*, p 341). And in *Grey Granite*, Ewan has even greater personal cause to feel aggrieved at the capriciousness of the populace of Duncairn: he complains in 'Epidote,' 'you can't blame a union if the chaps who belong to it won't attend its meetings' (*SQ*, p 390). His subsequent inability to persuade the complacent Gowans and Gloag's workers to take strike action prevents him from harbouring any illusions about those he is trying to help, so that finally Ewan and Jim Trease resolutely continue to 'hack out the road ahead', despite the fact that 'neither had a single illusion about the workers: they weren't heroes or gods oppressed, or likely to be generous and reasonable when their great black wave came flooding at last' (SQ, p 481).

Even assuming the communists were to overcome these worries in their own camp, however, the hostile forces directly opposing them, as Mitchell pointed out explicitly in his letter to The Left Review published in 1935, themselves add up to a quite formidable power. Ewan explains to Ellen in the final section of Grey Granite that 'capitalism had a hundred dodges yet to dodge its own end, Fascism, New Deals, Douglasism, War' (SQ, p 473).

Although Marxism is one of the major ideological and aesthetic influences in A Scots Quair, the trilogy nevertheless demonstrates that Mitchell could never have said with his friend Hugh MacDiarmid, 'I have found in Marxism all that I need.'[38] The Quair gradually discloses communism as the most promising political solution to the increasing destitution of modern society but, in keeping with the attitudes of the 'reformer', the author's approval of the communist line is not dogmatic, but guarded and restrained, balancing those factors recommending Ewan's political credo with reservations on its practical viability. Indeed, there is a perceptible sense of anti-climax when Ewan, honed to a political state of absolute immutability, finally disappears from the scene on his hunger march on the second last page of the volume. This subtle sense of bathos is most appropriate, in fact, because A Scots Quair is ultimately Chris's book, and as such, it should therefore end with her.

CHRIS

Mitchell's heroine is not directly involved in the main political theme of A Scots Quair, and she is not the political protagonist of any of the three novels. The political hero of Sunset Song is the peasant farmer, represented jointly by John Guthrie, Ewan Tavendale, Chae Strachan and Long Rob, whose passing from the scene Robert laments at the close of the book; Robert himself is the political protagonist of Cloud Howe, and young Ewan is his successor in Grey Granite. Although Chris herself has only a tenuous connection with the political theme, however, her personal intimacy with these individuals heightens the impact of their respective fates, all of which are attributed to social factors. 'God' kills her father (SQ, p 95), and the war kills Ewan, Chae and Rob in the first volume. 'The world' breaks Robert's heart and mind (SQ, p 447), and the strike action and Chris's miscarriage are tragically linked in the following volume. In the final book the Communist Party takes her son Ewan away from her, and leaves him pushing his onerous burden up the hill. However, although all these experiences are at the least extremely disturbing and more often devastating to Chris, she never alters her resolutely neutral political stance throughout the trilogy. Indeed, although her sympathies lie completely with the 'common folk', her ideological detachment appears exhaustive in Cloud Howe when she condemns the legacy left by the agricultural accident on the Nile to which Robert attributes civilisation itself:

. . . loyalty and fealty, patriotism, love, the mumbling chants of the dead old gods that once were worshipped in the circles of stones, christianity, socialism, nationalism—all—Clouds that swept through the Howe of the world, with men that took them for gods: just clouds, they passed and finished, dissolved and were done . . . (*SQ*, p 300).

Chris thus stands apart from the political theme of the trilogy, and yet her experience is not merely the connecting link between the volumes, it provides the dominant thematic strain of the whole work. Her political role in the proceedings may be passive but she responds to life and develops on a considerably deeper level than the political protagonists, ultimately representing the quasi-religious meaning that Mitchell himself found in life.

Mitchell has been done a disservice by critics such as Kurt Wittig and David Macaree who have foisted a heavily symbolic meaning upon the trilogy, holding Chris up as a national symbol, a kind of Scots Cathleen ni Houlihan . To restrict Mitchell's ideology to a purely national level is, as I indicated earlier, a denial of everything he stood for as a 'reformer', and likewise to force a nationalist message from *A Scots Quair* is to ignore those very factors which contribute most readily to the book's claims to greatness. When Mowat and Robert identify Chris with Scotland, apprehending her respectively as 'Scotland herself' (*SQ*, p 273) and 'Chris Caledonia' (*SQ*, p 298) they are merely casting her as the ultimate representative of her class, as the definitive peasant. The contexts in which the descriptions arise both confirm that the allusions apply to her character and indirectly reflect her political status, but there is nothing to indicate that either reference is symbolically suggestive or nationalistically inclined. Indeed, there is finally a far greater correspondence between Mitchell and the O'Casey of *The Plough and the Stars, The Silver Tassie* and *Red Roses for Me* than there is with the Yeats of *Cathleen ni Houlihan*.

Marxist theory has a particularly strong hold on the political theme of the trilogy, but it also spills over into the more profound areas of the book. As a 'blasphemer', Mitchell constantly approached life with unsentimental objectivity, and the 'Rank Materialism' which lands Ellen Johns in hot water with the education authorities in *Grey Granite* represents his own belief, outlined in the draft of one of his unfulfilled projects, in 'the apparently mechanical origin of life—an accident in a little by-pass of the chemical processes'.[39] Ellen's scientific rationalism thus stands in direct opposition to the traditional Christian belief in a divine intelligence standing behind life. She maintains that 'there wasn't a God at all. . . . He was just a silly old man the Jews worshipped and the world had really begun in a fire' (*SQ*, p 393).

Chris herself has compelling personal reasons for condemning the traditional Calvinist conception of God, as this is the very agency which 'kills' her father in the first volume, and this is the spectral figure to which Robert clings in the mental instability produced by his political disillusionment in the closing pages of *Cloud Howe*. Consequently, she criticises organised religion as a vain pursuit 'hurting life' as well as death, and in *Sunset Song* she defends her fellow Scots by playing down the part played in their lives by religious observance, affirming to her brother that the Scots folk, unlike other

European races, 'have never BELIEVED' (*SQ*, p 165). It is worth noting here also that the stances which Rob and Chae adopt in response to Mutch's orthodox Calvinist view of a stern God presiding over the world in *Sunset Song* are in turn atheistic and agnostic, Rob consciously trying to 'make a fool of God', while Chae 'was half on his side and half wasn't' (*SQ*, p 83). As his other books show, Mitchell the 'blasphemer' wavered between these two viewpoints.

In accordance with this unbelieving attitude, Mitchell affirms the material nature of existence throughout the trilogy, laying particular stress upon the physical realities of the human cycle of 'Birth, and life, and death' that he referred to in 1934. Thus, the Mowats of legendary times who make way for the modern social reality of Segget in *Cloud Howe* do so with an air of inevitability, as mere mortals who share the experience common to mankind. Mitchell's chronicler remarks with ironic abruptness, 'and they lived and they died and they went to their place' (*SQ*, p 203). The same view of human existence is later extended by Chris herself. She envisages the changes in the Howe which Trusta has perceived from its elevated vantage point with the passing of the ages, which finally welcomes man on to the natural scene as, 'the flicker of the little folk that came and builded and loved and hated and died, and were not, a crying and swarm of midges warmed by the sun to a glow and a dance' (*SQ*, pp 299–300).

Specific references to the cardinal events in the human cycle are frequently just as clinical. When Chris give birth in the final section of *Sunset Song*, the miracle of new life is apprehended with calm pragmatism, the mother describing her son as having 'a body as small and warm as a cat's, with a heart that beat steady and assured' (*SQ*, p 147). Six pages later, she expresses her contentment with life as a young wife and now also a mother again in physical terms, asking herself blissfully of her dependants, 'what more could she have or want than the two of them, body and blood and breath?'. And in *Cloud Howe*, Chris confines her view of the miracle of childbirth to its physical properties once more, again refusing to consider the greater spiritual implications of the event, remembering that Ewan 'had been your baby, been yours, been you, been less than that even' (*SQ*, p 295).

Mitchell is equally firm in his approach to the other pole of human experience, representing death time and again as the final reality. The spiritually disturbing image of skull and crossbones set against the figure of an hour-glass which Chris perceives inscribed on a Covenanter's gravestone early in *Sunset Song* looms over the trilogy in general as a grim reminder of the fate awaiting every human being. Chris herself in her youth is unaware of the morbid implications of the engravings, but it is pertinent that the girlish fear which comes upon her immediately afterwards in the graveyard is not a superstitious fear, rather a revulsion at the grizzly idea of the physical decay of the corpses beneath her feet, 'their bodies turned to skeletons now so that if you dug in the earth you'd find only their bones . . . and maybe there in the darkness worms and awful things crawled and festered in flesh grown rotten and black, and it was a terrifying place' (*SQ*, p 55). Subsequently in the trilogy, she dwells habitually and almost neurotically upon the physical significance of the deaths of her father, Ewan and Robert, repeatedly tormenting herself with the thought of their conclusive transformation from living quick to dead matter. And in *Cloud Howe*, this line of thought lurches uncertainly towards a general understanding of universal meaninglessness: Chris decides that her father 'died a coarse farmer in a little coarse house, hid in the earth and forgot by men, as forgot as your pains and your tears by God, that God that you knew could never exist' (*SQ*, p 235). Twice in *Cloud Howe* the sombre environment of the kirkyard fills Mitchell's heroine with further broodings upon death which, in the first instance, includes consideration of her own future fate, and in the second, inspires a formula for human life which is neat and compact, Chris thinking of, 'the folk that had once been bairns, and died, and nothing of them endured' (*SQ*, p 315).

John Muir, appropriately cast in the heavily Shakespearean role of the gravedigger, vigorously reinforces Chris's understanding of the futility of human life and the finality of death. His fatalistic outlook on life, embodied in his much-quoted catch-phrase that 'we all come to black flesh and a stink at the end', is his comic trademark as a character, but his final vision is sober and profound. Having expounded the social significance of Rob Moultrie's death as signifying the passing of an era in Segget, Muir goes on to apprehend the comprehensive principle of death and decay governing existence. This proves strangely reassuring to him, just as Chris's dying vision proves comforting to her. In the description of the gravedigger:

> . . . a queer calm came in the pit of his wame, he stopped in the sun to gley in a dream, 'twas as though they were shadows in the sunblaze he saw, nothing enduring and with substance at all, kirk and minister, and stones all around graved with their promised hopes for the dead, the ways and beliefs of all olden time—no more than the whimsies a bairn would build from the changing patterns that painted the hills (*SQ*, pp 336-7).

Mitchell's *Quair* is thus steeped in a candid materialism. As in the early novels, this produces a sharp note of despair. In his political and religious disillusionment, Robert is obviously the most suitable vehicle for the representation of the resultant sense of Absurdity which is the common response in Mitchell's early novels to the idea of the spiritual inconsequentiality of life. *Cloud Howe* is the most active book of the three in the exposition of this particular theme.

Even before embarking upon his ill-fated attempt to reform society, Robert experiences bouts of depression which intimate the futility of his mission in a world where the overriding reality is unpleasant. This despair is expressed in the renunciation of his Christian faith as 'a fantastic dream' in favour of a vision of quite horrific bleakness which introduces him to 'the fleshless grin of the skull and the eyeless sockets at the back of life' (*SQ*, p 212), a much more unnerving image than the sobering device which Chris perceived upon the Covenanter's gravestone in *Sunset Song*. In the following section, 'Cumulus', Chris articulates the same philosophical choice, using Robert's experience as the touchstone, between the Christian and an atheistic view of life, and she comes down firmly in favour of the latter: 'You knew that he knew he followed a dream, with the black mood REAL, and his hopes but mists' (SQ, p 236). In the final section of the intermediate book, she directly endorses this bleak vision of reality: 'There was neither direction, salvation, nothing but the storming black lour of the Clouds as the frosts and the fog of this winter came' (SQ, p 339). In view of Robert's experience in Cloud Howe, therefore, his black mood does indeed seem the most valid, and his conclusion at the end of the book that 'there is no hope for the world at all', unless a miraculous new faith should disclose itself, appears disturbingly accurate.

This sense of the hopelessness and meaninglessness of human existence persists in Grey Granite, in which Chris comes to appreciate much of the terrible desperation and loneliness that her husband had experienced. On the second page, she attempts to come to terms with the reality at the core of life, and again this reality offers little comfort, being perceived by her as 'those grim essentials' (SQ, p 358). At the close of the following section, she discovers what Mitchell later called, 'that remoteness of the human spirit that is man's terrible heritage', and just as with the author's sensitive hero Nansen, so with Chris also the knowledge 'sunk into the naked consciousness like a frozen knife', Mitchell writing in 'Sphene', 'and a feeling of terrible loneliness came on her standing so at that hour, knowledge of how lonely she had always been, knowledge of how lonely every soul was, apart and alone as she had been surely even at the most crowded hours of her life' (SQ, p 428). Four paragraphs later this impression of the vulnerability and isolation of the human spirit fills her with suppressed terror, when she considers her own situation and realises the privations which circumscribe her existence, concluding blackly that 'SHE HAD NOTHING AT ALL'.

The honesty with which Mitchell approaches life in A Scots Quair is often dauntingly frank. His materialistic attitude, involving an atheistic denial of spiritual meaning, constantly evokes despair. This makes the trilogy a thoroughly modern book, associating the author with those modern European writers from Kafka and Sartre to Camus and Beckett who have made high art out of the belief in the inherent hopelessness and incoherence of the human condition. However, although Mitchell partially shares the philosophical desolation of Kafka or Beckett in what Douglas Gifford calls his 'journey to despair', I believe he finally goes beyond the 'grotesque' to find a quasi-religious meaning denied these others.

The stern atheistic perspective tendered throughout the trilogy is balanced by a contrastingly sanguine affirmation of faith in the natural order, most frequently expressed as a simple land-love, though also manifested in Sunset Song through McIvor, the 'daft Highland poet' who is Ewan's best man, as a kind of Gaelic mysticism. The heroine, who in the persona of the 'Chris that was Murdoch, Chris of the land' (SQ, p 44) inherits an intuitive understanding of the 'earth-magic', is obviously the main proponent of this theme, although Ewan, who 'had fair the land in his bones' (SQ, p 29), and the Kinraddie crofters as a whole, for whom the earth represented their 'life and enduring love' (SQ, p 192), share this Wordsworthian intimacy with nature. The philosophical principles involved in the idyllic 'song' of life, in which man lives in harmony with his natural environment, and the insistent pantheistic refrain that 'nothing endures but the land' are both logical extensions of this fundamentally pagan theme, and yet, being based upon essentially romantic and intuitive factors, ultimately these proposals would be no more convincing in themselves than Gay Hunter's whimsies or Saloney's fanciful expression of faith in the benevolent omnipotence of nature in 'Daybreak'. However, Chris's experience forges a dynamic connection between the materialistic and 'naturistic' planes, between the pragmatic and romantic approaches to life, and this provides justification for Mitchell's vision, which consequently acquires a religious kind of assurance.

John Berger's personal detachment from the peasant society in France which is the subject of *Pig Earth* gives his study a capacity for objective insight which Mitchell, sentimentally attached to his Mearns peasants, could not hope to achieve. Berger is particularly astute on the unorthodox religious stance of the peasant farmer:

> Inexhaustibly committed to wresting a life from the earth, bound to the present of endless work, the peasant nevertheless sees life as an interlude. This is confirmed by his daily familiarity with the cycle of birth, life and death. Such a view may predispose him to religion, yet religion is not at the origin of his attitude and, anyway, the religion of peasants has never fully corresponded with the religion of rulers and priests.[40]

This diagnosis could fairly be applied to Mitchell himself for, over and above his hard pragmatic approach to both life and death, he finds a near-religious meaning. Unlike Berger's French peasants, however, Mitchell justifies his beliefs explicitly and convincingly.

In his trilogy, Mitchell denounces the traditional ways in which his secondary characters respond to life, and through Chris he advances what he considers to be the correct response. The key philosophical question occurs in the middle of the book when Mitchell's heroine considers the scepticism of the Kinraddie peasants and Robert's desperate belief in a Christian God and, appearing unhappy with them both, she ponders:

> The men of the earth that had been, that she'd known, who kept to the earth and their eyes upon it—the hunters of clouds that were such as was Robert: how much was each wrong and how much each right, and was there maybe a third way to Life, unguessed, unhailed, never dreamed of yet? (*SQ,* p 301).

Chris's search in *A Scots Quair,* therefore, is for an alternative approach which has the merit of pagan materialism and the spiritual reassurance of a religious faith. Her experience in the trilogy as a whole is thus authoritative and decisive, her search for 'her surety unshaken' (*SQ,* p 322) stretching throughout the volume.

This ritualistic search for 'surety' introduces a transcendental dimension to *A Scots Quair,* for Chris's experience takes place on a different plane from Ewan's, which exists in the normal mimetic contexts of time and place as Edwin Muir defines them in *The Structure of the Novel.* The political theme of the work hinges upon the principle of change, for Robert's aim in *Cloud Howe* and Ewan's in *Grey Granite* is to make sense of the historical process, to gain control over the factors which shape society and which brought about the demise of the peasant farmer in *Sunset Song*. Robert and Ewan thus operate in a historical dimension, each trying, with mixed success, to alter its course by political methods, but neither attempting to transform the actual nature of that plane itself. They want to influence what Chris calls 'the shifting sands of life' (*SQ*, p 235), but not to stop their movement altogether; to constantly rework society towards the ideal.

Robert and Ewan exist in a unilinear plane of history in which time has a past, a present and a future. Events are assumed to have a historical connectedness, and accordingly time appears as a single uniform line, as a 'tunnel' (*SQ*, p 59), in which all human behaviour is influenced by what has happened in the past and itself influences what happens in the future. This indeed is one of the chief axioms of Marxist philosophy, as the early proselytising Ellen Johns indicates in *Grey Granite* when she tells Ewan, 'You're a consequence and product as all of us are' (*SQ*, p 387). And Ake reinforces this idea in the following section when he observes to Chris that 'we're all on leading strings out of the past' (*SQ*, p 404).

However, this whole historical plane is of secondary importance within the *Quair*, just as the political theme itself is subsidiary. As the peasant narrator in *Sunset Song* implies when he says that the crofters 'had no history' (*SQ*, p 17), and when he refers later to the occasion when 'Time was clecked in Kinraddie' (*SQ*, p 53), the whole historical dimension is subsumed within the cyclical organic pattern of reality represented by Gibbon as a 'song'. As a cyclical motion, change is continuous but also repetitive. This cycle is epitomised in nature, in the repetition of birth, life and death, and in the constant revolution of the seasons. And on a lesser scale, Chris also perceives this permanence of change in her own physical development: although she matures in distinct stages, even in *Sunset Song* she constantly emphasises that, like the dimple beneath her breast, in essence she remains the same.

Chris finds a more generous and inspiring image of the eternal in the cyclical permanence of the Land. Thus, whereas the political theme of the book revolves around the principle of change, her experience has a religious quality in that it represents the search for stability and permanence. Where Robert and Ewan seek to control 'the shifting sands of life', Chris endeavours to still them, to work through the historical plane to the eternal. Whereas Ewan's destiny demands the sacrifice of his individuality in the mass political effort of the Communist Party, Chris's is to consolidate hers. To use the analogy Ewan makes on the second last page of the book, he continues the historical search for GOD, while his mother leaves the 'tunnel' of time altogether in her pursuit of personal FREEDOM.

Chris goes through four distinct incarnations in the course of the trilogy as a whole. Her first two selves are pre-adolescent—at the beginning, there is the spontaneous, nature-loving 'Chris Murdoch' and the ambitious, scholarly Chris Guthrie. After puberty, these are succeeded by the third romantic personage, which is a hybrid of Chris Tavendale, Chris Colquohoun and Chris Ogilvie, and the fourth and final Chris is the wholly independent figure who has sole responsibility to herself and who returns to Echt at the close of the trilogy, 'concerning none and concerned with none' (*SQ*, p 496).

Despite its apparently relentless progress, this pattern is quite symmetrical: Chris was born at Cairndhu, and her end is appropriately a return to the source. The incarnations which frame the middle sections of the novel contrast sharply with the central marital experience in that both involve a retreat, or at least a detachment, from the social and romantic concerns of life. In fact, Jean Guthrie's advice provides the key here, when she tells her daughter that 'there are better things than your books or studies or loving or bedding, there's the countryside your own, you its, in the days when you're neither bairn nor woman' (SQ, p 33).

At this time, early in *Sunset Song*, Chris is indeed 'neither bairn nor woman', as she has left her childhood behind but has yet to reach adolescence, and consequently, this first self, 'the Chris that was Murdoch, Chris of the land', is instinctually aware of the 'sweetness of the Scottish land and skies'. Chris's final incarnation is also 'neither bairn nor woman', as she ends with 'all the passion of living put by long ago' (SQ, p 409). However, the experience she has had of life has largely undermined her spontaneous appreciation of the security she found in nature. Adult life has cut her off from the sanctuary of her childhood, and therefore although she never loses her intimacy with the Land she must make a conscious effort to recover the awareness of its deeper significance. Chris's 'search for reality' is thus particularly convincing for being brought from a subconscious, intuitive level to a conscious level. This stands as the single most profound development in all of Mitchell's writing, for ultimately, through Chris's experience, he provides justification for his own deepest philosophical beliefs.

As the search for, and ultimate discovery of 'surety' in 'the shifting sands of life', Chris's experience is thus salutary. Her whole life builds up to her final reunion with the Land, and this act is viewed as a form of spiritual fulfilment. The structure of the trilogy helps to emphasise the climactic importance of this experience, as the conclusion of *Grey Granite* has an air of finality which stands in pointed contrast to the indeterminate endings of both *Sunset Song* and *Cloud Howe*. Chris's end is final and complete.

The more doctrinaire critics of the trilogy tend to ignore the smooth way in which Chris's experience develops and they deny its importance in the work. The Marxist critic Jack Mitchell tries to highlight the political significance of the trilogy by playing down Chris's role, asserting that 'Chris falls deeper into peasant fatalism and nostalgia'.[41] Ian J Simpson, writing in a less dogmatic vein, refers to the 'rawness and defeatism' which he feels mar *Grey Granite*.[42] In a more recent article, Ian Carter stresses the sociological issues raised in the trilogy to the detriment of the major philosophical themes, maintaining that the end of the trilogy is 'the ultimate cop-out', and that, 'Gibbon's grand design falls to pieces in the last few pages of his trilogy'.[43] But surely the trilogy's coda provides a totally satisfying conclusion to Chris's quest.

Even as a young girl, Chris has an unusual philosophical poise, apprehending death, for example, as 'that last dark silence', as the 'necessary' swift end to the sensuous experience of life. However, she still has to work through the 'passion of living' before she can face up to this final act, the positive assertion of her individuality allowing her eventually to find the God she is looking for at the end of *Grey Granite*. The spiritual haven, the castle that Kafka's hero seeks, remains elusive in the novel of that name, but Chris's spiritual journey is a successful one. The more self-assured she becomes throughout the trilogy, so the more tangible seems her God. The whole volume thus represents in its most exalted form the convergence of man and God, the attainment of an empirical rather than a superstitious vision, based upon 'knowledge' rather than 'faith'.

In order to face up to this spiritual reality at the end of life, Chris has to shed the superficial elements of her being and abnegate all responsibilities apart from the most basic personal responsibilities she has to herself, ending finally as something akin to Lear's 'unaccommodated man'. Mistress Mutch's advice to her when she is poised on the threshold of married life with Ewan in *Sunset Song* is thus prophetic in view of later developments: 'You belong to yourself, mind that' (*SQ*, p 127). In *Cloud Howe*, Mitchell's heroine continues to work towards this ideal of self-sufficiency, realising in 'Cumulus' that 'you'd been caught and ground in the wheels of the days, in this dour little Howe and its moil and toil' (*SQ*, p 250), which has cut her off from the simple harmony of life as it appeared to her in her youth. Later however, Chris looks forward to the fate awaiting her at the end of her life and realises what a deeply personal experience it is, forecasting from the prospect of the kirkyard that, 'she would die down there on a bit of land as deserted and left' (*SQ*, p 257). Nevertheless, on the following page, she still experiences difficulty in squaring up to this forbidding prospect, as she is meantime actively involved in the everyday business of living.

By the final section of *Cloud Howe*, however, Chris has begun to look beyond the pains and joys of her life to a time when she will be free from all but personal obligations. As yet, she lacks the courage of her convictions, but when she longs for 'Chris-alone, Chris-herself, with Chris Guthrie, Chris Tavendale, Chris Colquohoun dead' (*SQ*, p 317), she is defining in advance the sublime state she achieves at the end of the trilogy. Three pages after this, she appears altogether more sure of herself and sure in herself, lying 'aloof and sure and untroubled by things', and this self-assurance is directly set against Robert's desperate clinging to his Christian God on the following page, Chris interpreting this as a 'Fear he'd be left in the day alone, and stand and look at his naked self'.

As Robert becomes increasingly intent on finding God, Chris becomes more secure within herself, realising by the end of *Cloud Howe* that 'this life she lived now could never endure, she knew that well as she looked about her, however it ended it could not go on', and thus she casts herself, 'halted here, in these Segget years, waiting the sound of unhasting feet, waiting a Something unnamed, but it came' (*SQ*, pp 332–3). Chris is therefore content to wait until her destiny makes itself known, while Robert in his desperation frantically pursues his God beyond reality and into the realm of fantasy.

At the beginning of *Grey Granite*, not even the realisation of the 'grim essentials' at the base of life can disturb Chris unduly, who now appears 'neither sick nor sorry' at the harshness of life. Later in 'Epidote', the 'naked self' which she longs to attain is presented as being the state she was close to as a girl, and her subsequent experiences as an adult stand between her and this secure past, Chris imagining on her outing to the country with Ewan and Ellen:

> . . . you were again that quean in the sleet, all the world and living before you unkenned, kisses and hate and toil and woe, kisses at night when the byre-stalls drowsed, agony in long deserted noons, hush of terror of those moon-bright nights when you carried within your womb seed of men—for a minute they seemed no more than dreams as you drowsed, a quean, in the smore of the sleet . . . (SQ, p 384).

The physical return to the croft of Cairndhu where she was born is thus invested with a profound philosophical significance on the following page, as an attempt to regain the freedom and harmony that informed her days when she was 'neither bairn nor woman'. Mitchell describes how 'Chris wandered from place to place like one seeking that which she wouldn't know—maybe something of that sureness mislaid in the past, long ago, when she was a quean'. As yet, however, she is unable to find this 'sureness' at Cairndhu, observing that 'here was nothing, nothing but change that had followed every pace of her feet'. At the end of the book, Chris discovers that this very principle of change itself offers the 'sureness' she seeks.

In the following section, Chris is still tenuously involved in the physical concerns of life, and in obedience to Ma Cleghorn's maxim that 'a woman stopped living when she stopped having bairns' she is still disconcerted by the prospect of growing old, of existing with 'all the passion of living put by'. Later in the section, however, Ma's death shows Chris that there is something of far greater import to mankind than these comparatively superficial concerns, and, considering her late partner's case, she reflects that 'the dreich fight drew to its close, begun a sixty years before, ending in this', and asks more with curiosity than anguish, 'what for, what for?' (SQ, p 433). By the following page, however, she has begun to find a stoical kind of security in the prospect of death, echoing Lawrence's 'joy of moving on with the invisible' when she affirms that 'no worry could last beyond the last point'.

The final two sections of Grey Granite show a pointed contrast in Chris's appearance in the 'present' described in the opening and closing pages of the separate sections from which she reviews the events of the recent past. In 'Apatite', she appears decked out in all her finery on the steps of Windmill Brae, and, still haunted by the idea that to remarry would be to go back 'to a life again full and complete from a half-life, unnatural, alone and apart', she mistakenly considers that 'the fugitive Chris was imprisoned at last' (SQ, p 434-5). However, her abortive marriage with Ake Ogilvie puts paid to this illusion in the following pages, adding poignancy to the main difference she draws between herself and her previous husband, Robert, as she admits to herself, 'I've no patience with crowds or the things they want, only for myself I suppose I can plan. And I stand in the bareness, alone, tormented' (SQ, p 447).

In 'Zircon', however, Chris is finally stripped of the superficial concern with the 'passion of living' and fully asserts her individuality. From the top of the Barmekin, at the beginning of the section, she 'looked down with untroubled eyes at the world below' (SQ, p 467), and twenty pages later this personal freedom which she achieves is endowed with a religious significance, as the ritualistic process of self-discovery. How she is no longer afraid to face her 'unaccommodated' self:

> That dreadful storm she'd once visioned stripping her bare was all about her, and she feared it no longer, eager to be naked, alone and unfriended, facing the last realities with a cool, clear wonder, an unhating desire. Barriers still, but they fell one by one . . . .

By the final page of the volume, all these obstacles standing between Chris and the realisation of her personal destiny have disappeared, for 'she had found the last road she wanted and taken it, concerning none and concerned with none'. Thus, there is a gentle serenity and a tranquillity about her death, represented with implicit metaphysicality; it is pertinent, in fact, that Mitchell does not formally pronounce his heroine dead, merely relating that 'she still sat on as one by one the lights went out and the rain came beating the stones about her, and falling all that night while she still sat there, presently feeling no longer the touch of the rain or hearing the sound of the lapwings going by'.

It is therefore incorrect to regard Chris's experience as fatalistic, as her final 'naked' state of freedom is something that she has to work towards. Indeed, she herself indicates the affirmative nature of the act when, preparing to 'face the last realities' at Cairndhu, she looks back upon her life, and refers to 'attaining' this, her final state (SQ, p 468).

Chris's experience thus embodies what Mitchell takes to be the real religious experience. Religion to him is not something imposed from without, but something discovered within the individual—Freedom as opposed to God, as Ewan puts it. It is also an honest search, not for faith, but for truth, a coming to terms with the 'naked' self, a frank confrontation of 'the last realities' of life and death. Within this lexicon, true religion, or Freedom, involves the pursuit by the individual of spiritual meaning, whereas the traditional God, whether secular or religious, is seen as something imposed from outside which enslaves its followers, as Christianity enslaves Robert and Communism enslaves Ewan. Truly religious experience is a personal affair, whereas the traditional God is merely a general cause. Mitchell re-emphasises the positive nature of his heroine's experience by representing it as a search for divine meaning.

The major implication of the change in the metaphorical patterns governing the final two books of the trilogy is political, with Robert's ethereal political dreams in Cloud Howe giving way in Grey Granite to the much more practical and concrete measures of communism advocated by Ewan. However, on a more exalted plane, the symbolism reflects the difference between God and Freedom, between that which Robert and Ewan seek and the 'sureness' which Chris seeks, between the tyrannical God and the assertion of spiritual freedom. Mitchell found tacit support for this dichotomy in the diffusionist scheme, and yet even in the more glibly polemical passages in *Cloud Howe* he rises to a more sublime theme of religious import. Thus, from consideration of Robert's vision of the Golden Age, Chris moves on to apprehend the natural absolute of life, realising that, for all man's grand aims and pretentions, 'nothing endured but the Seeker himself, him and the everlasting Hills' (*SQ*, p 300). Again, then, the definitive relationship presented here is between man and his god.

In the following section, the heroine again stresses the legitimacy of her search for 'surety' when she reflects that 'she had found in the moors and the sun and the sea her surety unshaken, lost maybe herself, but she followed no cloud, be it named or unnamed' (*SQ*, p 322). The god she seeks is thus not merely a faith to latch on to in order to give meaning to life and death, but empirical truth—'knowledge' as opposed to 'faith', as Mitchell describes it in *Nine Against the Unknown*. In the trilogy, he establishes this quest as a religious one by identifying the object of this search as God itself.

In *Sunset Song*, Chris's religious beliefs are largely intuitive and reside in the subconscious. However, by *Cloud Howe*, she is able to consciously elucidate even her deepest thoughts and instincts. In 'Cumulus' especially, she gives the natural reality to which she has always been closely bound a directly divine aspect:

> There was something lacking or something added, something that was bred in your bones in this land—oh, Something: maybe that Something was GOD—that made folk take with a smile and a gley the tales of the gods and the heavens and the hells, the afterlives and the lives before, heaven on earth and the chances of change, the hope and belief in salvation for men—as a fairy-tale in a play that they'd play, but they knew the whole time they were only players, no Scots bodies died but they knew that fine, deep and real in their hearts they knew that here they faced up to the REAL at last, neither heaven nor hell but the earth that was red, the cling of the clay where you'd alter and turn, back to the earth and the times to be, to a spraying of motes on a raging wind when the Howe was happed in its winter storms, to a spray of dust as some childe went by with his plough and his horse in a morning in Spring, to the peck and tweet of the birds in the trees, to trees themselves in a burgeoning Spring (*SQ*, p 236).

I quote this astonishing paragraph in full because it seems to me to paraphrase the procedure by which Mitchell redefines religion in the *Quair*, moving from the traditional gnosticism and agnosticism through a pagan romanticism such as that which pervades the short story 'Clay'. And finally, he arrives at the concept of 'thoroughgoing Materialism', which reduces life to the atomic level of 'motes' and touches upon the eternal by considering the possibility of the infinite reworking of these primal cells.

Chris's philosophical understanding is described in more orthodox religious terms later on in the section, and Robert's assertion to Chris the sceptic that 'you will sometime [believe in God], however you find Him' (*SQ*, p 258) proves portentious, for although she does indeed employ an unorthodox method, there is no denying that the essence of her achievement is that she 'finds God'. And at the beginning of the final section of *Cloud Howe* Chris's faith is again described in a semi-devotional manner when she receives insight into the eternal plane existing beyond the dimensions of space and time after she has retreated to the sanctuary of the Kaimes and discovers that 'there was something beyond that endured, some thing she had never yet garbed in a name' (SQ, p 311). Eleven pages after this, Chris terms this 'her surety unshaken', and eleven pages later she is presented awaiting 'a Something unnamed', both of which add considerably to the impression that her quest is fundamentally a religious one.

At the beginning of Grey Granite, Chris expresses her antipathy towards formal religion by affirming her own impartiality:

> But then she'd never understood religion, thought it only a fairy-tale, not a good one, dark and evil rather, hurting life, hurting death, no concern of hers if others didn't force it on her, she herself had nothing to force in its stead (SQ, p 375).

Ewan reinforces this idea of his mother's neutrality in 'Apatite' when he tells Ellen that, 'you could go on living though you might believe in nothing at all—like Chris' (SQ, p 465). The inference here is that his mother lacks a formal discipline or creed, a God in his sense, but the utterly personal spiritual solution that she finds finally is more profoundly important than Ewan's communist god. Whereas he marches on thirled to history, at the end of the book attempting to alter 'space and time', for Chris time itself finally ceases, as she considers 'change that went on as a hurpling clock, with only benediction to ring at the end—knowledge that the clock would stop some time, that even change might not endure' (SQ, p 468). Finally, then, she looks forward to 'benediction', coming to appreciate this universal principle of change as the agency governing all life, and by coming to terms with this principle at the end of the book she is finally recognising the god she has been trying to name throughout the final two volumes of the trilogy. Thus finally she realises:

> And that was the best deliverance of all, as she saw it now, sitting here quiet—that that Change who ruled the earth and the sky and the waters underneath the earth, Change whose face she'd once feared to see, whose right hand was Death and whose left hand Life, might be stayed by none of the dreams of men, love, hate, compassion, anger or pity, gods or devils or wild crying to the sky. He passed and repassed in the ways of the wind, Deliverer, Destroyer and Friend in one (SQ, p 496).

Mitchell constantly represents the search for philosophical truth as a delving beneath the superficial layers of existence—most commonly presented as masks or veils—to the heart of reality. This stripping down to the bare essentials is the main philosophical exercise worked out in the Quair, constituting the only praiseworthy method of looking for universal truth; and yet it requires considerable courage to divest oneself of all the comforting creeds or 'clouds' which provide spiritual reassurance. In Cloud Howe, Robert loses this courage, seeking solace in the chimerical figure of Christ at the end of the book rather than facing up to 'the fleshless grin of the skull and the eyeless sockets at the back of life'. His fear that 'he'd be left in the day alone, and stand and look at his naked self' thus leads him to obscure the real existential issues, and he reacts by 'draping his dreams on the face of life' (SQ, p 321). In direct contrast to his step-father, Ewan is self-confident enough to forsake the comforts offered by such illusions, and when he is still a youth he faces up to the social squalor prevailing in Segget with such candour that Chris observes, 'He was turning to look in the face of Life'. After he has been won over by the communist ideal, however, Chris alone carries on the effort to win existential understanding by penetrating to the heart of reality.

Midway through *Cloud Howe*, Chris comes to realise that the human experience is subsidiary, that although the individual must seek his own spiritual fulfilment there is a greater reality beyond, that 'nothing endured but the Seeker himself, him and the everlasting Hills'. As is the case with Nansen in *Nine Against the Unknown*, it is only when Chris is in communion with the elements, when she is alone in the most deprived natural surroundings, that she gains the knowledge and enlightenment that she has been seeking in her 'search for reality'.

The historical plane which Robert and then Ewan inhabit is thus dismissed by Chris as spurious, in much the same way as George Mackay Brown, following Edwin Muir's example, discovers the 'REAL' in the natural base of life as it appears in his native Orkney, writing in *An Orkney Tapestry:*

> It often seems that history is only the forging, out of terrible and kindly fires, of a mask. . . . Underneath, the true face dreams on, and the Fable is repeated over and over again.[44]

Mackay Brown's 'Fable' is in essence the same as the natural 'song' which Mitchell perceives beneath the clouds in the 'Howe' of the world. In this constant revolution of the natural cycle, he finds an image of the eternal. The nihilism of Chris's conviction that 'nothing endures' thus generally relaxes when she contemplates the natural sphere, and throughout the trilogy she regularly wins epiphany from the consideration of this natural absolute. In the 'shifting sands of life', the Land offers security and sanctuary.

At the beginning of *Cloud Howe*, Chris represents the changes she apprehends in the human sphere against the permanence she finds in the constant regeneration of nature, remembering that 'once she had seen in these parks . . . the truth, and the only truth that there was, that only the sky and the seasons endured, slow in their change, the cry of the rain, the whistle of the whins on a winter night under the sailing edge of the moon' (SQ, p 207). The tone of the passage is romantic, and yet Chris's vision of the natural absolute has a philosophical pungency which Gay Hunter's for the most part lacks. The Scots heroine's final return to Cairndhu is thus the single most thematically important event in the whole book, representing the climax of her quest for 'surety', the discovery of 'the only truth that there was' in her union with the Land. In this final scene, Mitchell places his 'unaccommodated man' in the natural world, as a world of relentless change, a world of death and decay, of spiritual emptiness, and yet he still manages to find peace and security in the prospect, discovering that materialism does indeed promise, 'something/ Hardy to be distinguished from eternal life'. In the vision Chris herself perceives, 'looking far on that world across the plain and the day that did not die there but went east, on and on, over all the world till the morning came, the unending morning somewhere on the world', Mitchell imbues his heroine's death with an implicit spiritual promise, just as Mungo Park's fate in *Niger*, with his body being ushered from the Niger to ever greater expanses up to the sea itself, touches upon the eternal. Mitchell is less equivocal in his treatment of Chris's end than in Mungo Park's, however, for just before she finally becomes insensate to the feel of the rain and oblivious to the noise of the passing lapwings, she ultimately recognises God in the constant working and reworking of her natural surroundings, identifying the power of Change which holds sway over life as the final truth.

Chris's experience is thus of paramount importance in *A Scots Quair*, for through his heroine Mitchell presents the 'third way to Life', redefining the religious experience in a universe devoid of spiritual meaning, and providing an empirically valid conception of God. Where Ewan ends trying to conquer the future, Chris finally triumphs over all the forces of time.

In *A Scots Quair*, therefore, Mitchell, in true Joycean fashion, creates his own linguistic medium which, in addition to its poetic appeal, seems to have given him a greater intellectual clarity. This makes the volume his most coherent statement on political and philosophical matters, the efforts of both the 'reformer' and the 'blasphemer' climaxing quite magnificently in this work. The humanitarian politics of the 'reformer' are expressed most powerfully in Ewan's communist god which emerges in response to the compelling urge for social change, while the philosophical achievement of the 'blasphemer' comes to an even more inspiring climax in Chris's discovery of Freedom, in her visionary acceptance of the principle of change as the universal reality. In the *Quair*, Mitchell holds a mirror up to existence, representing the 'shifting sands of life' in their full complexity, but his 'free and undefiled illusion' is also an instructive exercise, for ultimately it also provides enlightenment.

Conclusion

In this study I have argued that Leslie Mitchell was a novelist of the very highest calibre. I rest my claim firmly upon the evidence of *A Scots Quair*, basing my judgement primarily upon an appreciation of the thematic merits of the volume, as opposed to its equally worthy technical accomplishments. John Garland's affirmation in *Stained Radiance* that the modern novel is only as good as the personal values held by the author provides the standard against which ultimately Mitchell's own writing should be judged, for those works which are most true to the forces which inspired him as a man—the Scottish stories 'Clay' and 'Forsaken', the early novels, *Spartacus* and *A Scots Quair*—have an enduring power beyond the slighter English stories and the more lightly conceived imaginative romances.

Neither Mitchell's political views nor his philosophical beliefs belong to the realm of the orthodox, but the designs of both the 'reformer' and the 'blasphemer' remain of the utmost relevance in the modern world. The humanitarian search for a political means of creating a better society, a society based securely upon egalitarian and libertarian principles, deservedly plays a major role in his work and thought, and this search comes to a truly inspiring climax in *Spartacus* and *A Scots Quair*.

The response of the 'blasphemer' is more complex. Mitchell shows fortitude in his approach to the major existential problems of human transience, and of a universe without a god. This avenue of his thinking comes to a wholly satisfying conclusion in the trilogy, in which he rises beyond the Absurd despair produced by recognition of the spiritual inconsequentiality of life to find reason in the apparent disorder of the material universe. Chris finally discovers an image of God at the end of the book, and remarkably Mitchell gives empirical justification for her vision.

Thus, in my emphasis upon the ideological developments to which Mitchell's work bears witness, the trilogy must take priority over all his other books; for finally, not only is it his finest work but it attests to his intellectual and philosophical maturity. The author's two-fold quest for political and spiritual enlightenment comes to fruition in this volume, and the intellectual merits of the work contribute significantly to its lasting vitality as a work of art. Indeed, the enduring power of the *Quair* rests finally not so much upon its technical virtues as upon the success with which the author approaches and resolves the most profound problems of human existence.

Leslie Mitchell ranks among the best novelists of the twentieth century, and not only in his native Scotland. He certainly occupies a unique position in the history of the Scottish novel, and modern Scottish fiction writers such as Gordon Williams, Fred Urquhart, David Toulmin and William McIlvanney have all at one time or another acknowledged his importance.[1] However, I have tried to show that Mitchell's greatness as a novelist actually rests upon the generosity of his outlook: the aesthetic and intellectual influences are international, and ultimately this gives his greatest work the universal appeal which is the mark of all great art. In the final analysis, the trilogy stands high in the history of the modern novel, and in its own right it ranks alongside *The Rainbow*, *Ulysses* and *The Waves* as one of the truly unique works of fiction produced in the early years of this century. As Hugh MacDiarmid observed, '*A Scots Quair* stands alone and has had no successors nor is it likely to have any.'[2] That the trilogy cannot be conveniently pigeonholed is the ultimate tribute to the originality of Mitchell's achievement.

Appendix A

The following five poems by Mitchell (*NLS*, Acc. 7900) are reproduced on account of their political themes, as a pointer to the radical views of the 'reformer', and in disregard of their dubious technical merits. These are arranged in loose chronological order, as far as this can be ascertained.

A COMMUNIST'S CREDO

Yesterday, yours; *To-day*—it is a sea
Where writhe and foam the tides of storm
    and shine
Mist-spume o'erhung; but in the still, stark
    hours
Reading the stars, I know *Tomorrow* mine!

THE COMMUNARDS OF PARIS

We shall not grieve, O splendid hearts of old!
When find we that for which ye dearly sought:
We labour in the Dawn; in blackest Night:
For this same Day full gloriously ye wrought.

From your red graves of treachery and woe
We hear the battle-song that stirred ye on:
And scaling the last barricade well know
Yours is the glory, Pioneers of Dawn!

ON THE MURDER OF KARL LIEBKNECHT AND ROSA LUXEMBURG

They gathered a Hundred Splendid Souls,
The Gods of the Heart's Day-Dreams,
And pointed adown the Verge of Space:
'See! Where yon Planet gleams!
Go down to the struggling Sons of Men,
And teach Them all Ye know,
And guide their Feet to the only Path
From the surging Pit below.'

Each Splendid Soul with a gladsome Heart
To its mighty Task went forth:
Some to the East, and Some to the West,
And Some to the Snow-capped North,
And Some where the luscious Southern Flowers
Are kissed by the burning Sun,
And Some where the Plains in the Gloaming lie,
And Some where the Morn is dun.

And Two of the Hundred Splendid Souls
Went back but Yester-Eve:
The Road well-paved, the Beacon lit—
Comrades, Ye need not grieve!
For the Ninety-and Eight shall marshall the Host
Ere the Night-Watch-Fires low burn,
And the longed-for Dawn shall glint our Spears,
And the Splendid Two return!

LENIN: 1919

'His shadow lies on Europe'—(Whisper low!)—
'Turning the day to blackest night below,
A shadow whereneath hell-fires belch and glow:
      The shadow of a sword.'

Your shadow, little man. I see your eyes,
Steadfast and cold, unutterably wise,
Look westward where the ling'ring sunset dies
      By ridge and ford.

I hear your voice—A prayer or a command?—
Wild helot-laughter fills a darkened land,
And old dreams die, and princes outcast stand
      Disrobed, abhorred.

You move, and all the nations of the Earth,
Shuddering in pangs of agonizing birth,
Cry to the skies through wrack of doom and dearth
      'How long, O Lord?'

How long? The years are sun-motes in your sight:
'It comes.' And still by daylight and by night
Hangs sky-obscuring, making faint the light,
      The shadow of a sword.

AN OLD THEME

On the surrender of the G.C. TUC on the 12th June 1926

How slow the spring! Through the long winter nights
We hear the whoom of hail on frozen heights.
How dream of May beside an ice-girt mere?—
    Yet Spring is near.

How slow the corn! No burgeoning of green
Where eastward slope the bare, brown fields is seen.
How dream of harvest and the curlew's cry?—
    Yet Autumn's nigh.

How slow the dawn! Oh God, how long the night
To hopeless hearts who pray the gift of light.
How dream the day when even dreams enumb?—
    Yet Morn will come.
How slow the march of Right! Yet, unforgot,
    It tarries not.

Appendix B

As is the case with the five political poems cited in Appendix A, this poem is reproduced solely on account of the themes it adumbrates rather than any aesthetic value it may possess. I quote the following poem (*NLS*, Acc. 7900) as a succinct embodiment of Mitchell's main initiative as a 'blasphemer'—the swing away from the gnostic stance towards a more pragmatic approach in which 'knowledge' has replaced 'faith' as the key to philosophical progress.

WHEN GOD DIED

God died one morn
As dawn sprang red,
And the sun arose
With flame-crowned head,
Nor aught of all its glory shed
Nor seemed to know
That God was dead.

The earth glowed to the light
That dawn's pale fingers led
By rivulet and rill,
By curtain-shadowed bed,
By whitening seas whence night-spume fled:
Nor any gladness lost
Though God was dead.

A lark sang clear
Against the sky
Of the gracious things
That would never die,
Being born of song and Eternity,
Fashioned of no sick dreams
Nor sprung of any lie.

In olden walks night-chilled
The sea-breeze shook and said:
'Oh, bloom, ye flowers of dawn!
Of skies and waters fed:
For Time and Fate are meetly wed,
And winters come no more
Now God is dead.'

And the cities' clamour rose,
And men for love and bread
Strove in the heats of day,
Strove until overhead
The arc-glares' light was sickly shed:
Nor any dreamt or knew
That God was dead.

But the forests whispered
Each eventide
And called by cliffs
Where the night-waves ride
With a star for lamp and guide:
'The world is better
Since God has died.'

Notes

INTRODUCTION

1 Letter, Mitchell to Mr & Mrs Alexander Gray, dated 29 September 1929, *NLS* (Acc.5325a).
2 Raymond Williams, *The Country and the City* (London, 1973), pp 268–71.
3 David Smith, *Socialist Propaganda in the Twentieth-Century British Novel* (London, 1978); Chapter Eight devoted to *A Scots Quair*.
4 Hugh MacDiarmid, 'A Drunk Man Looks at the Thistle', in *Complete Poems* (London, 1978), p 87.
5 J Leslie Mitchell, 'The Buddha of America', in *The Cornhill*, 72(1932), p 598. The importance of this phrase is reinforced by the fact that Mitchell repeats it in his article on 'Religions of Ancient Mexico', in *Religions*, no. 13(October 1935), p 17.
6 Matthew Arnold, 'The Function of Criticism at the Present Time', in *Selected Prose*, edited by P J Keating (Harmondsworth, 1970), p 133.
7 By, amongst others, Kurt Wittig in *The Scottish Tradition in Literature* (Edinburgh, 1958), p 333, and James Barke, in 'Lewis Grassic Gibbon', in *Left Review*, 2(1936), p 220.
8 Edwin Muir's definition of the term 'confession' in *The Structure of the Novel* (London, 1928), p 150, is derogatory, being used to describe a novel lacking in invention. I subscribe to Harry Levin's more complimentary reference to the increasing role autobiography plays in modern fiction, quoted by David Lodge in *The Novelist at the Crossroads and other essays* (London, 1971), p 14, as a welcome development. The reference to 'philosophical' fiction is Lodge's own, quoted in *The Novelist at the Crossroads*, p 15.

ONE   'REFORMER': MITCHELL'S POLITICAL THINKING

1 Quoted in *Munro,*, p 134.
2 Hugh MacDiarmid, 'Lewis Grassic Gibbon', in *Scottish Art and Letters*, no. 2(Spring 1946), p 41.
3 BBC Scotland, Post-production script of 'Places of the Sunset: The Land of Lewis Grassic Gibbon', *NLS* (Acc.5399).
4 Alexander Gray, 'His school essays even baffled the rector', in *People's Journal*, 16 May 1964, p 13.
5 James Leslie Mitchell, Arbuthnott School Essay Books, *NLS* (Acc.5325b).
6 I am grateful to Mr Andy Robertson of Nethercraighill, Arbuthnott, for providing me with this information in our conversation at his home on 5 December 1980.
7 Nan Milton, *John MacLean* (London, 1973); William Gallagher, *Revolt on the Clyde* (London, 1940); Harry McShane and Joan Smith, *No Mean Fighter* (London, 1978).
8 Quoted in *Munro*, p 131.
9 *William Morris: The Critical Heritage*, edited by Peter Faulkner (London, 1973), p 400.
10 William Morris, *News from Nowhere*, in *Three Works* (London, 1967), pp 247–8.

11   Quoted in *Munro*, p 37.
12   Letter, Mitchell to Helen B Cruickshank, dated 18 November 1933, *NLS* (Acc.5512).
13   Personal letter, Ray Mitchell to the present writer, dated 1 May 1978.
14   Letter, Mitchell to Neil Gunn, dated 2 November 1934, *NLS* (Acc.7900).
15   Personal letter, George Malcolm Thomson to the present writer, dated 8 February 1979.
16   Lewis Grassic Gibbon, 'News of Battle: Queries for Mr Whyte', in *The Free Man*, 3(17 March 1934), p 9.
17   Personal letter, Ray Mitchell to the present writer, dated 20 June 1978.
18   Letter, Mitchell to Mrs Gray, dated 13 June 1929, *NLS* (Acc.5325a).
19   Edwin Muir, *Scottish Journey* (London, 1935), p 79.
20   J. Leslie Mitchell, 'A Footnote to History', in *The Cornhill* 71(1931), p 208. (My general practice throughout this study will be to refer to Mitchell's English stories in the form in which they originally appeared, as those which were republished in *The Calends of Cairo* and *Persian Dawns, Egyptian Nights* were slightly abridged. As there are no such problems with the Grassic Gibbon stories, I will refer to the slightly more polished versions which appeared in *Scottish Scene*, as they are reprinted in *A Scots Hairst*.)
21   J Leslie Mitchell, 'The Epic', in *The Cornhill*, 67(1929), p 170.
22   Helen B Cruickshank, photocopy of PEN circular issued after Mitchell's death, undated, *NLS* (Acc.5284).
23   Acknowledged by Mitchell in a letter to Helen B Cruickshank, undated (1934), *NLS* (Acc.5512).
24   Letter, Mitchell to Mr &. Mrs Gray, dated 4 December 1933, *NLS* (Acc.5325a).
25   Lewis Grassic Gibbon, 'Book Reviews: Fiction. Scots Novels of the Half-Year', in *The Free Man*, 2(24 June 1933), p 7.
26   J. Leslie Mitchell, 'Grieve—Scotsman', in *The Free Man*, 2(9 September 1933), p 7.
27   Mitchell, 'Lowland Scots as a Literary Medium', *NLS* (Acc.7900).
28   Letter, Mitchell to Christopher Grieve, dated 12 January 1935, *NLS* (Acc.7900).
29   Lewis Grassic Gibbon, 'A Novelist Looks at the Cinema', in *Cinema Quarterly*, 3(1935), p 85.
30   *Ibid.* p 82.
31   Lewis Grassic Gibbon, 'Controversy: Writers' International (British Section)', in *Left Review*, 1(1935), pp 179–80.
32   I am referring in particular here to an article written by Gunn in *The Wick Mercantile Debating Society Magazine* in April 1929, reprinted in *Scottish Literary Journal*, 4, no.2(December 1977), pp 58–61.
33   See *Language, Thought, and Reality: Selected Writings of Benjamin Lee Whorf* (Massachusetts and New York, 1959), and introduction to this volume by John B Carroll.
34   Lewis Grassic Gibbon, *Sunset Song* (New York, 1933), p vii.
35   *Ibid.* p 303.
36   Hugh MacDiarmid, introduction to *The Golden Treasury of Scottish Poetry* (London, 1946), p xxv.
37   Marx and Engels, *The Communist Manifesto*, in *The Essential Left* (London, 1960), p 26.
38   Mitchell, 'Synopsis of THE STORY OF RELIGION', *NLS* (Acc.7900).
39   Mitchell, fragment of Wallace novel, *NLS* (Acc.7900).
40   Neil M Gunn, 'The Ghost's Story', in *The White Hour and other stories* (London, 1950), pp 222–30.
41   James Barke, *The Green Hills Far Away* (London, 1940), p 25.
42   *Ibid.* p 41.

43 Quoted in *Young*, p 22.
44 Quoted in Louis Katin, 'Author of *Sunset Song*', in *Glasgow Evening News*, 16 February 1933, p 6.
45 Neil M Gunn, *The Serpent* (London, 1978). p 175.
46 Hugh MacDiarmid, 'Politicians', in *Scottish Scene* (London, 1934), p 252.
47 Quoted in *The Anarchist Reader*, edited by George Woodcock (Glasgow, 1977), pp 82-3.
48 Dorothy Tweed, unpublished memory of James Leslie Mitchell, found in Mrs Mitchell's possession in September 1978.
49 J Leslie Mitchell, 'The Prince's Placenta and Prometheus as God', in *The Twentieth Century*, 2, no.12(February 1932), p 17.
50 Edwin Muir, 'Lewis Grassic Gibbon: An Appreciation', in *Scottish Standard*, March 1935, p 23.
51 Hugh MacDiarmid, *Lucky Poet* (London, 1943), p 67.
52 Letter, Mitchell to George MacDonald, dated 20 January 1924, *NLS* (Acc.5356).
53 Letter, Mitchell to Mr & Mrs Gray, dated 10 December 1926, *NLS* (Acc.5325a).
54 Letter, Mitchell to Mr & Mrs Gray, dated 13 July 1929, *NLS* (Acc.5325a).
55 Personal letter, Finlay Hart to the present writer, dated 14 January 1980.
56 Personal letter, Betty Reid to the present writer, dated 14 November 1979.
57 Quoted in *Munro*, p 43.
58 Letter, Neil Gunn to Mitchell, dated 30 October 1934, *NLS* (Acc.7900).
59 Personal letter, Cuthbert Graham to the present writer, dated 26 August 1978.
60 Mitchell, 'Synopsis of THE STORY OF RELIGION', *NLS* (Acc.7900).
61 Mitchell, 'Synopsis of MEMOIRS OF A MATERIALIST', *NLS* (Acc.7900).
62 This is contained among Mrs Mitchell's papers, *NLS* (Acc.7900).
63 Letter, Mitchell to Neil Gunn, dated 2 November 1934, quoted in *Munro*, p 173.
64 Letter, Mitchell to Mr and Mrs Gray, dated 13 February 1934, *NLS* (Acc.5325a).
65 Lewis Grassic Gibbon, 'News of Battle: Queries for Mr. Whyte'.
66 Lewis Grassic Gibbon, 'Controversy: Writers' International (British Section)', p 180.

TWO   'BLASPHEMER': MITCHELL'S PHILOSOPHICAL THINKING

1 D H Lawrence, 'Books', in *Selected Essays* (Harmondsworth, 1950), p 48.
2 Recalled by Mr & Mrs Jeams in conversation with the present writer at their home in Stonehaven on 5 December 1980.
3 Mitchell, 'Christmas', in Arbuthnott School Essay Book, *NLS* (Acc.5325b).
4 Sean O'Casey, *I Knock at the Door*, in *Autobiographies, 1* (London, 1980), p 28.
5 Mitchell, 'Christmas', in Arbuthnott School Essay Book, *NLS* (Acc.5325b).
6 Mitchell, 'Synopsis of THE STORY OF RELIGION', *NLS* (Acc.7900).
7 Mitchell, 'Brief Synopsis of A HISTORY OF MANKIND', *NLS* (Acc.7900).
8 Mitchell, 'Notes for DOMINA', untitled fragment and 'Outline of a Story', all *NLS* (Acc.7900).
9 Mitchell, 'Brief Synopsis of A HISTORY OF MANKIND', *NLS* (Acc.7900).
10 Mitchell, 'Synopsis of MEMOIRS OF A MATERIALIST', *NLS* (Acc.7900).
11 J Leslie Mitchell, 'Religions of Ancient Mexico', p 19.
12 Mitchell, 'Synopsis of THE STORY OF RELIGION', *NLS* (Acc.7900).
13 *Ibid.*
14 J Leslie Mitchell, 'The Prince's Placenta and Prometheus as God', p 17.
15 J Leslie Mitchell, 'Religions of Ancient Mexico', p 11.
16 Mitchell, 'Synopsis of MEMOIRS OF A MATERIALIST', *NLS* (Acc.7900).
17 Mitchell, 'Brief Synopsis of A HISTORY OF MANKIND', *NLS* (Acc.7900)
18 T S Eliot, *Sweeney Agonistes*, in *Collected Poems* (London, 1974), p 131.

19 James Bryce, *The Story of a Ploughboy* (London, 1912), pp 341–2.
20 D H Lawrence, *Collected Letters*, edited by Harry T Moore, 2 vols (London, 1962), vol 1, p 291.
21 Mitchell, 'Power', in Arbuthnott School Essay Book, NLS (Acc.5325b).
22 John Alcorn, *The Nature Novel from Hardy to Lawrence* (London, 1977), p x.
23 Mitchell, inscribed army notebook, NLS (Acc.7900).
24 D H Lawrence, 'Democracy', in *Selected Essays*, p 88.
25 These volumes, William Wallace's *The Logic of Hegel*, and H S Macran's *Hegel's Doctrine of Formal Logic*, were still in Mrs Mitchell's possession when I visited her in September 1978.
26 Friedrich Engels, *Socialism: Utopian and Scientific*, in *The Essential Left*, p 121.
27 *Ibid.* p 123.
28 J Leslie Mitchell, 'Near Farnboru', in *Reynolds's Illustrated News*, 12 July 1931, p 10.
29 Hugh MacDiarmid, 'Island Funeral', in *Complete Poems*, p 583.
30 *Ibid.* p 582.
31 Douglas F Young, 'Lewis Grassic Gibbon', in *Scottish Review*, no.14(May 1979), p 40.
32 Patricia J Wilson, 'Freedom and God: some implications of the key speech in *A Scots Quair*', in *Scottish Literary Journal*, 7, no.2(December 1980), p 71.
33 Martin Esslin, *The Theatre of the Absurd* (Harmondsworth, 1968), p 391.
34 Jan Kott, *Shakespeare Our Contemporary* (London, 1964), pp 101–37.

THREE THE ENGLISH STORIES

1   Lewis Grassic Gibbon, 'New Novels: Mr. Barke and Others', in *The Free Man*, 3(24 February 1934), p 6.
2   Mitchell, 'Outline of a Story', NLS (Acc.7900).
3   *Grim Death*, edited by Christine Campbell Thomson (London, 1928).
4   According to F R Hart and J B Pick, *Neil M. Gunn: A Highland Life* (London, 1981), p 69.
5   J Leslie Mitchell, 'One Man with a Dream', in *The Cornhill*, 66(1929), p 593.
6   *Ibid.* p 598.
7   J Leslie Mitchell, 'The Life and Death of Elia Constantinidos', in *The Cornhill*, 67(1929), pp 521–2.
8   J Leslie Mitchell, 'The Epic', p 160.
9   J Leslie Mitchell, 'The Road', in *The Cornhill*, 67(1929), p 347.
10 *Ibid.* p 342.
11 J Leslie Mitchell, 'Vernal', in *The Cornhill*, 68(1930), p 258.
12 J Leslie Mitchell, 'He Who Seeks', in *The Cornhill*, 67(1929) p 102.
13 J Leslie Mitchell, 'The Road', p 342.
14 J Leslie Mitchell, 'A Volcano in the Moon', in *The Cornhill*, 67(1929), p 466.
15 J Leslie Mitchell, 'The Road', p 342.
16 J Leslie Mitchell, 'Daybreak', in *The Cornhill*, 68(1930), p 388.
17 J Leslie Mitchell, 'Gift of the River', in *The Cornhill*, 68(1930), p 19.
18 *Ibid.* p 19.
19 J Leslie Mitchell, 'It is Written', in *The Cornhill*, 68(1930), p 523.
20 *Ibid.* p 515.
21 *Ibid.* p 513.
22 *Ibid.* p 521.
23 *Ibid.* p 526.
24 J Leslie Mitchell, 'The Passage of the Dawn', in *The Cornhill*, 68(1930), pp 642–3.
25 *Ibid.* p 651.

26   *Ibid.* p 655.
27   J Leslie Mitchell, *The Calends of Cairo* (London, 1931), p 282.
28   J Leslie Mitchell, 'Gift of the River', p 17.
29   J Leslie Mitchell, 'Daybreak', p 387.
30   *Ibid.* p 391.
31   *Ibid.* p 392.
32   *Ibid.* p 395.
33   *Ibid.* p 396.
34   Letter, Mitchell to Helen B Cruickshank, dated 3 November 1932, *NLS*
      (Acc.5512).
35   J Leslie Mitchell, 'The Refugees', in *The Millgate*, 27(1931), p 33.
36   J Leslie Mitchell, 'Thermopylae', in *The Cornhill*, 71(1931), p 684.
37   *Ibid.* pp 689–90.
38   *Ibid.* p 699.
39   *Ibid.* p 692.
40   J Leslie Mitchell, 'The Lost Constituent', in *The Cornhill*, 71(1931), p 355.
41   J Leslie Mitchell, 'Cartaphilus', in *The Cornhill* 73(1932), p 344.
42   J Leslie Mitchell, 'The Floods of Spring', in *The Cornhill*, 71(1931), p 623.
43   J Leslie Mitchell, 'Cartaphilus', p 344.
44   J Leslie Mitchell, 'A Footnote to History', p 202.
45   *Ibid.* p 212.
46   J Leslie Mitchell, 'The Lost Constituent', p 359.
47   J Leslie Mitchell, 'The Last Ogre', in *The Cornhill*, 72(1932), p 710.
48   J Leslie Mitchell, 'The Floods of Spring', p 625.
49   *Ibid.* pp 637–8.
50   *Ibid.* p 638.
51   Fionn MacColla, *At the Sign of the Clenched Fist* (Edinburgh, 1967), *passim*.
52   Mitchell, 'Lenin: 1919', *NLS* (Acc.7900). Quoted in full in Appendix A.
53   J Leslie Mitchell, 'Cartaphilus', p 348.
54   *Ibid.* p 357.
55   *Ibid.* p 348.
56   J Leslie Mitchell, 'Dawn in Alarlu', in *The Cornhill*, 74(1933), p 197.
57   Geoffrey Wagner, 'James Leslie Mitchell/ Lewis Grassic Gibbon', in *The
      Bibliotheck*, 1(1956), p 12.
58   According to the American *National Union Catalog: pre-1956 imprints*.

FOUR   THE SCOTS STORIES

1   Mitchell, Synopsis of 'The Lost Whaler', *NLS* (Acc.7900).
2   *Young,* p 157.
3   Lewis Grassic Gibbon, *Smeddum: Stories and Essays*, with commentary and notes
     by D M Budge (London, 1980), p xiii.
4   I am grateful to Mr Andy Robertson of Nethercraighill and Miss Nellie Riddoch of
     Arbuthnott for providing me with this information.
5   Mitchell, Synopsis of 'Gypsy', *NLS* (Acc.7900).
6   Mitchell, notebook, *NLS* (Acc.7900).
7   Mitchell, army notebook, *NLS* (Acc.7900).
8   J Leslie Mitchell, 'Cartaphilus', pp 348, 350.
9   Matthew 25. 31–46.

FIVE   THE ENGLISH NOVELS

1 Letter, Mitchell to Mr &. Mrs Gray, dated 4 January 1928, *NLS* (Acc.5325a).
2 See *Munro*, p 55.
3 Letter, Mitchell to Mr &. Mrs Gray, dated 6 September 1930, *NLS* (Acc.5325a).
4 Letter, Mitchell to Mr &. Mrs Gray, dated 14 November 1930, *NLS* (Acc.5325a).
5 Quoted in David Lodge, *The Novelist at the Crossroads*, p 15.
6 I am relying here in particular upon the recollections of Mr &. Mrs Jeams of Stonehaven, given to me in conversation at their home on 5 December 1980.
7 Letter, Mitchell to George MacDonald, dated 20 January 1924, *NLS* (Acc.5356).
8 Mentioned in *Library Review*, November 1932, p 391.
9 Letter, Mitchell to Mr &. Mrs Gray, dated 14 November 1930, *NLS* (Acc.5325a).
10 Letter, Mitchell to Mr &. Mrs Gray, dated 9 March 1928, *NLS* (Acc.5325a).
11 Letter, Mitchell to Mr &. Mrs Gray, dated 14 November 1930, *NLS* (Acc.5325a).
12 *Ibid.*
13 *Young*, p 39.
14 J Leslie Mitchell, 'It is Written', p 513.
15 Letter, Mitchell to Rebecca Middleton, dated 20 December 1921, quoted in *Munro*, p 38.
16 The novel was originally subtitled, 'Portrait and Saga of Malcom Maudslay in his adventure through the dark corridor', although this has inexplicably been dropped in Paul Harris's reprint.
17 *Young*, p 45.
18 Douglas F Young, 'Introduction', in *The Thirteenth Disciple* (Edinburgh, 1981), p 3.
19 Letter, Mitchell to Mr &. Mrs Gray, dated 14 November 1930, *NLS* (Acc.5325a). fact, not fiction.'
21 Lewis Grassic Gibbon, 'Book Review—In Oor Kailyaird', in *The Free Man*, 2(7 October, 1933), p 9.
22 Mitchell, unpublished manuscripts, all *NLS* (Acc.7900).
23 Frank Kermode, *D. H. Lawrence* (Suffolk, 1973), p 67.
24 *Young*, p 46; Gifford, *Gunn and Gibbon* (Edinburgh, 1983), pp 52–3.
25 Ian Campbell, 'The Science Fiction of James Leslie Mitchell', in *Extrapolation*, 16(1974), p 54.
26 Letter, Mitchell to George MacDonald, dated 15 February 1932, *NLS* (Acc.5356).
27 Hugh MacDiarmid, 'Lewis Grassic Gibbon', in *Scottish Art and Letters*, p 43.
28 D H Lawrence, *Women in Love* (Harmondsworth, 1960), p 216.
29 Maxim Gorky, *Mother* (Moscow, 1954), p 246.
30 Mitchell, 'Precis of THE LOST TRUMPET', *NLS* (Acc.7900).
31 Jan Kott, *Shakespeare Our Contemporary*, p 105.
32 J Leslie Mitchell, *The Lost Trumpet* (Indianapolis, 1932).
33 Letter, Mitchell to Helen B Cruickshank, undated (1934), *NLS* (Acc.5512).
34 Friedrich Engels, *Socialism: Utopian and Scientific*, in *The Essential Left*, p 114.
35 Letter, Mitchell to Helen B Cruickshank, undated (1934), *NLS* (Acc.5512).
36 Hugh MacDiarmid, 'Lewis Grassic Gibbon', in *Scottish Art and Letters*, p 44.
37 J Leslie Mitchell, 'A Volcano in the Moon', p 473.
38 Ivor Brown, in *The Observer*, 12 November 1933.
39 Arnold P. Hinchliffe, *The Absurd* (London, 1977), p 36.

SIX   *A SCOTS QUAIR*

1 Hugh MacDiarmid, *The Company I've Kept* (London, 1966), p 226.
2 Ian Campbell, *Kailyard: A New Assessment* (Edinburgh, 1981).

3   Letter, Mitchell to George MacDonald, dated 15 February 1932, *NLS* (Acc.5356).
4   Personal letter, Ray Mitchell to the present writer, dated 1 May 1978.
5   See *Munro*, p 71.
6   Letter, Mitchell to Helen B Cruickshank, dated 2 December 1932, *NLS* (Acc.5512).
7   Letter, Mitchell to Helen B Cruickshank, dated 4 June 1934, *NLS* (Acc.5512).
8   Personal letter, Ray Mitchell to the present writer, dated 25 January 1978.
9   J Leslie Mitchell, 'The Epic', p 167.
10   *Young*, pp 146–53.
11   Erich Maria Remarque, *All Quiet on the Western Front* (St Albans, 1977), pp 179–80.
12   Ignazio Silone, *Fontamara* (London, 1975), p 9.
13   Ian J Simpson, 'Lewis Grassic Gibbon', in *Scottish Educational Journal*, 2 April 1954, p 222.
14   Marion Nelson, 'The Kailyard Comes to Life', in *New Frontier*, January 1937, p 21.
15   Edwin Muir, *Scottish Journey*, p 23.
16   Lewis Grassic Gibbon, 'New Novels: Mr. Barke and Others'.
17   J Leslie Mitchell, 'Vernal', p 265.
18   J Leslie Mitchell, 'Grieve—Scotsman'.
19   Lewis Grassic Gibbon, 'Controversy: Writers' International (British Section)', p 179.
20   Georg Lukács, *The Meaning of Contemporary Realism* (London, 1963), p 103.
21   David Lodge, *The Novelist at the Crossroads*, p 7.
22   Edwin Muir, 'Lewis Grassic Gibbon: An Appreciation', p 23.
23   Louis Katin, 'Author of *Sunset Song*'.
24   Mitchell, 'Curtain Raiser', *NLS* (Acc.7900).
25   Lewis Grassic Gibbon, *The Speak of the Mearns* (Edinburgh, 1982), p 22.
26   Letter, Mitchell to Mr & Mrs Gray, dated 16 July 1930, *NLS* (Acc.5325a).
27   Quoted in James Veitch, *George Douglas Brown* (London, 1952), p 150.
28   Letter, Mitchell to Helen B Cruickshank, dated 4 June 1934, *NLS* (Acc.5512).
29   Jessie Kesson, *Glitter of Mica* (London, 1963), p 104.
30   Edwin Muir, *Scottish Journey*, p 25.
31   Thomas Hardy, *A Pair of Blue Eyes* (London, 1975), p 119.
32   John MacLean, *In the Rapids of Revolution*, edited by Nan Milton (London, 1978), p 193.
33   Maxim Gorky, *Mother*, p 15.
34   *Ibid.* p 146.
35   Fyodor Gladkov, *Cement* (New York, 1977), p 114.
36   J Leslie Mitchell, 'Grieve—Scotsman'.
37   Fyodor Gladkov, *Cement*, p 65.
38   Hugh MacDiarmid, 'Further Passages from "The Kind of Poetry I Want"', in *Complete Poems*, p 615.
39   Mitchell, 'Brief Synopsis of A HISTORY OF MANKIND', *NLS* (Acc.7900).
40   John Berger, *Pig Earth* (London, 1979), p 200.
41   Jack Mitchell, 'The Struggle for the Working-Class Novel in Scotland, 1900–39', in *Zeitschrift Fur Anglistik und Amerikanistik*, 21(1973), p 401.
42   Ian J Simpson, 'Lewis Grassic Gibbon', p 223.
43   Ian Carter, 'Lewis Grassic Gibbon, *A Scots Quair*, and the Peasantry', in *History Workshop*, Part 6(1978), p 183.
44   George Mackay Brown, *An Orkney Tapestry* (London, 1973), p 2.

CONCLUSION

1   Gordon Williams pays homage to *A Scots Quair* by name in *From Scenes Like These* (London, 1978), p 152, and Fred Urquhart makes complimentary reference to the narrative powers of 'that man, Grassic Gibbon' in the story 'The Prisoners', in *The Ploughing Match* (London, 1978), p 78. Mitchell's influence is even more strongly felt in David Toulmin's *Blown Seed* (Edinburgh, 1976), and in William McIlvanney's *Docherty* (London, 1975), and both these authors have registered their sincere affection for Mitchell's work: in a letter to myself, dated 8 April 1980, Mr Toulmin acclaims Mitchell as a 'master craftsman' and a 'great man', and in a discussion I had with Mr McIlvanney in December 1980, during his year as writer in residence at the University of Aberdeen, he was particularly fulsome in his praise of Mitchell's 'love of the ordinary people'.

2   Hugh MacDiarmid, 'Lewis Grassic Gibbon', in *Selected Essays*, edited by Duncan Glen (London, 1969), p 192.

Bibliography

For full details of Mitchell's published works, the reader is directed to the check-lists by Geoffrey Wagner (*The Bibliotheck*, 1(1956), pp 3–21), W R Aitken (*The Bibliotheck*, 1(1957), pp 34–5), Douglas F Young (*The Bibliotheck*, 5(1969), pp 169–73), James Kidd (*The Bibliotheck*, 5(1969), pp 174–7), and myself (*The Bibliotheck*, 11 (1983), pp 149–56).

Unless otherwise stated, the following were published under Mitchell's own name:

1 NOVELS

Stained Radiance: A Fictionist's Prelude, London, 1930
The Thirteenth Disciple: Being Portrait and Saga of Malcom Maudslay in his Adventure through the Dark Corridor, London, 1931
Three Go Back, London, 1932
The Lost Trumpet, London, 1932
Lewis Grassic Gibbon, *Sunset Song*, London, 1932
Image and Superscription, London, 1933
Lewis Grassic Gibbon, *Cloud Howe*, London, 1933
Spartacus, London, 1933
Gay Hunter, London, 1934
Lewis Grassic Gibbon, *Grey Granite*, London, 1934
Lewis Grassic Gibbon, *A Scots Quair*, London 1946
(comprising *Sunset Song*, *Cloud Howe* and *Grey Granite*)

2 OTHER BOOKS

Hanno: or The Future of Exploration, London, 1928
The Calends of Cairo, London, 1931
Persian Dawns, Egyptian Nights, London, 1932
Lewis Grassic Gibbon, *Niger: The Life of Mungo Park*, Edinburgh and London, 1934
The Conquest of the Maya, London, 1934
Lewis Grassic Gibbon and Hugh MacDiarmid, *Scottish Scene: or The Intelligent Man's Guide to Albyn*, London, 1934
J Leslie Mitchell and Lewis Grassic Gibbon, *Nine Against the Unknown: A Record of Geographical Exploration*, London, 1934
Lewis Grassic Gibbon, *A Scots Hairst: Essays and Short Stories*, edited by Ian S Munro, London, 1967
Lewis Grassic Gibbon, *Smeddum: Stories and Essays*, edited by D M Budge, London, 1980
Lewis Grassic Gibbon, *The Speak of the Mearns*, Edinburgh, 1982

3 STORIES

'Siva Plays the Game', in *T. P.'s and Cassell's Weekly*, 18 October, 1924, pp 849–50
'If You Sleep in the Moonlight', in *Grim Death*, edited by Christine Campbell Thomson, London, 1928, pp 11–18

'For Ten's Sake', in *The Cornhill*, 66(1929), pp 38-51
'One Man with a Dream', in *The Cornhill*, 66(1929), pp 589-600
'He Who Seeks', in *The Cornhill*, 67(1929), pp 97-107
'The Epic', in *The Cornhill*, 67(1929), pp 160-70
'The Road', in *The Cornhill*, 67(1929), pp 341-52
'A Volcano in the Moon', in *The Cornhill*, 67(1929), pp 463-76
'The Life and Death of Elia Constantinidos', in *The Cornhill*, 67(1929), pp 513-26
'Cockcrow', in *The Cornhill*, 67(1929), pp 641-54
'Gift of the River', in *The Cornhill*, 68(1930), pp 17-30
'East is West', in *The Cornhill*, 68(1930), pp 129-43
'Vernal', in *The Cornhill*, 68(1930), pp 257-70
'Daybreak', in *The Cornhill*, 68(1930), pp 385-96
'It is Written', in *The Cornhill*, 68(1930), pp 513-26
'The Passage of the Dawn', in *The Cornhill*, 68(1930), pp 641-55
'Roads to Freedom', in *The Millgate*, 26(1931), pp 547-50
'Near Farnboru', in *Reynolds's Illustrated News*, 12 July 1931, pp 10, 18
'A Footnote to History', in *The Cornhill*, 71(1931), pp 195-212
'The Lost Constituent', in *The Cornhill*, 71(1931), pp 355-64
'The Refugees', in *The Millgate*, 27(1931), pp 33-8
'The Floods of Spring', in *The Cornhill*, 71(1931), pp 623-38
'Thermopylae', in *The Cornhill*, 71(1931), pp 684-703
'O Mistress Mine!', in *The Millgate*, 27(1932), pp 491-4
'The Last Ogre', in *The Cornhill*, 72(1932), pp 699-711
'Cartaphilus', in *The Cornhill*, 73(1932), pp 344-57
'Camelia Comes to Cairo', in *Persian Dawns, Egyptian Nights*
'The Children of Ceres' in *Persian Dawns, Egyptian Nights*
'Dawn in Alarlu', in *The Cornhill*, 74(1933), pp 185-97
Lewis Grassic Gibbon, 'Greenden', in *The Scots Magazine*, December 1932, pp 168-76
Lewis Grassic Gibbon, 'Smeddum', in *The Scots Magazine*, January 1933, pp 248-56
Lewis Grassic Gibbon, 'Clay', in *The Scots Magazine*, February 1933, pp 329-39
Lewis Grassic Gibbon, 'Sim', in *The Free Man*, 2(10 June 1933), pp 5-7
Lewis Grassic Gibbon, 'Forsaken', in *Scottish Scene*
'Lost Tribe', in *The Millgate*, 29(1934), pp 199-202
'Busman's Holiday', in *Masterpiece of Thrills*, edited by R. Huson, London, n.d.
J Leslie Mitchell and Fytton Armstrong, 'Kametis and Evelpis', in *Masterpiece of Thrills*
Lewis Grassic Gibbon, 'A Stele from Atlantis', in *Masterpiece of Thrills*
Lewis Grassic Gibbon, 'The Woman of Leadenhall Street', in *Masterpiece of Thrills*

4 NON-FICTION ARTICLES

'The End of the Maya Old Empire', in *Antiquity*, 4(1930), pp 285-302
'Yucatan: New Empire Tribes and Culture Waves', in *Antiquity*, 4(1930), pp 438-52
'The Diffusionist Heresy', in *The Twentieth Century*, 1, no.1(March 1931), pp 14-18
'Inka and pre-Inka', in *Antiquity*, 5(1931), pp 172-84
'The Prince's Placenta and Prometheus as God', in *The Twentieth Century*, 2, no.12(February 1932) pp 16-18
'William James Perry: A Revolutionary Anthropologist', in *The Millgate*, 27(1932), pp 323-6
'The Buddha of America', in *The Cornhill*, 72(1932), pp 595-604
Lewis Grassic Gibbon, 'Sunset Song: Author's Reply to the Editor', in *The Fife Herald and Journal*, 28 September 1932, p 2
Lewis Grassic Gibbon, 'Book Reviews: Fiction. Scots Novels of the Half-Year', in *The Free Man*, 2(24 June 1933), p 7

'Grieve—Scotsman', in *The Free Man*, 2(9 September 1933), p 7
'Book Review—Man and the Universe', in *The Free Man*, 2(7 October 1933), p 9
Lewis Grassic Gibbon, 'Book Review—In Oor Kailyaird', in *The Free Man*, 2(7 October 1933), p 9
Lewis Grassic Gibbon, ' "Canting Humbug!" To the Editor of *The Mearns Leader*', in *The Mearns Leader and Kincardineshire Mail*, 8 February 1934, p 1
Lewis Grassic Gibbon, 'New Novels: Mr. Barke and Others', in *The Free Man*, 3(24 February 1934), p 6
Lewis Grassic Gibbon, ' "I Kent his Faither!" A Scots Writer Reviews his Reviewers', in *Glasgow Evening News* (Saturday Supplement), 24 February 1934, p 1
Lewis Grassic Gibbon, 'News of Battle: Queries for Mr. Whyte', in *The Free Man*, 3(17 March 1934), p 9
Lewis Grassic Gibbon, 'Controversy: Writers' International (British Section)', in *Left Review*, 1(1935), pp 179–80
Lewis Grassic Gibbon, 'A Novelist Looks at the Cinema', in *Cinema Quarterly*, 3(1935), pp 81–5
'Religions of Ancient Mexico', in *Religions*, no.13(October 1935), pp 11–20

5   MISCELLANEOUS

'Introduction', in Heinrich Mann, *The Blue Angel*, London, 1932, pp 5–7
'Introduction', in Peter Freuchen, *Mala the Magnificent*, London, 1932, p 5
Louis Katin, 'Author of *Sunset Song*', in *Glasgow Evening News*, 16 February 1933, p 6, is based upon an interview with Mitchell conducted at his home in Welwyn Garden City in the wake of the success of the first Grassic Gibbon novel

Further Reading

The books by Ian S Munro, Douglas F Young and Douglas Gifford are mandatory reading for those interested in Leslie Mitchell's life and work. I offer the following suggestions as useful secondary material. Particularly warm and sympathetic pen-portraits of Mitchell are as follows:

Helen B Cruickshank, 'Lewis Grassic Gibbon: A Man of the Mearns', in *Octobiography* (Montrose, 1976), pp 87–90

Cuthbert Graham, 'The Man Who Wrote *Cloud Howe*: Lewis Grassic Gibbon—An Intimate Sketch', in *Aberdeen Bon-Accord*, 2 February 1934, p 9

Alexander Gray, 'His school essays even baffled the rector', in *People's Journal*, 16 May 1964, p 13

Ray Mitchell, 'So Well Remembered: Lewis Grassic Gibbon', in *New Scot*, 4, no.6(June 1948), pp 16–17

Edwin Muir, 'Lewis Grassic Gibbon: An Appreciation', in *Scottish Standard*, March 1935, pp 23–4

Willa Muir, *Belonging: A Memoir* (London, 1967), pp 193–4

Mitchell's work is regularly examined in critical surveys, most successfully, in my estimation, in Raymond Williams's *The Country and the City* and David Smith's *Socialist Propaganda in the Twentieth-Century British Novel*. Other general studies which reserve a special place for Mitchell's achievement are:

Walter Allen, *Traditional and Dream* (London, 1964), pp 249–52

Alan Bold, *Modern Scottish Literature* (London, 1983), pp 123–39

David Craig, *Scottish Literature and the Scottish People, 1680–1830* (London, 1961), pp 291–3

Francis R Hart, *The Scottish Novel: A Critical Survey* (London, 1978), pp 229–41

Jack Lindsay, *After the Thirties* (London, 1956), pp 48–54

Kurt Wittig, *The Scottish Tradition in Literature* (Edinburgh, 1958), pp 330–3

Among the wealth of minor criticism, the following articles are particularly meritorious:

James Barke, 'Lewis Grassic Gibbon', in *Left Review*, 2(1936), pp 220–5

David Craig, 'Novels of Peasant Crisis', in *Journal of Peasant Studies*, 2(1974), pp 47–68

Neil M. Gunn, 'Nationalism in Writing: Tradition and Magic in the Work of Lewis Grassic Gibbon', in *The Scots Magazine*, October 1938, pp 28–35

Ian Milner, 'An Estimation of Lewis Grassic Gibbon's *A Scots Quair*', in *Marxist Quarterly*, 1(1954), pp 207–18

Geoffrey Wagner, 'The Other Grassic Gibbon', in *Saltire Review*, 2, no.5(Autumn 1955), pp 33–41

Index